The Making of Methodism

Exploring Methodism

The Making of Methodism

Barrie W. Tabraham

EPWORTH PRESS

0 7162 0499 1

Ab urso ad vulpem

First published 1995
by Epworth Press
20 Wyatt Way
Peterborough PE3 7PG

Second impression 1997

Typeset at The Spartan Press,
Lymington, Hants
and printed in Great Britain by
Redwood Books, Trowbridge, Wiltshire

Contents

Preface to the Series

What is Methodism and how did it begin? What did John Wesley teach? We sing Charles Wesley's hymns but what can we discover about his life? What is the character and work of the Methodist Church today? What have Methodists had to say about social issues? What place have women had in Methodism? These are the kind of questions which *Exploring Methodism* is aiming to answer.

All of the contributors are experts in their field, and all write in an attractive way that will appeal to both church members and everyone interested in the life and history of the churches. The format of the books enables each writer to introduce extracts from the writings of the main characters and official church documents, and in this way to bring the reader close to what was actually said and written by the leaders of the church and church members. It is hoped that the books will be studied in house groups and other discussion groups as well as read by individuals, and questions for discussion, directly related to the present day, are included at the end of each chapter. Each volume contains an annotated list of books for further reading.

Barrie Tabraham opens the series with a general overview of Methodist history, concentrating on the origins and early development. Future volumes will cover the Methodist Church today, official statements by the Church on social and political issues, the activity of women in early Methodism, the life and work of Charles Wesley, and Methodism outside Great Britain.

Cyril S. Rodd

Foreword

In *The Making of Methodism*, Barrie Tabraham has produced a valuable and attractive handbook, for both the student and the general reader. The book is based on wide reading, though the scholarship does not obtrude. The author brings to his narrative all his skills as an experienced teacher of history, both in the classroom and through distance learning.

The book is eminently user-friendly, because it presupposes no previous detailed knowledge of the subject. It includes a glossary of technical terms, and is admirably lucid in presentation. At the same time, the author never talks down to the reader. He includes a generous selection of first-hand material – drawn from letters, journals, hymns and sermons – which give the flavour of the period, and kindle the imagination of the reader.

The book is designed for group discussion as well as personal study, and the questions appended to each chapter relate the historical study to the contemporary living of the Christian life.

I warmly commend the book as a reliable and stimulating account of Methodism from its eighteenth-century origins to the present day, and hope that it will have the wide readership it deserves.

John A. Newton
Liverpool

Preface

Why another book on Methodism and the Wesleys?

Apart from Rupert Davies' classic short study written in the early 1960s, there has been little to offer the serious but *busy* reader who wants more than a brief historical summary of how Methodism came into being. This introduction to Methodism is set within a historical framework, but considerable space is devoted to the study of ideas (in particular John Wesley's theology), and the worship and life of 'the people called Methodists'. The idea originated from a correspondence course which I wrote a few years ago entitled *Methodism and Wesley Studies*, and a number of the students who followed the course encouraged me to make the material available to a wider readership. This little book is the result. The discussion starters at the end of each chapter and the short study guide in Appendix 3 indicate that it can be read in a variety of ways – by groups, as part of an individual study scheme, or just for enjoyment.

Where it differs from other short surveys is in the inclusion of primary source material alongside the text. The documentary extracts can give us a much better flavour of the period than narrative by itself. However, the space which they occupy has meant that I have had to be very selective, otherwise the book's size would have defeated its main purpose – to whet the reader's appetite. Some themes such as overseas missions are merely touched upon, while the final chapter covers enormous ground only very briefly. In this respect I have tried not to sacrifice critical comment at the expense of narrative detail. If you become frustrated with the omissions, the suggestions for further reading in Appendix 2 will, I hope, encourage you to delve a little deeper. This book does not pretend to contain original research. Indeed, I have relied heavily upon the work of generations of scholars. What I hope it will do, however, is to open up a vast treasury which I believe is worth exploring – a treasury consisting of the sources contemporary with the Wesleys that are available for study, and of the immense amount of material produced since their deaths.

It has been said that the best form of ecumenical co-operation involves a 'sharing of treasures', and this can best be done if we understand our own treasures as well as those of other churches. We shall then be less like strangers and more truly pilgrims together. Whether you have always been a Methodist, or have recently joined and want to understand something of its background, or belong to another tradition and are simply interested in knowing more about Methodism as a denomination, then I hope this short study will make a contribution to that process of enrichment which all of us need in order to grow in our faith.

In the course of writing this book I owe a great debt of gratitude to many people. My own interest in Methodism was kindled by Donald English, whose inspirational lectures at Wesley College, Bristol, introduced me to the riches of Methodist history and theology. Cyril Rodd and Graham Slater have painstakingly read and checked the manuscript, and I have found their help and advice invaluable. I also wish to thank the late Rupert Davies whose wisdom was of great assistance in the compiling of the original course, and John Newton – my Chairman of District when I worked in Merseyside – for kindly agreeing to write the Foreword. The life of a circuit minister is an exceedingly busy one, and therefore I am indebted to the Methodist Church for granting me a three-month sabbatical, during which much of the work was done. Finally, the support of my wife Joan, and my sons John and Paul, have been a constant source of encouragement. Without them *The Making of Methodism* would not have been possible.

Barrie Tabraham

Introduction

Why hast thou cast our lot
In the same age and place,
And why together brought
To see each other's face,
To join with loving sympathy,
And mix our friendly souls in thee?[1]

You are about to take a rapid journey through the history of Methodism from the early years of the eighteenth century to our own day, but you need have no expertise in church history or Christian theology to understand or enjoy this book. Indeed, it does not matter whether you have read any history or theology at all. The appendices at the back will help you. Appendix 1 is a glossary of terms which, while not exhaustive, gives the meaning of various technical terms which theologians and historians love to use, and includes some of those rather puzzling expressions which have altered in meaning since the eighteenth century. Appendix 3 is a section on reading techniques which may be useful if you have not done any reading for a while. Whether or not we are newcomers to history and theology, both are important subjects of which we should strive to gain at least some understanding.

First, the study of history is of immense value, and what we refer to as 'church history' is no different in that sense from any other kind. That is not to say that we should draw direct parallels from the past. History rarely, if ever, repeats itself. The past, however, can teach us something of human behaviour and the processes of change and development, enabling us to come to a better understanding of ourselves and of today's complex world with all its challenges and frustrations. It was Cicero who once said that the person who remains ignorant of the past 'remains forever a child'. We need to know whence we have come in order to understand where we are now, both individually and corporately. Studying human situations is also very interesting and rewarding for its own sake, and first and foremost this book is about people. John and Charles Wesley may now be regarded as giants by some, but they were men of flesh and blood, and their story, along with that of their followers, is a fascinating one.

Secondly, theology belongs to us all, not just the 'professionals' or the ordained. It is quite simply, 'thinking about God' – a task too important to be left to the few.

When we study theology, we engage in a process of reflection in which we seek to discern God's loving purposes for us as individuals and for the world which he has made. We need to use all available resources if we are to make sense of the times in which we live, and not become detached observers of what is happening around us. John Wesley told his preachers, 'You will need all the sense you have, and to have your wits about you.'[2] There is nothing new about linking history and theology, of course, and though we may be more than two hundred years distant from the Wesleys, our human predicament remains very similar.

John Wesley is the most prominent person discussed in the following chapters and three of them deal primarily with his theological ideas. This is not, however, a book only about John and the Methodist movement. It is a pity that his younger brother Charles has seemed to occupy a subordinate position in the history of Methodism. The concurrence of their early careers, the superficial similarities of their 'conversions' in 1738, and Charles' own inclination towards self-effacement,[3] all tend to reinforce this impression. The primary and secondary sources concerning Charles are a fraction of the quantity of those relating to John. His letters have not survived in a plentiful supply, and what we have of his journal covers only the years from 1736 to 1756, though hymns there are in abundance! Nevertheless, his contribution to Methodism and the universal church deserves more than a passing mention.

The term 'Methodist' itself needs a little clarification. Although it came into use while the Wesleys were active in the 'Holy Club' in Oxford in the 1720s (as we shall see in chapter 2), and was originally applied to John and Charles' followers, it could also be used in a much wider sense. George Whitefield, who parted company with the Wesleys on theological grounds, was regarded as a 'Methodist', along with his adherents, as were certain evangelical groups in Wales. So too were similar groups within the Church of England, and, as Henry Rack points out in his recent biography of John Wesley, the term 'Methodist' could even at times be used to describe anyone who seemed to be religiously 'serious'.[4] This broader use of the word had been developed by Rupert Davies who examined the basic characteristics of Methodism and of parallel groups in the history of the Christian church, such as the Montanists in the second century, and came to the conclusion that it was a 'recurrent form of Christianity'.[5] He warns against pushing comparisons too far, and says that 'the setting in which it (i.e. eighteenth-century Methodism – ed.) arose placed on it the stamp which makes it different from anything which has happened before or since.'[6] This is certainly true, but so is the gentle reminder to those Christians who fondly imagine their own denomination to be unique, that many 'new' developments have been anticipated in Christian history.

It is worth noting at this stage that, in church history generally, there have been two ways in which writers have tended to be guilty of bias. These have been far less common in recent years, but are ever-present banana skins waiting to trip the unwary or uncritical!

One is to slide into hagiography – in other words, to make most of the central characters too saintly. Many *were* saints, of course, but that should not blind us to the natural failings of the people concerned. To underplay or ignore these weaknesses does disservice not only to the persons in question, but also to the basic principles of historical method, which must always involve the search for truth based on evidence that is as reliable as possible. Furthermore, it makes it more difficult for us to empathize with the particular characters, who become remote and unreal. Myths surround John Wesley along with most other important historical figures, and authors of recent years who have been concerned to reveal his more human side are undeserving of the criticsm they have occasionally received. Therefore when we discover less attractive aspects of the lives of the 'saints', we should neither be surprised nor disappointed.

The other way in which bias has affected the writing of church history is just as understandable, but more subtle. This is to suppose that church history is somehow different from any other kind of historical inquiry, on the grounds that it deals with a divine institution – the church. The result has been that much church history written in the last century and the first part of this one is regarded somewhat dubiously by secular historians, because they felt that it fails properly to take into account things that were happening in the rest of the country and the world at large. This is why the chronological table in the appendices contains a broad range of events, and not simply 'church' ones. In the eighteenth century alone, major developments such as the Enlightenment, the changes in industry and agriculture, and the French Revolution had a profound influence on the history of Christianity which cannot be ignored.

The changes that we have seen in our own lifetimes – particularly in the past few years – have been even more cataclysmic, and we can only begin to grapple with the questions they pose if we study the history of the church in this wider context. In this situation, with his keen interest in everything human and his understanding of the way in which sacred and secular are intertwined, John Wesley can be one of our best teachers.

I

The England of the Wesleys

Didst thou not make us one,
That we might one remain,
Together travel on,
And share our joy and pain,
Till all thy utmost goodness prove,
And rise renewed in perfect love?

Into what kind of world were John and Charles Wesley born? So very different from ours, that we can do no more than sketch an outline of some of its basic characteristics. It was an age of contrasts and extremes, some of which no doubt horrify, others simply puzzle us. Before we look at some of the main features of early eighteenth-century England, however, a note of caution.

When studying any period of history (and the eighteenth century is no different in this respect from any other), there is a temptation to suppose that, because people of the time were less advanced technologically than we are, they were therefore less sophisticated in *every* aspect of life. For example, it would be a mistake to think that John Wesley was somehow more 'primitive' than we are today because he did not use a word-processor when writing his letters and sermons, knew nothing of modern methods of communication, and had some ideas concerning medicine that strike us as being very odd. This notion rests on the fallacy that technology is the sole criterion for judging the extent to which people are civilized or advanced in mental and spiritual terms. There has been sufficient evidence in the twentieth century to dispel that idea.

'When John Wesley was born in 1703 some of the most significant turning-points in English and European history had just been passed,' writes the historian Herbert Butterfield.[1] Landmarks there were indeed. The turn of the century saw the beginning of what came to be known as the 'Age of Reason'.[2] The publication of Isaac Newton's *Principia* in 1687 ushered in what we would recognize now as modern scientific method. A year later the 'Glorious Revolution', as it was called – in which James II was deposed and replaced by William and Mary – opened the way for the future transition to parliamentary government in this country. In 1694–5 the establishment of the Bank of England and the National Debt marked the increasing importance of economics and finance in government. In 1702 the first daily newspaper was published in Britain – a small but significant step towards mass communication, despite the current low level of literacy.

What then were the most significant areas of change?

Imagine now that we have a camera which we can point at different spheres of life in Britain at the turn of the eighteenth century. The camera has a wide-angle lens, because we are more interested in taking a few broad snapshots than in using a whole roll of film on any one aspect. In any case there is a whole range of material available in print which can give a fuller picture, a selection of which can be found in Appendix 2. For the moment, a brief look at five areas will give us a sufficient overview.

The political scene

In 1700 Britain had a constitutional monarchy and an active Parliament, but a very small fraction of the population had the vote. Elections and the way in which Parliament conducted its affairs were very different from today, and most public offices were controlled by a vast system of royal and aristocratic patronage.[3] Many constituencies were 'in the gift' of their patrons (usually wealthy landowners) who were able to control the electors (their tenants, by and large) because voting was open until the secret ballot was introduced in 1872. This might seem corrupt to us, but in the eighteenth century it was an accepted feature of British political life. The historian J. H. Plumb writes that 'in any case, the age did not believe in democracy; the world of authority belonged to the owners of property, and not to the dispossessed'.[4]

There were political parties, but not as we would recognize them. Whigs and Tories represented great clans of family and landed interests, and the distinctions between them were often quite blurred. Although party rivalries were intense, party discipline as we understand it was unknown. The 1720s and 1730s did see the emergence of a 'prime minister' as a strong leading figure, together with the beginnings of a cabinet system, and radical political groups grew slowly as the century wore on. For much of this period, however, the country was virtually run by about seventy great families. Until the end of the century 'in reality there was no big political issue to produce an effective basis for genuine party-conflict'.[5]

Abroad, the eighteenth century saw Britain become an economic and colonial power to be reckoned with, thanks largely to her supremacy at sea. A succession of wars with other European powers, especially France and Spain, though resulting in the loss of the American Colonies in 1783, confirmed Britain's arrival as a major power with world-wide colonial interests. For the greater part of this period Britain was a medium-sized power with aspirations to greatness.

The economy

The eighteenth century witnessed enormous changes in agriculture, industry and communications. Expansion only accelerated from about the middle of the century onwards, but from the lord to the labourer, the people of this country were quite aware that they were living in rapidly changing times.

In 1700 England's wealth was built on woollen cloth, which was made in practically every village in the country. As the century progressed, the 'Agrarian Revolution', as it has been termed, saw new techniques of crop-rotation, breeding, cultivation methods and farm management being introduced to cope with Britain's rising population and the expansion of her overseas markets.

These factors helped bring about a revolution in industry, with factories gradually superseding the domestic system in the production of textiles, and a series of inventions making possible great strides in the manufacture of iron, steel and pottery, and in the mining of coal.

A series of rapid improvements in communications involving canals and roads – railways did not pose a serious challenge until well into the next century – constituted another important advance. Its impact, however, should not be exaggerated. For, during much of the eighteenth century, travel between Manchester and Leeds was impossible in winter, and many areas remained almost completely isolated. Even at the end of the century this was still true. When Sydney Smith became curate of the village of Netheravon on Salisbury Plain in 1794, he noted grimly that the most exciting event of the week for the local inhabitants was the arrival of the butcher's cart from Salisbury.

Society

Late twentieth-century England would seem very crowded to John Wesley and his contemporaries. In his home county of Lincolnshire the population density was probably little more than fifty persons per square mile when he was born in 1703. Although the first official census was not taken until 1801, we can reasonably estimate that in 1700 the population of England and Wales was barely five million, little more than it had been centuries earlier. By the 1740s it started to grow rapidly, rising to over eight and a half million by the end of the century.

From what we have noted concerning the economy, it will not be difficult to realize that British society in 1700 contained startling contrasts, with an unbelievably wide gulf between the life-styles of the aristocracy at the top, and the common people at the bottom, of the social pyramid. Recent historians while not wishing to minimize the contrasts, have shown that in reality society in Britain was finely graded. In his good introduction to the social history of this period, Roy Porter points out that 'partly because the crevasses between the ranks were in theory bridgeable, personal mobility upwards and downwards acted as a safety-valve, preserving the overall profile of society'.[6]

He also cites a comment by David Robinson, a contemporary observer, which forms the first extract from 'primary sources' [1] – in other words, material which dates from the particular time in question, as opposed to 'secondary sources' which date from a later period. In fact, the first three documents are all taken from Porter's book, partly to demonstrate that one does not always have to research the archives in order to study contemporary evidence. In this excerpt, Robinson praises the flexibility of English society in the eighteenth century.

---

1. In most other societies, society presents hardly anything but a void between an ignorant labouring population and a needy and profligate nobility . . . But with us the space between the ploughman and the peer is crammed with circle after circle, fitted in the most admirable manner for sitting upon each other, for connecting the former to the latter, and for rendering the whole perfect in cohesion, strength and beauty.

Source: Roy Porter, *English Society in the Eighteenth Century*, Penguin 1982, p. 64.

This observation is worth noting, since it has been asserted by some historians that Methodism was an important factor in helping ordinary people to move up the social order and to 'better themselves'. Whether being a Methodist meant that a person became more 'respectable' is, as we shall see later, a debatable point!

At the beginning of the century most people lived in the countryside in extreme squalor. Apart from London, which was of disproportionate size with nearly 750,000 inhabitants, the largest city in 1700 was Bristol, with a mere 20,000. Townspeople fared little better than their rural counterparts, and though the economic changes brought prosperity to the country as a whole, life was still 'nasty, brutish and short'[7] for the vast majority of the population, who lived in a world of disease, high infant mortality, lack of education, drunkenness, promiscuity, and generally appalling living conditions.

On a brief visit to this country, the German traveller Lichtenberg made no attempt to hide his true feelings when describing the lot of London's poor [2]. The 'old Adam' to which he refers is another way of describing an individual's primitive base instincts, rather in the way St Paul used the term in his letters.

---

2. . . . persons born in the fields, generally near the brick-kilns round London . . . They grow up without learning to read or write, and never hear the words 'Religion' or 'Belief', and not even the word 'God', excepting the phrase 'God damn it'. They gain their livelihood by all kinds of work in the brick-kilns, helping the drivers of hackney coaches, and so forth, until the old Adam in them is aroused: then they take to stealing and are generally hanged between the ages of 18 and 26. A short life and a merry one is their motto, which they do not hesitate to proclaim in court.

Source: Roy Porter, op. cit., p. 111.

We should also remember that the poor were not alone in their suffering. It is true that the growing numbers of merchants and tradesmen were able to take advantage of the progress in agriculture and industry, and join the landed classes in achieving relative prosperity. However, the middle ranks of society were not immune from hardship, either. This can be seen by Revd John Howlett's summary of the plight of the small tenant farmer [3], whose life-style – apart from periods of super-abundant harvests – was generally one of squalid mediocrity.

---

3. The small farmer is forced to be laborious to an extreme degree; he works harder and fares harder than the common labourer; and yet with all his labour and with all his fatiguing incessant exertions, seldom can he at all improve his conditions or even with any degree of regularity pay his rent and preserve his present situation. He is confined to perpetual drudgery, which is the source of profound ignorance, the parent of obstinacy and blind perseverance in old modes and old practices, however absurd and pernicious.

Source: Roy Porter, op. cit., p. 84.

The realm of thought

Every age sees new developments, but the eighteenth century was a little different in that people felt that they were living in more 'modern' times. The century itself came to be known as the 'Age of Reason', and thinkers began to apply scientific methods to processes of thought. Isaac Newton (1642–1727) had given England a high place in the estimate of European thinkers in the area of scientific method, and his contribution was paralleled by the philosophical writings of John Locke (1632–1704)[8] on the study of man and human understanding. Such work was developed with different implications by scholars such as David Hume (1711–1776), another outstanding philosopher, who laid the foundations of modern humanism.

We can only sketch these developments in the faintest detail here, of course, but the new generation of thinkers were not concerned only with the realms of science and political theory. When they turned their attention to Christianity and questioned whether religious faith and reason could be reconciled, they were opening up a debate that would shake the foundations of the established church. David Hume in particular launched a devastating attack on those who claimed that religion could be based on a combination of reason and revelation. Neither, he argued, could prove the existence of God. In Hume's opinion all perceptions of the human mind could be simply reduced to a series of impressions, none of which had any real validity. We can gain an insight into this area of contention by looking at a brief passage from one of Hume's books, in which he advocates a 'sceptical' approach to religion [4].

---

4. The sceptic is another enemy of religion, who naturally provokes the indignation of all divines and graver philosophers . . . This begets a very natural question. What is meant by a sceptic? And how far is it possible to push these philosophical principles of doubt and uncertainty?

. . . to have recourse to the veracity of the Supreme Being in order to prove the veracity of our senses is surely making a very unexpected circuit. If his veracity were at all concerned in this matter, our senses would be entirely infallible, because it is not possible that he can ever deceive. Not to mention that, if the external world be once called into question, we shall be at a loss to find arguments by which we may prove the existence of that Being, or any of his attributes.

This is a topic, therefore, in which the profounder and more philosophical sceptics will always triumph when they endeavour to introduce a universal doubt into all subjects of human knowledge and inquiry.

Source: David Hume, *An Inquiry Concerning Human Understanding*, Ch. XII

Religion

Many people in eighteenth-century England rarely darkened the door of a church between being baptized and getting buried. Yet, curiously, most of the population seems to have had a faith of a sort, even though much of it was what we would term 'folk religion'. After the violent events of the English Reformation of the sixteenth century which saw the Church of England established as a national Protestant church, persecution became less widespread. Religious divisions nonetheless continued to run very deep. The three main groups – Anglicans, with Roman Catholics and Dissenters on either side – shared mutual feelings of distrust, fear, and often sheer hatred.

The Church of England enjoyed great status as the most important religious body, not only as an accepted part of the English constitution, but because in many ways it was a 'resource'. In the absence of state provision for education and social welfare, the church fulfilled an informal but important benevolent role. It provided, for example, most of the teaching staff of the main universities, and was widely expected by the populace to be engaged, not only in much charitable work, but also in medical care. Judging the Church of England's faithfulness and efficiency is difficult, because it was so diverse in character. Examples of excessive wealth, corruption, ignorance or neglect can be set alongside just as many others which give the opposite impression. For the most part, Anglican clergy went about their duties quietly and conscientiously, but with perhaps little enthusiasm or conviction. There is a general sense of the Church of England having lost its 'nerve', and being ill-equipped to respond to the developments that were soon to change the face of the country.

What of the other Protestant groups known as the Dissenters?

These were a collection of denominations, probably numbering about a third of a million in the early part of the eighteenth century, who wished to remain separate from the Church of England. Most had their origins in seventeenth-century Puritanism, and among them we can include Presbyterians, Independents (or Congregationalists), Baptists and Quakers.

A little progress towards complete freedom of religious expression had been made by 1700. When William and Mary took James II's place in 1689 a Toleration Act allowed Dissenters (Roman Catholics, too) the right to worship in their own buildings according to their own beliefs, provided that fairly stringent legal and doctrinal conditions were met. In practice, the various laws regarding religious practices outside the Church of England were inefficiently administered and infrequently enforced. Nevertheless, the toleration granted to Protestant Dissenters was — in theory, at any rate – of a very limited and grudging nature, as we can see from a portion of the Occasional Conformity Act of 1711 [5].

This placed the Dissenters in a strange and difficult position. They could worship in their own communi-

ties, yet could only be baptized, married or buried in Anglican churches. In many ways the fact that this limited toleration took the form of legal statutes made it objectionable, irrespective of how efficiently it was

---

5. An act for preserving the protestant religion, by better securing the Church of England, as by law established; and for confirming the toleration granted to protestant dissenters by an act, intituled, An act for exempting their Majesties' protestant subjects, dissenting from the Church of England, from the penalties of certain laws, and for supplying the defects thereof . . .

And whereas it is or may be doubted whether a preacher or teacher or any congregation of dissenting protestants, duly in all respects qualified according to the said act, be allowed . . . to officiate in any congregation in any county, other than that in which he so qualified himself, although in a congregation or place of meeting duly certified and registered as is required by the said act; Be it . . . enacted . . . that any such preacher or teacher, so duly qualified . . . is hereby allowed to officiate in any congregation . . . provided that the said congregation, or place of meeting, hath been before such officiating duly . . . registered . . . and such preacher or teacher shall, if required, produce a certificate of his having so qualified himself, under the hand of the clerk of the peace for the county or place where he so qualified himself . . .

Source: E. N. Williams, *The Eighteenth Century Constitution*, CUP 1960, pp. 334–336.

---

enforced. Yet in spite of these and other constant sources of irritation to Dissenters, the presence and steady growth of English nonconformity, which constituted a bridge between the old and new ways of thinking, may have made religious extremism less likely as the century wore on. It would be a mistake, however, to see Methodism as Nonconformist: Wesley distinguished Methodists very carefully from Dissenters, as we shall see later, and history has shown how Methodism has stood between the Church of England and Nonconformity, sometimes leaning towards one, sometimes towards the other.

These, very briefly, were the main characteristics of England at the beginning of the eighteenth century, and it was in this religious climate that John Wesley came to faith, preached the gospel and worked out his theological position.

For Discussion

1. Would you have wished to live in the eighteenth century, or not? What aspects of life then either interest or appal you?

2. In what respects do you think Roy Porter's comments on the flexibility of eighteenth-century society are applicable to Britain today?

3. How fair/unfair do you feel the level of religious toleration to have been in those days? Are we significantly more tolerant in this country today?

2

The Wesleys: Background and Early Life

The beginnings

Where shall my wondering soul begin?
How shall I all to heaven aspire?
A slave redeemed from death and sin,
A brand plucked from the eternal fire?
How shall I equal triumphs raise,
Or sing my great Deliverer's praise?

In a world which to some seemed so godless, John and Charles Wesley had the advantage of being born into a strongly religious family, which naturally exerted a very important influence upon their subsequent development. Both the Wesleys' grandfathers were Dissenting ministers, one of them being imprisoned on more than one occasion for his opposition to the Act of Uniformity.[1] This did not mean, however, that John was bound to share this attitude to the Church of England. His parents, Samuel and Susanna Wesley – the former educated in a Dissenting academy – had returned to the Anglican fold of their own free will. Each was an extremely interesting character.

Samuel Wesley was a Tory and a high churchman who was the Rector of the parish of Epworth in Lincolnshire from 1697 until his death in 1735. He was a man of great principle, but rather pedantic and prone to obstinacy. Political disagreements with Susanna were common – Samuel was a staunch supporter of House of Orange, whereas his wife remained loyal to the exiled King James, even refusing to say 'Amen' at the close of evening prayers for King William. In 1701, following another after-supper row, Samuel declared petulantly that 'You and I must part; for if we have two Kings, we must have two beds.' Despite periods of estrangement, however, they had nineteen children,[2] ten of whom survived. The accession of Queen Anne in 1702 ended the couple's political squabbles, and it is quite likely that John's conception was the result of their reconciliation.

Apart from a little poetry Samuel's main literary achievement was a dull, multi-volume commentary on the Book of Job, which not surprisingly was hardly read by anyone. Samuel's rigidity in discipline contrasted with his carelessness in money matters. Epworth was, by eighteenth-century standards, a modest living which carried an annual stipend of £160 together with £60 from nearby Wroot, where Samuel served as curate. However, he found it difficult to make ends meet and in 1705 spent three months in a debtors' prison, being bailed out eventually by the Archbishop of York.

This hard-working, fiery but kindly man was unable to relate to the needs of the time or of his flock, with whom he had a tempestuous relationship. Yet Samuel was a man of deep faith, and an indication of the quality of his spirituality may be seen in the comments of his son John, in a letter written to a friend in March 1748. The 'first Reformers' is a reference both to the great European figures of the Reformation period such as Luther and Calvin, and also to the architects of the Reformation in England, such as Archbishop Cranmer who was burned at the stake in the reign of Queen Mary. The phrase 'inward witness' describes a believer's personal experience of the presence of God [6].

> 6. My father did not die unacquainted with the faith of the gospel, of the primitive Christians, or of our first Reformers; the same which, by the grace of God, I preach, and which is just as new as Christianity. What he experienced before, I know not; but I know that during his last illness, which continued eight months, he enjoyed a clear sense of his acceptance with God. I heard him express it more than once, although at that time I understood him not. 'The inward witness, son, the inward witness,' said he to me, 'that is the proof, the strongest proof, of Christianity.' And when I asked him (the time of his change drawing nigh), 'Sir, are you in much pain?' he answered aloud, with a smile, 'God does chasten me with pain — yea, all my bones with strong pain; but I thank Him for all, I bless Him for all, I love Him for all!' I think the last words he spoke, when I had just commended his soul to God, were, 'Now you have done all.' And, with the same serene, cheerful countenance, he fell asleep, without one struggle or sigh or groan. I cannot therefore doubt but the Spirit of God bore an inward witness with his spirit that he was a child of God.
>
> *Source*: J. Wesley, *Letters*, Vol. 2, pp. 134–135.[3]

Susanna Wesley had an enormous influence upon John, more so than her husband. In contrast to Samuel's volatile temperament, she 'was competent, businesslike and possessed of a cool, rational mentality'.[4] Samuel's frequent absences placed heavy responsibilities upon Susanna, not just for bringing up the children, but also for the spiritual life of the parish — and these she willingly accepted.

In 1709 the Epworth rectory was completely destroyed by fire. There had been a previous alert in 1702 which Susanna felt had been divine retribution for Samuel's political views. The exact cause of the second fire has been the subject of considerable speculation, and it has even been suggested that disgruntled parishioners were responsible. John, who was six years old at the time, was rescued from an upstairs window and as a result the conviction grew that he had been spared for some special purpose. The verse from one of Charles' most famous hymns which heads this chapter is a reminder that John was regarded as 'a brand plucked from the burning'.[5]

Whilst the rectory was being rebuilt, the children were farmed out to live with other families, and on their return Susanna made special efforts to bring them back to a 'proper mode of living'. When Samuel was away in 1712, for instance, she set up a house meeting in the rectory kitchen to cover for the lack of a Sunday afternoon service. This was initially for the family, but before long the sessions attracted servants, parishioners and neighbours, until she had a congregation of two hundred. Needless to say, this did not meet with Samuel's approval.

Susanna saw the fire of 1709 as sign from God concerning young 'Jacky', as he was known, and afterwards vowed to be 'more particularly careful of the soul of this child'. Consequently she identified special qualities in the young John Wesley that would destine him for greatness. Her interest lay in *all* her children's welfare, and she ruled the whole family with a rod of iron, as much a result of necessity as of her own natural inclinations. As far as John was concerned, her first step was to 'break his will' (i.e. his self-will), in order that she might 'instil into his mind the true principles of religion and virtue'. Susanna combined a keen intellect (with an inclination towards scepticism) and a deep devotion to her faith. She taught the surviving children with a strictness that seems unduly severe to us today, though a careful reading of a letter written to her son John in July 1732, reveals that justice was tempered with mercy [7]. The word 'chid' towards the end of the extract is a shortened form of the word 'chided'.

---

7. When turned a year old (and some before), they were taught to fear the rod, and to cry softly, by which means they escaped abundance of correction which they might otherwise have had; and that most odious noise of crying of children was rarely heard in the house . . .

Our children were taught, as soon as they could speak, the Lord's Prayer, which they were made to say at rising and bedtime constantly; to which, as they grew bigger, were added a short prayer for their parents, and some collects, a short catechism, and some portion of Scripture, as their memories could bear. They were very early made to distinguish the Sabbath from other days . . .

There was no such thing as loud talking or playing allowed of; but everyone was kept close to business for the six hours of school. And it is almost incredible what a child may be taught in a quarter of a year by vigorous application . . . Rising out of their places, or going out of a room, was not permitted, except for a good cause; and running into the yard, garden, or street, without leave, was always esteemed a capital offence.

There were several bye-laws observed among us . . . That whoever was charged with a fault, of which they were guilty, if they would ingenuously confess it, and promise to amend, should not be beaten . . . That no sinful action . . . should ever pass unpunished . . . That no child should ever be chid or beat twice for the same fault . . . That every signal act of obedience . . . should always be commended, and frequently rewarded.

Source: Maldwyn Edwards, *Family Circle*, Epworth Press 1949, pp. 58–62.

John Wesley's personal development to 1725

> *Lord, that I may learn of thee,*
> *Give me true simplicity;*
> *Wean my soul, and keep it low,*
> *Willing thee alone to know.*

In 1714 John entered Charterhouse, where his religious devotion and intellectual potential were already apparent. Only the barest facts are known of his experience there. Discipline was severe, but though Charterhouse toughened John, it did not coarsen him. In 1720, having obtained a scholarship worth £40 a year, he went up to Christ Church, Oxford where, it

seems, the quality of both teaching and spiritual life left much to be desired. John's first five years at Oxford were comparatively uneventful, and religion was still 'a habit'. Nonetheless his search for truth – and, in particular, for the assurance that his soul would be spared eternal damnation – had already begun.

The year 1725 was to be one of great significance in John's spiritual development, for two reasons.

On 14 April 1725 John Wesley met 'Varanese'. It was common in the tradition of the eighteenth century for correspondents to adopt rather fanciful pen names, and 'Varanese' was the literary nickname given to Sally Kirkham, the daughter of the Rector of Stanton in Gloucestershire, with whom he struck up a deep friendship. They corresponded regularly, even after her marriage to Revd John Chapone in December 1725 (with the latter's consent, of course!). Despite her marriage, John remained very close to Sally, who proved to be the first of a number of women whom he might have married. In their correspondence, in which Wesley was addressed as 'Cyrus', Sally had a great influence upon his thinking and faith, and as a consequence he was led to a greater awareness of the inward spiritual life and of the love of God in the heart of the believer.

Two other ladies, Mary and Anne Granville, later to be 'Aspasia' and 'Selina' in the letters, became friends; and when John's brother, Charles, joined the letter-writing circle, he became known rather quaintly as 'Araspes'. These female friendships, while not leading to any engagements of a permanent nature, deepened and perhaps softened John Wesley's spiritual perceptions as a young man.

The second event of importance in 1725 was John Wesley's ordination as deacon on 19 September. His father had advised waiting, but Susanna approved, thinking that it would accelerate John's spiritual development. This was a far-reaching step whose significance has only fairly recently been acknowledged by historians. Hitherto, the well-documented event at Aldersgate Street in May 1738 had been regarded as marking John Wesley's 'conversion', as we shall see in chapter 4, and 1725 was given no more than a passing mention. In later life Wesley described some of the influences which led to the deepening of his faith and personal commitment from 1725, while at Oxford [8].

---

8. In the year 1725, being in the twenty-third year of my age, I met with Bishop Taylor's *Rules and Exercises of Holy Living and Dying*. In reading several parts of this book I was exceedingly affected, by that part in particular which related to 'purity of intention'. Instantly I resolved to dedicate *all my life* to God, *all* my thoughts and words and actions, being thoroughly convinced there was no medium, but that *every* part of my life (not *some* only) must either be a sacrifice to God, or to myself; that is, in effect, to the devil . . .

In the year 1726 I met with Kempis's *Christian Pattern*. The nature and extent of *inward religion*, the religion of the heart, now appeared to me in a stronger light than ever it had done before. I saw that giving even *all* my life to God (supposing it possible to do this and go no further) would profit me nothing unless I gave my *heart*, yea *all my heart* to Him.

I saw that 'simplicity of intention and purity of affection', *one design* in *all* we speak or do and *one desire* ruling all our tempers, are, indeed, 'the wings of the soul', without which she can never ascend to the mount of God.

A year or two after, Mr Law's *Christian Perfection* and *Serious Call* were put into my hands. These convinced me more than ever of the absolute impossibility of being *half a Christian*, and I determined, through His grace (the absolute necessity of which I was deeply sensible of) to be *all-devoted* to God: to give Him *all* my soul, my body and my substance.

Source: J. Wesley, *Works* (ed. Thomas Jackson), London 1872, Vol. VIII, pp. 366–367.

Such words leave us in no doubt as to Wesley's sincerity and devotion. When, after all, does any person 'become a Christian'? Wesley himself later wrote that in 1725 he had the faith 'of a slave', whereas after 1738 it was the faith 'of a son' – yet he makes surprisingly little reference to the Aldersgate experience in his later writings. He even added a footnote to one of his Journal entries of 1738, which seems to suggest that he might have over-emphasized his lack of faith prior to that year.[6] The author Robert Tuttle speaks of 1725 in terms of a 'religious conversion', as opposed to his 'evangelical conversion' thirteen years later.[7] Other writers have given differing emphases to the two dates, but we should beware

of putting Wesley's experiences (or anyone's, for that matter) into pigeon-holes of our own making.

In addition to the influence of his family and home and contact with people such as Sally Kirkham, there were other factors which made John Wesley acutely aware of the importance of personal holiness. From his earliest years John was a prolific reader and both the Cambridge Platonists[8] and the mystics influenced him greatly. From the former, such as John Smith and Ralph Cudworth, he came to recognize the importance of the spiritual over the material side of religion, and the need to harmonize reason and faith. His reading of the mystics, such as Jeremy Taylor, William Law and Thomas à Kempis, taught him that spiritual reality could be found in personal experience, the life of God expressing itself in the life of the believer. He did not, however, agree with all that the mystics had to say, as we can see in a letter he wrote to his mother in May 1725, in which he set out his impressions of the writings of Thomas à Kempis [9].

---

9. I was lately advised to read Thomas à Kempis over, which I had frequently seen, but never much looked into before. I think he must have been a person of great piety and devotion, but it is my misfortune to differ from him in some of his main points. I can't think that when God sends us into the world He had irreversibly decreed that we should be perpetually miserable in it. If it be so, the very endeavour after happiness in this life is a sin; as it is acting in direct contradiction to the very design of our creation. What are become of all the innocent comforts and pleasures of life, if it is the intent of our Creator that we should never taste them?

Another of his tenets, which is indeed a natural consequence of this, is that all mirth is vain and useless, if not sinful. But why, then, does the Psalmist so often exhort us to rejoice in the Lord and tell us that it becomes the just to be joyful? . . . he seems to carry the matter as much too far on the other side afterwards, where he asserts that nothing is an affliction to a good man, and that he ought to thank God even for sending him misery. This, in my opinion, is contrary to God's design in afflicting us; for though He chasteneth those whom He loveth, yet it is in order to humble them: and surely the method Job took in his adversity was very different from this, and yet in all that he sinned not.

Source: J. Wesley, *Letters*, Vol. I, pp. 15–16.

A further example of John Wesley's recollections can be found in an entry in his Journal on 24 January 1738, when he was engaged in a deep spiritual struggle with his own fears and anxieties. Desperately searching for the peace of mind which he lacked, he reflected upon the influence which the mystic writers had had upon his devotional progress in the mid-1720s [10]. We would expect him to applaud their precept that a person can have a constant awareness of God's presence in this life, even though his own doubts prevented him from enjoying this fully. What is interesting is his sharp disagreement with other aspects of their teaching, and in particular with what he considered to be their spiritual introspection.

---

10. . . . I grew acquainted with the Mystic writers, whose noble descriptions of union with God and internal religion made everything else appear mean, flat and insipid. But, in truth, they made good works appear so, too; yea, and faith itself, and what not? These gave me an entire new view of religion – nothing like any I had before. But, alas! it was nothing like that religion which Christ and His apostles lived and taught. I had a plenary dispensation from all the commands of God. The form ran thus: 'Love is all; all the commands besides are only means of love; you must choose those which you feel are means to you and use them as long as they are so.' Thus were all the bands burst at once. And though I could never fully come into this, nor contentedly omit what God enjoined, yet, I know not how, I fluctuated between obedience and disobedience. I had no heart, no vigour, no zeal in obeying; continually doubting whether I was right or wrong and never out of perplexities and entanglements. Nor can I at this hour give a distinct account how or when I came a little back toward the right way. Only, my present state is this: all the other enemies of Christianity are triflers – the Mystics are the most dangerous of its enemies. They stab it in the vitals, and its most serious professors are most likely to fall by them. May I praise Him who hath snatched me out of this fire likewise, by warning all others that it is set on fire of hell.

Source: J. Wesley, *Journal*, Vol. 1, p. 420: 24 January 1738.[9]

At this stage we should say something about John's brother, Charles.

Charles Wesley's early life

Thou callest me to seek thy face;
'Tis all I wish to seek;
To attend the whispers of thy grace,
And hear thee inly speak.

Much less has been written about Charles, apart from various books dealing with his talents as a hymn writer, which we shall be looking at in a later chapter. We have noted already that, his hymns aside, Charles wrote comparatively little compared with his elder brother. Many of his surviving letters contain shorthand insertions as well as passages of Latin and Greek, and this can deter the casual reader. There are few biographies of him, and histories of Methodism have tended to pass over his very different spiritual journey. Although the two brothers shared a bond of mutual loyalty and affection throughout their lives, they were not without their differences.

It has been frequently pointed out that John was more like his mother, Susanna, while Charles inherited his father's volatile, emotional nature. He was not a natural leader, but his lack of driving energy and ambition was balanced by a greater capacity for contentment and a more sensitive understanding of human nature than are found in his brother. Family ties were very important to Charles, and when a distant (and rich) relative named Garrett Wesley offered him the opportunity of going to live with him in Ireland as his heir, the young man refused after careful consideration. One wonders what would have happened if he had not done so. The eventual heir became the grandfather of the Duke of Wellington, following a change of the family's name from Wesley to Wellesley. John Russell's portrait of Charles, perhaps the best of the few we have, suggests a kindly, gentle nature. True, he could be obstinate at times, and was given to periods of severe depression, but in his sociability, warmth and compassion Charles was in many ways a more attractive personality than John.[10] He comes across as a far less intimidating character, and was in a sense, a 'Barnabas' to John's 'Paul'.

Until he went to Oxford, Charles' development as a Christian had consisted of eight years' firm but loving instruction at home, followed by ten years at Westminster School in London, to which he was sent in 1716. His elder brother Samuel, seventeen years his senior and senior usher at Westminster for the first half of Charles' stay there, exerted a great influence upon him. Samuel was for some years his unofficial guide and tutor, and it was probably to him that Charles owed his lifelong high churchmanship. Charles was an average student, but good enough to gain a place at Christ Church, Oxford, in 1727, where he was a popular undergraduate.

In his biography of John Wesley, Stanley Ayling writes that 'until he was past twenty Charles Wesley, though he paid conventional allegiance to Christian beliefs and observances, showed no pronounced evidence of piety'.[11] It was not his intention as an undergraduate 'to be a saint all at once', as he playfully remarked to John, and he wrote later that 'my first year at College I lost in diversions'.[12] It seems that a brief infatuation with an older woman (an actress named Molly) helped Charles to be 'less addicted to gallantry', as he himself put it. However, the life of devotion soon beckoned. Many people have been surprised to discover that it was Charles, not John, who founded the group of Oxford undergraduates popularly known as the 'Holy Club', and who therefore can lay fair claim to being the 'first Methodist'. In a letter later in life he reflected:

> Diligence led me into serious thinking. I went to the weekly Sacrament and persuaded two or three young scholars to accompany me, and to observe the method of study prescribed by the Statutes of the University. This gained me the harmless nickname of Methodist.[13]

Of the two brothers, John appears to be much the more serious-minded (though as a young man he had no objection to playing cards and other social activities), but Charles' first conscious steps in deepening his faith were taken independently and in John's absence. So far, the two brothers' paths had diverged. It was the 'Holy Club' that saw the beginning of their partnership.

The Holy Club and developments to 1735

> Meet it is, and just, and right,
>   That we should be wholly thine,
> In thine only will delight,
>   In thy blessed service join:
> O that every work and word
>   Might proclaim how good thou art,
> Holiness unto the Lord
>   Still be written on our heart!

In March 1726 John was unanimously elected as Fellow of Lincoln College Oxford, which stood out from the various other colleges for the quality of its teaching and scholarship. As a tutor of Greek and logic, and later philosophy, he was ardent and methodical, and applied the same standards of discipline as he himself had received. This was to be interrupted in 1727 when he responded to his father's appeal for help at home. For two years John acted in a part-time capacity as Samuel's curate at Wroot, being ordained priest on 22 September 1728.

This short interlude was notable for two things. First, in his pastoral work, tending to the needs of the poor, visiting prisoners and so on, Wesley saw the necessity for combining a deep inward faith with its practical outworking. Wesley was not uncritical of his father, but his somewhat severe and head-strong nature was tempered by the honesty to admit when he was wrong. A sincere compassion for other people's feelings could also be seen in his care for the often difficult members of the parish. Secondly, these years were also characterized by further difficulties with women friends. Whether his childhood or his ideal of womanhood had been over-influenced by his mother, or whether he was simply a 'ditherer', it is impossible to say. What we do know is that his marriage, when it came at long last in 1751, did not prove to be a happy one. In September 1729 he returned to Oxford, where he joined the group of undergraduates and young men which was to become known as the 'Holy Club'.

The Holy Club was already in existence, as we have seen, but John quickly became its natural leader, and Charles was happy to give place to his elder brother. The group's activities consisted of regular meetings for private devotion, prayer, the reading and discussion of scripture and other sacred works, the taking of communion (weekly), and various excursions to the town and the local prison for charitable work. The nicknames they were given by other students – 'Methodists', 'Bible Moths', 'Enthusiasts' and rather quaintly, 'Supererogationists' – were all offered mockingly, though it was 'Methodist' that proved the longest-lasting. Their aim was, primarily, to save their own souls, but the Holy Club was not entirely inward looking. A few years later in October 1732, John wrote a letter to Richard Morgan, the father of William, one of the members of the Holy Club. In it he defends the activities of 'that ridiculous Society', as it had been dismissively described [11]. Although John was prone to write in exaggerated terms in his journal, we have no reason to doubt either his honesty or the reliability of his memory in this instance, and the passage gives an accurate impression of the group's purpose and emphases.

It was here, interestingly, that the brothers met George Whitefield, but it is significant that it was Charles, and not John, who was the main influence in his conversion – further evidence of the fact that Charles was 'his own man' as a Christian.

In 1734 Samuel invited John to succeed him at Epworth. At the age of seventy-one he relinquished his watery parish of Wroot, but he had hoped that John would take over at Epworth (his main living), and provide security of tenure for himself in his declining years. The eldest of the Wesley brothers, Samuel, was now headmaster at Blundell's School at Tiverton in Devon, and Charles had not yet been ordained. John's reply in December 1734, refusing his father's invitation, was possibly one of the most unattractive things that he ever wrote. His main objective, he was at pains to explain, was to foster holiness in himself and lead to his own 'self-improvement'. The reasons he gives for staying in Oxford provide a very interesting comment on his 'spiritual temperature' at the time [12].

---

11. In November 1729, at which time I came to reside at Oxford, your son, my brother and myself, and one more agreed to spend three or four evenings in a week together. Our design was to read over the classics, which we had before read in private, on common nights, and on Sunday some book in divinity. In the summer following, Mr Morgan (*William – Ed.*) told me he had called at the jail, to see a man that was condemned for killing his wife; and that, from the talk he had with one of the debtors, he verily believed that it would do much good if any one would be at the pains now and then of speaking with them. This he so frequently repeated, that on the 24th of August, 1730, my brother and I walked down with him to the Castle. We were so well satisfied with our conversation there, that we agreed to go thither once or twice a week; which we had not done long, before he desired me, August 31, to go with him to see a poor woman in the town who was sick. In this employment too, when we came to reflect upon it, we believed that it would be worth while to spend an hour or two in a week; provided the minister of the parish in which any such person was were not against it . . .

As for the names of Methodists, Supererogation Men, and so on, with which some of our neighbours are pleased to compliment us, we do not conceive ourselves under any obligation to regard them, much less to take them for arguments . . .

Source: J. Wesley, *Letters*, Vol. 1, pp. 124–132.

---

12. I therefore believe that, in the state wherein I am, I can most promote this holiness in myself, because I now enjoy several advantages which are almost peculiar to it.

The first of these is daily converse with my friends. I know no other place under heaven where I can have always at hand half a dozen persons nearly of my own judgement and engaged in the same studies . . . Another invaluable blessing which I enjoy here in a greater degree than I could anywhere else is retirement. I have not only as much, but as little, company as I please . . . Freedom from care I take to be the next greatest advantage to freedom from useless and therefore hurtful company. And this too I enjoy in greater perfection here than I can ever expect to do anywhere else . . . To quicken me in making a thankful and diligent use of all the other advantages of this place, I have the opportunity of public prayer twice a day and of weekly communicating . . .

From all this I conclude that, where I am most holy myself, there I could most promote holiness in others; and consequently that I could more promote it here than in any place under heaven. But I have likewise other reasons besides this to think so; and the first is, the plenteousness of the harvest. Here is, indeed, a large scene of various action. Here is room for charity in all its forms . . . I cannot quit my first conclusion, that I am not likely to do that good anywhere, not even at Epworth, which I may do at Oxford . . .

Source: J. Wesley, *Letters*, Vol. 1, pp. 168–175.

In 1735 John came into contact with General James Oglethorpe, a remarkable individual who managed to combine successful careers in both the army and the world of philanthropy in a way that few have done before or since. His great design was the rehabilitation of criminals, particularly debtors, and in 1732 he founded the colony of Georgia in America. Samuel Sr had had contact with Oglethorpe through correspondence already (their subject of mutual interest being rather obvious!), and when the General decided that the colony needed a pastor, he approached the two brothers. They agreed to accompany him, John as pastor to the colonists, and Charles as his private secretary. Why did they go?

Charles was more influenced by John's enthusiasm than by his own ambitions to be an administrator. He would personally have preferred to have spent the remainder of his days in Oxford, though it seemed to him right at the time to engage in this venture. He was a God-fearing young man with a strong sense of duty, rigorous in his devotions, possessed of a budding social conscience and a loving concern for the spiritual welfare of his fellows. Charles' ordination as deacon two Sundays before they left and his consecration as priest the Sunday immediately prior to their departure were the result of pressure from John. 'I exceedingly dreaded entering into Holy Orders,' he wrote later, 'but he overruled me . . .'

Three factors help to explain why John himself decided to leave England in October 1735. First, his father's death in 1735 inevitably resulted in upheavals at home. It might have seemed an inopportune moment to go, but Susanna quickly banished John's reluctance to leave his newly-widowed mother. His sisters Emily and Patty were both married shortly after their father's death, leaving only Kezziah a spinster, and therefore family responsibilities were no objection. Secondly, John's relationship with 'Aspasia' (Mary Pendarves) became unhappy after 1731 and may well have encouraged him to seek a change of surroundings. Finally, his desire and quest for personal holiness had not yet given him the peace of mind for which he so much longed. Could a stay in Georgia provide the answer?

Time Line of Events

1688	Samuel Wesley marries Susanna Annesley
1697	Samuel becomes Rector of Epworth
1703	Birth of John Wesley
1707	Birth of Charles Wesley
1709	Second rectory fire
1714	John enters Charterhouse
1716	Charles enters Westminster School
1720	John begins studies at Christ Church, Oxford
1725	John ordained as deacon
1726	John elected Fellow of Lincoln College
1727	Charles elected Student of Christ Church
1727–9	John serving as curate at Wroot
1728	John ordained priest
1729	Charles founds the 'Holy Club; John returns to Oxford
1734	John declines Epworth living
1735	Death of Samuel Wesley; the Wesleys leave for Georgia

For Discussion

1. In what ways can parents help their children to have a faith of their own? Are there any obvious pitfalls which should be avoided?

2. From what you have read, which do you feel were the strongest influences which helped shaped John Wesley's early spiritual development?

3. Do you think John was right to say 'No' to his father's request to succeed him at Epworth in 1734?

4. Which do you consider comes first – cultivating the inner spiritual life or reaching out in service to others?

3

Wesley's Theology 1: His Sources of Authority

Far off we need not rove
To find the God of love;
In his providential care,
Ever intimately near,
All his various works declare,
God, the bounteous God is here.

We now move from pure history to the study of ideas, and begin to examine Wesley's basic beliefs. In chapter 5 we shall see how John Wesley developed a coherent picture of the relationship between God and his people, and chapter 7 explores the contribution he and his brother made to the development of worship. These sections will enable us to have a clearer understanding of the distinctive features of Methodism itself. For the moment, however, we turn to the sources from which Wesley drew his religious ideas.

If your faith has ever been challenged by a theological or ethical problem, you may have asked yourself, 'How *do* I know that what I believe is actually true?' Responses such as 'The Bible says . . .', or 'It stands to reason', simply will not do, because we must be wary of the danger of over-simplifying situations and coming to hasty judgments. As we know, making sense of our faith in a complex world is a demanding task.

Although John Wesley lived over two hundred years ago, he had a method of working out his theology in a very practical way that can still be applied today. Our times may be different from his, but human nature remains much the same. We shall find that the fundamental questions of belief were just as common in the eighteenth century.

There are three preliminary matters to note.

First, the context in which John Wesley was writing. Sometimes he was addressing a national scene in which Roman Catholic, Anglican and Calvinist traditions were firmly established and well-defined. At others, he was writing to individuals about specific issues, often arising out of pastoral problems. In either case, it is important not to take his words out of context, especially in those areas where he modified his views over the passage of time.

Secondly, the absence of a single, all-embracing theological statement from Wesley. Although he remained an active and serious theologian throughout his life, he produced no systematic theology in the way that Karl Barth or Paul Tillich were to do. He was an exceedingly busy and much-travelled man. Thousands of words poured from his pen on countless issues. Wesley was primarily interested in meeting people's practical needs, and therefore his theology had a dynamic quality which evolved over the years.

Thirdly, Wesley's concentration on particular doctrines. He was not concerned to cover every single aspect of belief. There is little in his works, for example, about the Trinity,[1] or specific teaching concerning the Holy Spirit – though his writings contained much teaching about the Spirit's work. Being a practical man, he did not spend time in going over ground that had been well trodden by others. Rather, he brought new insights into the way in which the individual could experience God's salvation.

There were four sources of authority which Wesley believed underpinned his whole theology. They were **Scripture**, **Experience**, **Reason** and **Tradition**.

To illustrate how these four sources operated in Wesley's thinking, imagine a mobile, hanging from a ceiling in a hallway,[2] and rotating slowly in the moving air. In the centre is Scripture, and around it are Tradition, Reason and Experience. Like the mobile, Wesley's theology was a dynamic thing which was always moving and developing. Each element could be defended, but only in relation to the other three. Most scholars would agree that for Wesley, scripture and experience were the most important, with reason and tradition having slightly lesser importance. There was nothing new in this, simply that Wesley combined and expounded the elements in a distinctive way.

This, as we shall see, was a method of *doing* theology in a way that had a useful, practical application. Many Methodists have found that, suitably updated, the four 'pillars' make a good foundation for theology today.

1. Scripture

Still we believe, almighty Lord,
Whose presence fills both earth and heaven,
The meaning of the written word
Is by thy inspiration given;
Thou only dost thyself explain
The secret mind of God to man.

We know that scripture can, if studied in isolation, be made to prove almost anything. You may have come across the story of the Sunday School teacher who asked her class what they had learned from the story of Goliath. 'To duck,' came one boy's reply. Enough said. Wesley's theology centred on the Bible. He was, as he himself put it, *homo unius libri* – 'a man of one book', and he accepted its verbal inspiration.

However, when he said that he believed all that was in the Bible 'as far as I understand it', he was expressing the view of a man who had not been exposed to what we know as modern biblical criticism. Had he read the later theories – of the multiple authorship of Genesis and Isaiah, for instance – he would no doubt have subjected them to the same sharp scrutiny as the scholarship of his own day.

In the next document [13], Wesley explains how the Holy Spirit helps Christians to use and understand the Bible. In February 1748 he wrote a letter to a Quaker, probably Thomas Whitehead whom he had met in Bristol nine years earlier. He answers the question, 'Is there any difference between Quakerism and Christianity?' and in the following extract points to the need for a balanced approach to scripture. Note how Wesley is careful to draw a distinction between the words 'rule' and 'guide', in order to avoid extremes.

---

13. 'Yet the Scriptures are not the principal ground of all truth and knowledge, nor the adequate, primary rule of faith and manners. Nevertheless they are a secondary rule, subordinate to the Spirit. By Him the saints are led into all truth. Therefore the Spirit is the first and principal leader.'

If by these words . . . be only meant that '*the Spirit is our first and principal leader*', here is no difference between Quakerism and Christianity.

But there is great impropriety of expression. For though the Spirit is our principal leader, yet He is not our rule at all; the Scriptures are the rule whereby He leads us into all truth. Therefore, only talk good English; call the Spirit our 'guide', which signifies an intelligent being, and the Scriptures our 'rule', which signifies something used by an intelligent being, and all is plain and clear.

Source: J. Wesley, *Letters*, Vol. 2, p. 117.

Of course, Wesley accepted that there were bound to be slight inaccuracies in scripture, or 'corruptions in the received text', as he put it. However, proper study of the Bible involved more than just understanding the bare text. It was important to know both the context in which a particular passage had been written, and the levels at which the text was meant to be understood, given that some verses could have more than one meaning. Wesley was not, therefore, a literalist!

The method of biblical interpretation which Wesley advocated was two-fold. First, mastery of the *literal* meaning of the text – in other words, the plain meaning or sense of the words and phrases within the context in which they were written. Secondly, an understanding of the *spiritual* meaning of the passage, and its significance for the life of faith.

In the following document, Wesley states clearly how he believes scripture is an all-important authority as 'a complete rule of faith'. It is a short extract from a lengthy letter which he wrote to Dr Conyers Middleton in January 1749. Middleton, who was a Fellow of Trinity College Cambridge, had written a book in which he attacked aspects of the church's teachings, particularly in their reliance upon the authority of the Bible. Wesley is quick to defend his position [**14**].

---

14. You proceed: '*If the Scriptures are a complete rule* (I reject the word 'sufficient', because it is ambiguous), *we do not want the Fathers as guides, or, if clear, as interpreters. An esteem for them has carried many into dangerous errors: the neglect of them can have no ill consequences.*' (Page 97). I answer: (1) The Scriptures are a complete rule of faith and practice; and they are clear in all necessary points. And yet their clearness does not prove that they need not be explained, nor their completeness that they need not be enforced. (2) The esteeming the writings of the first three centuries not equally with but next to the Scriptures never carried any man yet into dangerous errors, nor probably ever will. But it has brought many out of dangerous errors, and particularly out of the errors of Popery. (3) The neglect in your sense of the primitive Fathers – that is, the thinking they were all fools and knaves – has this natural consequence (which I grant is no ill one, according to your principles), to make all who are not real Christians think Jesus of Nazareth and His Apostles just as honest and wise as them.

Source: J. Wesley, *Letters*, Vol. 2, p. 325.

---

2. Experience

> O *that with all thy saints I might*
>   *By sweet experience prove*
> *What is the length, and breadth, and height,*
>   *And depth of perfect love!*

Wesley tested all truth, including Christian truth, by experience. This did not mean that he over-emphasized mere feelings. There had been too many tragic examples in the seventeenth century of mis-guided religious zeal for Wesley to be unaware of the dangers of relying on experience alone. He knew only too well that it was possible to convince oneself of almost anything if one tried hard enough. Rather, what he understood by 'experience' was an awareness of the will and purpose of God which addressed an individual's whole personality. There was a subtle difference in Wesley's view, therefore, between simply having a *feeling* that a particular course of action was right, and allowing religious intuition in its broadest sense to guide one's perceptions.

Of course, Wesley himself was careful not to equate 'experience' in this sense with merely 'the wisdom of years'. This can be seen in the following extract from one of his letters, written when he himself was well past seventy. It was addressed to a Miss March, with whom he corresponded on a number of occasions. She has been described as 'a lady of good education' who, 'having a small independent fortune, devoted her life and all she had in doing good'. In a letter to her dated 27 December 1774 [**15**], Wesley sets down some of

---

15. A few minutes I spent with Miss M—— when she was in town two or three years ago . . . From her letters I should judge that she had still many convictions and strong desires to be a real Christian. At the same time it is plain she is surrounded with hindrances and is sometimes persuaded to act contrary to her conscience. It is extremely difficult to advise a person in such circumstances what to do. Methinks the first thing I would advise her to, at all events, is, 'Do nothing against your conscience. 2. At a proper opportunity, after praying for courage, tell your lady you scruple such and such things. And I doubt not but she will take effectual care that no one shall press you . . .' Leaving her place is the last step to be taken if she finds she cannot save her soul therein.

You know it is very natural for me to estimate wisdom and goodness by years, and to suppose the longest experience must be the best. But, although there is much advantage in long experience and we may trust an old soldier more than a novice, yet God is tied down to no rules; He frequently works a great work in a little time. He makes young men and women wiser than the aged; and gives to many in a very short time a closer and deeper communion with Himself than others attain in a long course of years . . .

Source: J. Wesley, *Letters*, Vol. 6, p. 132.

his thoughts regarding the nature of experience in the Christian faith. His advice concerning the pastoral problems he refers to in the first paragraph makes it quite clear that important decisions cannot be made without careful reflection.

It was experience, therefore, which confirmed the truth of doctrine, but Wesley never said that experience by itself proved anything. This would lead to the dangers of what he called 'speculative religion' in which people could believe almost what they liked. In this way, by linking experience to the other three main sources of religious authority, he guarded against the very thing of which eighteenth-century Methodists were so often wrongly accused – 'enthusiasm', or purely emotional religion. It is worth noting in this context that what Wesley often referred to as 'experimental' religion, we would now term 'experiential'. This is a pity, since the modern expression has lost the original sense of 'testing', clearly illustrated by the course of action which Wesley advised in the letter to Miss March.

We can summarize Wesley's teaching, then, by saying that experience confirms a doctrine that is already grounded in scripture, its truth being seen in the practical outworking of faith in our lives.

3. Reason

> To thee, inseparably joined,
>   Let all our spirits cleave;
> O may we all the loving mind
>   That was in thee receive.

This next source of Wesley's religious authority should be seen against the background of two extremes that were particularly evident in the eighteenth century. He was concerned to steer a middle course.

One extreme has been referred to already: 'Enthusiasm' – a term of reproach which in the eighteenth century meant religious fanaticism.[3] We can readily understand why 'enthusiasm' was widely feared in church circles in Wesley's day. The previous two centuries had seen the deaths of countless thousands of Protestants and Catholics throughout Europe as the result of an excess of religious zeal. When, after Queen Anne's reign, the move towards religious toleration increased, many of Wesley's contemporaries breathed a deep sigh of relief!

At the other end of the spectrum was Rationalism – which developed from the Enlightenment. We should not think of it as identical with twentieth-century humanism or atheism; rather, it was an appeal to the unaided use of the mind. Eighteenth-century rationalists inevitably questioned the nature of revelation and their ideas were seen as a threat to spiritual inspiration.

For Wesley, the use of 'reason' had to avoid both these extremes. He defined the term carefully, using it in three slightly different senses:

First, 'reasonable' in the sense of being 'logical'. For example, Wesley saw that reason, being a God-given faculty, was an essential part of every Christian's equipment – in order to search the scriptures, make moral decisions, and to 'seek after true religion'. He explains this in the following extract [16], taken from

---

16.   28. But one question still remains to be asked, 'What do you mean by *reason*?' I suppose you mean the eternal reason, or the nature of things: the nature of God and the nature of man, with the relations necessarily subsisting between them. Why, this is the very religion *we* preach: a religion evidently founded on, and every way agreeable to, eternal reason, to the essential nature of things . . .

29. It is in every way suited to the nature of man, for it begins in man's knowing himself, knowing himself to be what he really is – foolish, vicious, miserable. It goes on to point out the remedy for this, to make him truly wise, virtuous, and happy, as every thinking mind (perhaps from some implicit remembrance of what it originally was) longs to be. It finishes all by restoring the due relations between God and man . . .

30. But perhaps by reason you mean the faculty of reasoning, of inferring one thing from another . . .

. . . the strongest reasoner whom we have ever observed (excepting only Jesus of Nazareth) was that of Paul of Tarsus – the same who has left that plain direction of all Christians: '*In malice* (or wickedness) *be ye children, but in understanding* (or reason) *be ye men*' [cf. I Cor. 14:20].

31. We therefore not only allow but earnestly exhort all who seek after true religion to use all the reason which God hath given them in searching out the things of God.

Source: J. Wesley, *An Earnest Appeal to Men of Reason and Religion*, pp. 11–12.

An Earnest Appeal to Men of Reason and Religion, written in 1744. This was the first of a series of four *Appeals*, and in it Wesley presents a clear statement of the reasonableness of the Christian faith.

There are dozens of practical questions which every Christian has to face each week, the answers to which are not immediately apparent from reading the Bible. The church has been divided over many issues – recently, for example, over the ordination of women to the priesthood, gambling and the responsible use of alcohol. Wesley was right, therefore, to be concerned that we should think through the problems and issues that face us.

Secondly, Wesley used the word 'reason' to describe a human faculty in contrast to faith. He acknowledged that human reason had its limitations, and needed to be complemented by what he called the 'seeing eye' and the 'hearing ear' – spiritual senses developed by a life of faith through an intimate relationship with God.

Thirdly, by 'reason' he also meant an approach to belief which was in accord with orthodox faith and practice. In his *A Farther Appeal to Men of Reason and Religion*, Wesley examined the doctrines he taught, enquiring whether they were reasonable, and concluding in each case that they were and that together they constituted a reasonable and coherent system of belief.

Wesley always insisted that the faith he was teaching was 'agreeable to eternal reason, to the essential nature of things', and he was therefore anxious to avoid difficulties of two kinds. On the one hand, there were those created by 'Quietism' – which resulted from devaluing reason and waiting quietly to 'feel' the touch of God upon the soul; on the other, there were those produced by 'Deism' – which resulted from overvaluing reason and thus excluding the possibility of inspiration and revelation. In a letter to Dr Rutherforth in March 1768, Wesley summarized his position succinctly: 'It is a fundamental principle with us that to renounce reason is to renounce religion, that religion and reason go hand in hand, and that all irrational religion is false religion.' Passionate he might be, but never a woolly emotionalist!

4. Tradition

> *Head of thy Church, whose Spirit fills*
> *And flows through every faithful soul,*
> *Unites in mystic love, and seals*
> *Them one, and sanctifies the whole.*

This fourth pillar of John Wesley's theology was also very important, and one which reflected his upbringing and family background. Writing in June 1775 to the Earl of Dartmouth, who was the Secretary of State for the Colonies, Wesley asserted 'I am an high churchman, the son of an high churchman', and in all his writings he stressed the importance of the traditions of the church. This did not mean, of course, that all Methodists had to embrace Anglican *churchmanship* (i.e. its ceremonial and liturgical style). Rather, Wesley urged they should respect and value its doctrines and laws.

The following two extracts show how much importance Wesley gave to tradition or, as we might put it today, 'the collective wisdom of the centuries'. Notice how in the first passage [17], Wesley takes care to define exactly what he means by 'the church'.

---

17. You still think we are secretly undermining, if not openly destroying, the Church.

What do you mean by the Church? A visible church (as our Article defines it) is 'a company of faithful (or believing) people: *coetus credentium*'. This is the essence of a church, and the properties thereof are (as they are described in the words that follow) 'among whom the pure Word of God is preached, and the sacraments duly administered.' Now, then (according to this authentic account), what is the Church of England? What is it, indeed, but the 'faithful people, the true believers, of England'? It is true, if these are scattered abroad, they come under another consideration. But when they are visibly joined by assembling together to hear 'the pure Word of God preached' and to eat of one bread and drink of one cup, they are then properly the visible Church of England . . .

Others object that we do not observe the *laws* of the Church, and thereby undermine it. What laws? The rubrics or canons? In every parish where I have been curate yet, I have observed the rubrics with a scrupulous exactness, not for wrath, but for conscience's sake.

Source: J. Wesley, *An Earnest Appeal to Men of Reason and Religion*, pp. 30–32.

In that excerpt Wesley sees the church operating at different levels: the universal Catholic Church consisting of believers throughout the world; 'National Churches' represented in Britain by the Church of England; and, at the local level, companies of believers, no matter how few in number, meeting together in Christ's name. It was this common love for Jesus Christ that made the church holy in Wesley's view – not the church's laws and regulations, nor the relative virtue of its individual members. Rupert Davies has observed that because he thought in these terms, Wesley was actually calling into question Article 19 of the Church of England.[4] This article presupposed that the preaching of the pure Word of God and the proper administration of the sacraments had to take place for a church to exist in a particular place. Wesley did not consider that these conditions were always observed in the Roman Catholic Church, yet he was quite prepared to accept faithful Catholics as brothers and sisters in Christ.

The second of the two documents in this section is part of a letter John Wesley wrote to a Revd William Dodd, who had questioned him on certain doctrinal points. Dodd, who at various times was a lecturer and a hospital chaplain, eventually became convicted of forgery, and was visited in prison just before his execution in 1777. This excerpt [18], dated 12 March 1756, gives a brief insight into Wesley's views on the value of church tradition, particularly in its relationship to scripture.

> 18. In your last paragraph you say, 'You set aside all authority, ancient and modern.' Sir, who told you so? I never did; it never entered my thoughts. Who it was that gave you that rule I know not; but my father gave it me thirty years ago (I mean concerning reverence to the ancient Church and our own), and I have endeavoured to walk by it to this day. But I try every Church and every doctrine by the Bible. This is the word by which we are to be judged in that day. Oh that we may then give up our account with joy! Whatever farther thoughts you are pleased to communicate will be seriously considered by, reverend dear sir,
>
>   Your affectionate brother and fellow labourer.
>
> Source: J. Wesley, Letters, Vol. 3, pp. 172–3.

The reasons why Wesley laid such stress on tradition are not difficult to see: his own family upbringing, his experience at Oxford, and his strong belief in the church as the inheritor of the traditions of the Early Christian Fathers. In his great study *John Wesley and the Church of England* Dr Frank Baker has asserted that Wesley's views underwent a subtle but significant change over the years. Having started from a position in which he saw the church as an institution to be preserved with a traditional rule, Wesley came to see it as the company of the faithful with a mission to the world. In other words, while retaining his respect for and support of the church, Wesley recognized the need to transform a tradition which, in the case of the Church of England, had become over-preoccupied with the church as an institution. He was not blind to its faults! That part of the story will be told in a later chapter.

We should note that Wesley accepted that Christians from various denominations might hold different 'opinions'. This term has a far more general meaning today than it did in the eighteenth century. Wesley used it to mean views which different Christians might sincerely hold about religious matters over and above the 'core' of their faith. He acknowledged that for the most part, Christians were bound to think, worship and act differently.

If we want a brief insight into the 'irreducible minimum' which Wesley held to be necessary for genuinely belonging to the company of believers, we can do no better than to turn to his sermon on 'The Catholic Spirit', in which he preached on the text: 'Is thine heart right, as my heart is with thy heart? And Jehonadab answered: It is. If it be, give me thy hand' (II Kings 10.15), an extract of which is reproduced here [19]. Wesley examines what it is that Christians must believe and do to be 'of one heart'. He accepts the inevitable variety of opinion and practice amongst Christians, and then goes on to explore the implications of the text. Purists will no doubt want to question the way in which Wesley lifts the verse out of its context, but his ideas are both thought-provoking and surprisingly up to date.

19. The first thing implied is this: Is thy heart right with God? Dost thou believe His being and His perfections? His eternity, immensity, wisdom, power? His justice, mercy, and truth? . . . Dost thou believe in the Lord Jesus Christ, 'God over all, blessed for ever'? Is He revealed in thy soul? Dost thou know Jesus Christ and Him crucified? . . . Is thy faith . . . *filled with the energy, of love*? Dost thou love God 'with all thy heart, and with all thy mind, and with all thy soul, and with all thy strength'? . . . Art thou employed in doing, 'not only thy own will, but the will of Him that sent thee'? . . .

Is thy heart right toward thy neighbour? . . . Do you show your love by your works? . . .

'If it be, give me thy hand.' I do not mean, 'Be of my opinion' . . . You need not even endeavour to come over to me, or bring me over to you . . . I do not mean, 'Embrace my modes of worship' . . . We must both act as each is fully persuaded . . . I mean, first, love me . . . as a brother in Christ . . . I mean, secondly, commend me to God in all thy prayers . . . I mean, thirdly, provoke me to love and good works . . . I mean, lastly, love me not in word only, but in deed and in truth . . .

If, then, we take this word in the strictest sense, a man of a catholic spirit is one who, in the manner above mentioned, gives his hand to all whose hearts are right with his heart.

Source: J. Wesley, *Sermons*, Vol. 2, pp. 346–359.

For Discussion

1. Why is religious fanaticism so dangerous? What are some of the ways in which it can be avoided?

2. How would you justify your belief in the existence of God to an unbeliever?

3. In what sense can scripture be 'a complete rule of faith', when so many of the problems we are faced with today are not referred to specifically in the Bible?

4. A friend tells you that he is proposing a course of action (which you feel is unwise) because he has had 'a word from the Lord'. What would be your reply?

5. In a debate concerning some aspect of Christian belief, a person says 'It doesn't make sense!' How can you respond as one rational person to another, knowing that much of what you believe cannot be proved?

6. What is *your* 'tradition', and how has the church influenced your own pilgrimage as a Christian?

The important thing, which Wesley never neglected, was to link these four pillars together. He was only too aware of the problems that can be created by basing belief and practice on any one by itself. As we know, a reliance upon scripture to the exclusion of the other elements can lead to a dogmatic and sterile fundamentalism. Letting experience be the only guide to our actions can result in a spiritual outlook which becomes simply a matter of what we happen to feel is right at the time – a pragmatic, whimsical approach which will not do. A faith based solely on reason, by contrast, can end up by being a cold, formal, intellectual system of belief, without the warmth of a genuine experience of the love and presence of God. Too much emphasis upon tradition can lead to a fossilizing of attitudes in the church.

By allowing these four pillars to complement each other, Wesley was showing a way forward to a lively, balanced approach to faith that would help his contemporaries and provide his heirs with useful tools in their search for truth and meaning.

4

From Georgia to Aldersgate Street

The vineyard of their Lord
Before his labourers lies;
And, lo! We see the vast reward
Which waits us in the skies.

In this chapter we take the story of John and Charles Wesley from October 1735 when they embarked on their voyage to Georgia to May 1738, the occasion of the brothers' 'evangelical' conversions.

The 'great experiment'

The Georgian episode is one of the most thoroughly documented periods in the history of Methodism, since we have the journals of both the brothers available in print, as well as John's own manuscript diaries. The factors which led to John going to Georgia have already been discussed, but his *motives* make an interesting study. Undoubtedly his sense of disillusionment with Oxford was balanced by a naïve view of life in the New World. He conveniently set aside the arguments he had recently used as an escape from a future at Epworth,[1] and pictured an unsullied community in which he would be free from personal entanglements to preach the pure gospel to the native inhabitants – a 'Paul to the gentiles'. In a letter written to Dr John Burton on 10 October 1735, John explains his motives in typically methodical style [20].

20. My chief motive, to which all the rest are subordinate, is the hope of saving my own soul. I hope to learn the true sense of the gospel of Christ by preaching it to the heathen . . . They are as little children, humble, willing to learn, and eager to do the will of God; and consequently they shall know of every doctrine I preach whether it be of God. By these, therefore, I hope to learn the purity of the faith which was once delivered to the saints . . .

I then hope to know what it is to love my neighbour as myself, and . . . I am assured, if I be once fully converted myself, He will then employ me both to strengthen my brethren and to preach His name to the Gentiles, that the very ends of the earth may see the salvation of our God . . .

But perhaps you will ask, 'Cannot you save your own soul in England as well as in Georgia?' I answer, – No; neither can I hope to attain the same degree of holiness here which I may there; neither, if I stay here, knowing this, can I reasonably hope to attain any degree of holiness at all . . .

To the other motive – the hope of doing more good in America – it is commonly objected that 'there are heathens enough in practice, if not theory, at home; why, then, should you go to those in America?' Why? For a very plain reason: because these heathens at home have Moses and the Prophets, and those have not; because these who *have* the gospel trample upon it, and those who have it not earnestly call for it; 'therefore, seeing these judge themselves unworthy of eternal life, lo, I turn to the Gentiles.'

Source: J. Wesley, *Letters*, Vol. 1, pp. 188–191.

It is interesting that, on Wesley's own admission, the reasons for his leaving England focus first on his own spiritual needs. What he could do for others in Georgia was clearly a secondary consideration.

The outward voyage was an eventful one. On board the *Simmonds*, John not only led the normal services, but also introduced a careful regime of devotional activities – in essence a 'mini' Holy Club. The most significant aspect of the voyage, however, was his contact with a group of twenty-six Moravian Christians. Since they were to have a considerable influence upon both John and Charles, it will be worth digressing briefly to examine their background.

The Moravians were a Protestant evangelical community originating in Germany where they broke away from the Roman Catholic Church in 1467. In 1715, having suffered a history of persecution, they experienced a revival centred at Herrnhut in Saxony under a new leader, Count Nicholas Zinzendorf, and in 1727 they officially became a group within the Lutheran Church. It was August Gottlieb Spangenberg, the son of a Lutheran clergyman and a professor at Halle University, who obtained Oglethorpe's permission to take a group of twenty-seven Moravians from Saxony to Georgia. They established a community near Savannah, on the lines of the one in Germany at Herrnhut ('The Lord's watch'), and preached to the Creek Indians – with such success that a second group joined them, sailing on the same vessel as the Wesleys.

The Moravians placed great emphasis on the authority of the Bible and the need for personal salvation, their theology focussing on the death of Christ on the cross and, in particular, on the sacrificial element of the atonement.[2] They were concerned to revive the customs and faith of the early church, and their life-style was characterized both by deep inward devotion and by a determination to preach the gospel to all who would listen.

In mid-Atlantic the *Simmonds* encountered a storm which at one point threatened to sink the ship. The calm behaviour of the Moravian passengers in this crisis made a deep impression on John Wesley, who in contrast was consumed by the fear of losing his life [21].

---

21. At seven I went to the Germans. I had long before observed the great seriousness of their behaviour. Of their humility they had given continued proof, by performing those servile offices for the other passengers, which none of the English would undertake; for which they desired, and would receive no pay, saying, 'it was good for their proud hearts', and 'their loving Saviour had done more for them.' And every day had given them occasion of showing a meekness which no injury could move. If they were pushed, struck, or thrown down, they rose again and went away; but no complaint was found in their mouth. There was now an opportunity of trying whether they were delivered from the spirit of fear, as well as from that of pride, anger, and revenge. In the midst of the psalm wherewith their service began, the sea broke over, split the mainsail in pieces, covered the ship, and poured in between the decks, as if the great deep had already swallowed us up. A terrible screaming began among the English. The Germans calmly sung on. I asked one of them afterwards, 'Was you not afraid?' He answered, 'I thank God, no.' I asked, 'But were not your women and children afraid?' He replied mildly, 'No; our women and children are not afraid to die.'

Source: J. Wesley, *Journal, 25 January 1736.*

This was John's first experience of Moravian piety, and it influenced the emphasis he gave to the doctrine of 'assurance' in his later writings. In fact Nehemiah Curnock who edited the standard edition of Wesley's Journal said that 'the storm was one of the crucial facts in early Methodism'. Of course, as with any single incident its importance can be exaggerated, but bearing in mind John Wesley's status as senior clergyman on board and chaplain both to the crew and the passengers, his Journal does make remarkable reading, as the excerpt shows.

Charles was dreadfully sea-sick on the voyage, but his journal reveals feelings of delight and anticipation on his arrival in Georgia. This relatively brief document, written in quite a different style from that of his elder brother, makes absorbing reading. Initially, Charles clearly saw the whole experience as thrilling, though the idyll was soon shattered. Homesickness, disillusionment with the colonists, a breakdown in his none too robust health, quarrels with Oglethorpe, and an inability to make a success of his secretarial duties – all sapped Charles' initial enthusiasm. His stay in

Georgia, however, taught him much about human nature and deepened his devotional life. His journal entry for 23 March 1736 provides just one example of his continuing spiritual growth. 'In reading Hebrews XI,' he wrote, 'I felt my faith revive; and I was confident that God would either turn aside the trial, or strengthen me to bear it.'[3] In the end the experience proved too much for him and he returned to England in August 1736, a chastened but wiser man.

Charles' voyage home from Massachusetts was as eventful as the outward crossing, and saw an incident which provides an interesting parallel to his brother's experience of the Moravians on board the *Simmonds*. Almost inevitably the ship was struck by a storm, so severe that the mizzen mast had to be chopped down to prevent the boat from foundering. However, this time it was Charles who was able to give his fellow passengers comfort and reassurance. His comment at the time says much about his own spiritual progress:

> In this dreadful moment, I bless God, I found the comfort of hope; and such joy in finding I could hope, as the world can neither give nor take away. I had that conviction of the power of God present with me, overruling my strongest passion, fear, and raising me above what I am by nature, as surpassed all rational evidence, and gave me a taste of the divine goodness.[4]

John had even greater problems than Charles whilst in Georgia. He saw himself as a missionary, but never really got to grips with the work owing to his duties in Savannah, where he was rector at St James Church and pastor to the colonists, most of whom didn't want one! After his brother's departure John took over Charles' secretarial work, which he performed capably but which he found frustrating in that it diverted him from the 'main design', his mission to the Indians. He also found the Europeans, many of whom were from the dregs of English society, very disappointing. They, for their part, found this former Oxford don almost unbearable, and Southey is probably right when he writes that John treated his congregation like members of the Holy Club, and 'drenched them with the physic of an intolerable discipline'.[5]

Perhaps the most unrealistic of all John's expectations concerned women, with whom he showed a guileless simplicity. A certain Mrs Hawkins proved to be one of the greatest sources of trouble for him, both on the voyage and in Georgia itself, and John was too naïve to be able to cope with her. His relationship with the seventeen-year-old Sophia Hopkey was equally disastrous, but for different reasons. He fell in love with this charming, seemingly devout young lady, but his sense of duty caused him to procrastinate for so long that she gave up waiting for his expected proposal. Her subsequent marriage to another colonist provoked a bitter quarrel, resulting in John unwisely refusing her communion. It was a sad episode.

The 'great experiment', as Wesley termed it, taught him much about the inadequacies of his faith, though he could not yet fully accept the solution which the Moravians offered and which he and his brother admired. An idea of his spiritual uncertainties may be gained from looking at a conversation which he had with the Moravian leader, August Spangenberg, in early 1736 [22].

---

22. Mr Oglethorpe returned from Savannah with Mr Spangenberg, one of the pastors of the Germans. I soon found what spirit he was of; and asked his advice with regard to my own conduct. He said, 'My brother, I must first ask you one or two questions. Have you the witness within yourself? Does the Spirit of God bear witness with your spirit, that you are a child of God?' I was surprised, and knew not what to answer. He observed it, and asked, 'Do you know Jesus Christ?' I paused, and said, 'I know He is the Saviour of the world.' 'True,' replied he; 'but do you know He has saved you?' I answered, 'I hope He has died to save me.' He only added, 'Do you know yourself?' I said, 'I do.' But I fear that they were vain words.

Source: J. Wesley, *Journal*, 7 February 1736.

None of us likes being put on the spot in this way, and John's reaction was perhaps understandable. Spangenberg's use of the word 'witness' may well have caused John to remember his father's dying words, which now seemed to be directed at himself. Life seemed full of difficulties. Two months later, on

20 April 1736, he wrote a letter to General Oglethorpe summing up some of the problems he was encountering [23].

---

23. Savannah never was so dear to me as now. I believe, knowing by whom I send, I may write as well as speak freely. I found so little either of the form or power of religion at Frederica, that I am sincerely glad I am removed from it. Surely never was any place, no, not London itself, freer from one vice; I mean hypocrisy . . .

'Jesus, Master, have mercy upon them!' There is none of those who did run well whom I pity more than Mrs Hawkins. Her treating me in such a manner would indeed have little affected me, had my own interests only been concerned. I had been used to be betrayed, scorned, and insulted by those whom I had most laboured to serve. But when I reflect on her condition, my heart bleeds for her. Yet with Thee nothing is impossible!

With regard to one who ought to be dearer to me than her, I cannot but say that the more I think of it, the more convinced I am that no one, without a virtual renouncing of the faith, can abstain from the public as well as the private worship of God. All the prayers usually read morning and evening at Frederica and here, put together, do not last seven minutes. These cannot be termed long prayers; no Christian assembly ever used shorter; neither have they any repetitions in them at all. If I did not speak thus plainly to you, which I fear no one else in England or America will do, I should by no means be worthy to call myself, sir,

Yours, etc.

Source: J. Wesley, *Letters*, Vol. 1, pp. 200–1.

While not being an 'enthusiast', Oglethorpe was nevertheless a convinced and philanthropic Christian who cared deeply about the welfare of his people. The above note was probably occasioned by Oglethorpe's irregular attendance at worship, but to give him credit he accepted Wesley's gentle chiding. After Charles had left for England he relied ever increasingly upon John's efficiency as a secretary, sometimes for up to six hours a day.

Another interesting aspect of the Georgia experience was that we can see the prototypes of later Methodist institutions being explored and used, though of course in embryonic form. The use of lay people to assist in pastoral duties and the employment of deaconesses was introduced. Both John and Charles experimented with extempore prayer and preaching, initiated the occasional celebration of the Love-feast,[6] and began the practice of keeping lists of names for communion and pastoral purposes. The idea of small core-groups or 'classes' also finds its origin in the brothers' work in Georgia. Moreover, their contact with the Moravians confirmed for John and Charles the importance of hymnody in worship.

The Georgia interlude was therefore not all loss. Charles, as we have seen, returned to England more aware of himself and the nature of the 'real world'. John had learned a great deal, too. The foundation of much of his later writing; the *Notes* on both Old and New Testaments, his sermons and the *Christian Library*, which he edited,[7] were all developed in his Oxford and Georgia years. The rough and tumble of colonial life and the unexpected opposition he had received from almost everyone in Savannah forced Wesley to modify his rigid outlook. He would always be methodical and disciplined, but future years saw him become more adaptable and perhaps more understanding of human nature. Possibly this came naturally with the passage of years, but Georgia removed some of his rougher edges. Above all, John Wesley had had some of his mostly deeply seated notions concerning the nature of faith and salvation challenged, and it is this area of his personal development that we now turn.

The return from Georgia

Loosed from my God, and far removed,
Long have I wandered to and fro,
O'er earth in endless circles roved,
Nor found whereon to rest below:
Back to my God at last I fly,
For O the waters still are nigh.

'I shook the dust off my feet, and left Georgia, after having preached the gospel there not as I ought, but as I was able, one year and nearly nine months.'[8] Such were John's feelings as he left on 2 December 1737. On his arrival in England a few months later he reflected in characteristically strong terms on the time he had spent in the New World [24]. The footnotes which he added later to this entry in his journal are almost as important as the text itself, for they point to the fact that he sometimes tended to write about his own spiritual state in extreme terms, which he later modified. The first comment in particular, as we shall see later, sheds important light on the way in which Wesley viewed the whole process of conversion.

---

24. It is now two years and almost four months since I left my native country, in order to teach the Georgian Indians the nature of Christianity: but what have I learned myself in the meantime? Why (what I the least of all suspected), that I who went to America to convert others, was never myself converted to God.[1] 'I am not mad,' though I thus speak, but 'I speak the words of truth and soberness' . . .

If it be said that I have faith (for many such things have I heard, from many miserable comforters), I answer, So have the devils, – a sort of faith; but still they are strangers to the covenant of promise. So the apostles had even at Cana in Galilee, when Jesus first 'manifested forth His glory'; even then they, in a sort, 'believed on Him'; but they had not then 'the faith that overcometh the world.' The faith I want is,[2] 'A sure trust and confidence in God, that, through the merits of Christ, my sins are forgiven, and I reconciled to the favour of God.' . . .

'1. I am not sure of this.' – Wesley's own footnote, added later.

'2. The faith of a son.' – Ditto.

Source: J. Wesley, *Journal*, 29 February 1738.

Back in England John first had thoughts of returning to Oxford, but decided instead to visit the Moravian settlement at Herrnhut. In February 1738 he and Charles met a young Moravian called Peter Böhler, who had considerable influence upon both brothers. Böhler was a young Moravian pastor staying in London en route for Georgia. He was a devout, plain-speaking man with a simple faith, who was not afraid to tell the Wesleys a few home truths about their spiritual state. Charles, who was in Oxford in February and not in the best of health, spent some time helping Böhler with his English. On 24 February he recorded in his journal a conversation with the young German who had come to visit him in his sick bed. It provides an interesting insight into the younger Wesley's character, as well as his spiritual condition [25].

---

25. At six in the evening, an hour after I had taken my electuary, the toothache returned more violently than ever. I smoked tobacco; which set me a-vomiting, and took away my senses and pain altogether. At eleven I waked in extreme pain, which I thought would quickly separate soul and body. Soon after Peter Böhler came to my bedside. I asked him to pray for me. He seemed unwilling at first, but, beginning very faintly, he raised his voice by degrees, and prayed for my recovery with strange confidence. Then he took me by the hand, and calmly said, 'You will not die now.' I thought within myself, 'I cannot hold out in this pain until morning. If it abates before, I believe I may recover.' He asked me, 'Do you hope to be saved?' 'Yes.' 'For what reason do you hope it?' 'Because I have used my best endeavours to serve God.' He shook his head, and said no more. I thought him very uncharitable, saying in my heart, 'What, are not my endeavours a sufficient ground of hope? Would he rob me of my endeavours? I have nothing else to trust to.' . . .

Source: J. Telford (ed), *The Journal of Rev. Charles Wesley MA*, London 1909, pp. 134–135.

John, for his part, did not escape Böhler's probing. The month or so after his return to England had been spent in London preaching and visiting friends, but still searching for the peace of mind for which he longed. As in Charles' case, Böhler seemed to speak straight to John's condition. John had not yet realized the importance of 'revealed' as opposed to 'natural' religion – in other words, he had yet to commit himself to finding personal rather than philosophical solutions to his spiritual problems. 'That philosophy of yours must be purged away', Böhler pointed out, and encourged Wesley to continue preaching in spite of his misgivings [26].

---

26. I found my brother at Oxford, recovering from his pleurisy; and with him Peter Böhler; by whom, in the hand of the great God, I was, on Sunday, the 5th, clearly convinced of unbelief, of the want of that faith whereby alone we are saved.

Immediately it struck into my mind, 'Leave off preaching. How can you preach to others, who have not faith yourself?' I asked Böhler, whether he thought I should leave it off or not. He answered, 'By no means.' I asked, 'But what can I preach?' He said, 'Preach faith till you have it; and then, because you have it, you will preach faith.'

Accordingly, Monday, 6, I began preaching this new doctrine, though my soul started back from the work . . .

Source: J. Wesley, *Journal*, 4 March 1738.

Peter Böhler helped the Wesley's to understand and recognize 'unbelief', which at that time meant, in John's words: 'the want of that faith whereby alone we are saved'. Böhler also showed them the different quality of living that was possible for those who were at peace with God. On 23 March 1738 John Wesley wrote in his journal: 'I met Peter Böhler again, who now amazed me more and more by the account he gave of the fruits of living faith, – the holiness and happiness which he affirmed to attend it.' The quest for holiness and the lack of happiness in his faith were exactly the things which troubled John's spirit.

This remarkable Moravian, furthermore, convinced John that instantaneous conversion was biblical, and John, much to his own surprise, found little else when he examined the New Testament for evidence. 'I searched the Scriptures again,' wrote John in his journal on 22 April 1738, 'touching this very thing, particularly the Acts of the Apostles; but, to my utter astonishment, found scarce any instances there of any other than instantaneous conversions . . . What reason have I to believe He works in the same manner now?

Charles Wesley's evangelical conversion, 21 May 1738

> 'Tis love! 'tis love! Thou diedst for me!
>   I hear thy whisper in my heart;
> The morning breaks, the shadows flee,
>   Pure, universal love thou art;
> To me, to all, thy mercies move:
> Thy nature and thy name is love.

The fifteen months prior to May 1738 saw Charles engaged in an unremitting spiritual struggle. In one of the few scholarly biographies of him to have been written, Frederick Gill aptly titles his chapter on this phase in Charles' life 'Wrestling Jacob'.[9] It is also fitting that this should be the name given to the tune composed by Charles' grandson, Samuel Sebastian Wesley, which is sometimes sung to the hymn quoted above. Charles' letters to his brother and to Count Zinzendorf, even his sermons, all bore witness to his longing for a deeper experience of the love and forgiveness of God. William Law, whose mysticism Charles was later to reject, spent a great deal of time counselling the increasingly unhappy man and advised him to 'be not impatient'. The younger Wesley's journal of this period amply testifies to his inner conflict. On Saturday 18 December 1736 we find him 'in a murmuring, discontented spirit'; on 15 September of the following year 'with earnest desires of resigning myself up entirely to God'; on 9 October, 'still growing in humility and love', and on 4 December, 'much melted at the Sacrament'.[10]

It is significant and not always mentioned by historians that, just as Charles had been before John in the Holy Club at Oxford, so he experienced 'conversion' before him. Like his brother, he was strongly influenced by Peter Böhler and, also like John, found new insights in reading Luther – though from a different section of his writings. In the event their 'conversion experiences' were separated by just three days. Yet there the superficial similarities end. John, with his more reasoned and logical approach, engaged in 'the intellectual struggles of a man who will not make his judgement blind'.[11] Charles, on the other hand, was in many ways more receptive and his quest for peace of mind a much more emotional one. Despite his reluctance to accept Peter Böhler's arguments, he still clung to the idea of salvation by faith alone. After reading Luther's preface to the Galatians, he wrote in his journal: 'I am astonished I should even think this a new doctrine.'[12] The weeks before his 'conversion' found him beset by pleurisy, continuing in prayer, reading the scriptures, and alternating between periods of relative peace of mind and deep dejection, the latter being accompanied by much shedding of tears.

The circumstances surrounding Charles' conversion are less well known than John's experience at

Aldersgate Street, but make an interesting story. He was finally helped to the peace of mind for which he longed by a Mr Bray, in whose house he was lodging at this time. Charles described him as: 'a poor ignorant mechanic, who knows nothing but Christ; yet by knowing Him, knows and discerns all things.'[13] During the night of 20 May, ill again with pleurisy, Wesley heard a woman come into his room and say, 'In the name of Jesus Christ of Nazareth arise and believe, and thou shalt be healed of all thy infirmities.'[14] This was Bray's sister, and through this ordinary, devout family Charles experienced the assurance for which he had hungered.

'I now found myself', he wrote on the morning of 21 May 1738, 'at peace with God, and rejoiced in the hope of loving Christ.'[15] It was Whit Sunday, and he immediately composed the famous hymn, 'Where shall my wondering soul begin', though his later 'Come O Thou Traveller unknown', as we have already noted, is a far better description of the spiritual conflict through which he had passed. Charles therefore followed a distinct and individual path during his 'years of preparation', and what went on in each brother's mind was essentially unique. 'What John reasoned', writes Rattenbury, 'Charles saw.'[16] It is interesting to note that, while many of Charles' later hymns harked back to this occasion, John only occasionally referred to his experience on 24 May in later years.

Aldersgate Street, 24 May 1738

> O how shall I the goodness tell,
>   Father, which thou to me hast showed?
> That I, a child of wrath and hell,
>   I should be called a child of God,
> Should know, should feel my sins forgiven,
> Blest with this antepast of heaven!

John had wanted to be convinced by Peter Böhler's words, but how was he to achieve this sense of assurance? He knew in his mind that *faith*, not works was the prerequisite, but what could he do if he lacked it? As we have seen, Böhler encouraged him to persevere and not leave off preaching, but John's response was far from enthusiastic. March and April saw him wrestling with this problem. Was faith, then, a gift? If so, would he receive it at a particular point in time?

After the Aldersgate experience Wesley preached at St Mary's, Oxford on 18 June on the text 'By grace ye are saved through faith' (Eph. 2.8). Appropriately the sermon became the first in the collection that was eventually published, where it was given the title *Salvation by Faith*. In it Wesley described various kinds of inadequate faith – the faith of 'a heathen', 'a devil' and even the faith 'the Apostles themselves had while Christ was yet upon earth'. Clearly speaking from recent personal experience, Wesley concluded his sermon by emphasizing that true faith which saved the individual from guilt, fear and the power of sin was something that could be enjoyed 'even in this present world'. Moreover, it was 'the free, undeserved gift' of God.[17]

On 4 May Peter Böhler left England for America, with Wesley still engaged in his great internal struggle. He woke early on the morning of 24 May 1738, and was encouraged by the words he read in II Peter 1.4. 'Thou art not far from the kingdom of God.' In the afternoon he went to St Paul's, but the anthem – 'Out of the deep have I called unto Thee, O Lord' – failed to lift him. The moment of truth came in the evening, when he visited a small group of Moravians who were holding a meeting in Aldersgate Street in London. It is significant and probably no coincidence, that both Wesley brothers found the answer to their quest by learning what Luther had written about salvation when interpreting the teaching of St Paul.

Wesley describes what happened in his case in words that have become familiar to Methodists throughout the world, and have been inscribed on a black memorial in the shape of a flame that has been erected near the original site [27].

27. In the evening I went very unwillingly to a society in Aldersgate Street, where one was reading Luther's preface to the Epistle to the Romans. About a quarter before nine, while he was describing the change which God works in the heart through faith in Christ, I felt my heart strangely warmed. I felt I did trust in Christ, Christ alone, for salvation; and an assurance was given me, that He had taken away my sins, even mine, and saved me from the law of sin and death.

I began to pray with all my might for those who had in a more especial manner despitefully used me and persecuted me. I then testified openly to all there, what I now first felt in my heart. But it was not long before the enemy suggested, 'This cannot be faith; for where is thy joy?' Then was I taught, that peace and victory over sin are essential to faith in the Captain of our salvation; but that, as to the transports of joy that usually attend the beginning of it, especially in those who have mourned deeply, God sometimes giveth, sometimes witholdeth them, according to the counsels of His own will.

After my return home, I was much buffeted with temptations; but cried out, and they fled away. They returned again and again. I as often lifted up my eyes, and He 'sent me help from His holy place'. And herein I found the difference between this and my former state chiefly consisted. I was striving, yea, fighting with all my might under the law, as well as under grace. But then I was sometimes, if not often, conquered; now I was always conqueror.

Source: J. Wesley, *Journal*, Wednesday 24 May 1738.

Until now we have used the word 'conversion' in inverted commas to describe what happened to the Wesley brothers in May 1738. But what was he converted from, and what was he converted to? He certainly wasn't converted from a pagan to a Christian. Nor was he converted from a nominal, 'almost' Christian to a committed one. Even less was he converted from an Anglican to a Methodist! We should remember that throughout his early years, John's will was entirely devoted to serving God in every part of his life.

It will be recalled that thirteen years earlier, when he became ordained as deacon in the Church of England he wrote:

In the year 1725, being in the twenty-third year of my age, I resolved to dedicate *all my life* to God, *all*

my thoughts and words and actions . . . A year or two after, I saw the absolute impossibility of being *half a Christian*, and I determined, through His grace to be *all-devoted* to God: to give Him *all* my soul, my body and my substance.[18]

He was a decent, respectable Anglican clergyman, who had lived a devout religious life. He had been an honest, conscientious, hard-working servant of God. Someone once said with a fair amount of truth that, 'if John Wesley was not a true Christian (when in Georgia) God help millions of those who call and profess themselves Christians'. Wesley did not suddenly become a devout believer in May 1738. It was rather a change of emphasis, and a deepening of perception. Dr John Newton has summed up Wesley's condition by saying that 'he had a will of iron, great physical toughness, and one of the best educations through scholarships, that the eighteenth century could give. He was handsome, charming, full of grace as a character. And because all these varied gifts were bound together by religious zeal, John Wesley had the makings of a first-class – *pharisee*.'[19]

Some might consider this analysis too harsh, but only because Pharisees in the New Testament have all been tarred with the same over-critical brush. Indeed, it has been suggested that 1725, not 1738, was the more significant year in John Wesley's spiritual pilgrimage. Maximin Piette in his *John Wesley and the Evolution of Protestantism* has been one of the chief proponents of this theory, which at least has the merit of placing the Aldersgate experience in a much wider context.[20] It is perhaps understandable that the events of May 1738 have been isolated and given too much significance, because loyal Methodists over the years have wanted a particular date on which to focus. Certainly, as we have mentioned previously, Wesley himself made remarkably few references to Aldersgate subsequently. This is in marked contrast to his brother, whose hymns bear constant witness to his own experience on 21 May. We should, therefore, guard against supposing that Wesley's career thereafter was based solely upon this single event, and see it in a broad perspective.

No doubt the controversy will continue. What happened on 24 May was the culmination of a series of developments that stretched back to 1725 and earlier. At the Aldersgate Street meeting, it finally dawned on the unhappy John – the 'penny dropped', as we would say – that he was a child of God, loved and accepted by him, and he found forgiveness, peace and assurance. It is hardly surprising that, as we shall see in the next chapter, Wesley should later emphasize the possibility of every Christian experiencing 'assurance'.

Finally, it should be noted that Aldersgate Street marked an important theological, as well as a psychological, turning point in Wesley's life. Being released from the introspection which had characterized his earlier years, Wesley was now able to combine the notion of personal holiness with personal faith. It was as if he now had the best of both worlds. There was a sense in which the fervour and simplicity of faith in the grace of God, so characteristic of evangelical Protestantism, was now integrated with a deep concern for holiness and the importance of the sacramental life, emphasized by the Roman Catholic tradition. In many ways, this harmonization of grace and holiness has provided Roman Catholics and Methodists with an important point of contact in their ecumenical conversations, and has been the most significant of Wesley's many legacies to future Christians.

Time Line of Events

1715	Moravian revival at Herrnhut
1732	Charter granted to found the colony of Georgia
1733	The first settlers land
1735 (Oct)	Charles' ordination; the brothers set sail
1735 (Dec)	The storm incident
1736 (Feb)	The Wesleys arrive at Savannah
1736 (Aug)	Charles returns home; the Grand Jury meets to hear charges against John
1737 (Dec)	John leaves Savannah
1738 (Feb)	John arrives back in England; he and Charles meet Peter Böhler
1738 (May)	The Wesleys' conversion experiences

For Discussion

1. How far do you think John's motives for going to Georgia to have been naïve?

2. On balance, would you say that the brothers 'gained more than they lost' whilst in America?

3. Why do you think John had so many apparent problems with women?

4. What do you think John meant by the footnotes he added to his journal entry on his return from Georgia? (Box 24)

5. When looking at the events prior to May 1738, with which of the brothers do you most easily identify?

6. What, for you, is the most significant aspect of John Wesley's experience at Aldersgate Street?

5
Wesley's Theology 2:
His 'Order of Salvation'

To him that in thy name believes
Eternal life with thee is given;
Into himself he all receives,
Pardon, and holiness, and heaven.

Reflection on the experience of the Wesleys in May 1738 leads naturally to detailed examination of the nature of salvation, the central concept of Methodist theology. John Wesley could now bear witness to the activity of God's grace in the individual believer, and to understand how this work is possible he developed an outline of the whole process of salvation. In this chapter we shall examine his 'order of salvation', beginning with the basic need of sinful humanity and progressing to the ultimate goal of Christian perfection.

'Methodism', wrote Maximin Piette, 'has no confession of faith; its founder did not draw up any articles.'[1] In other words, John Wesley did not provide a single, systematic account of the 'Order of Salvation'. Rather, his understanding grew out of his developing ministry, and he stated his views in response to specific needs, enquiries and challenges. It is thus no surprise to discover that his teaching contains a number of internal tensions. He was trying to relate biblical teaching to the developing religious experience of his congregations. In the preface to the first volume of the *Sermons*, Wesley wrote in March 1771 that his purpose was 'to guard those who are just setting their faces towards heaven, from formality, from mere outside religion, which has almost driven heart religion out of the world . . .' And he added later, 'but I trust, wheresoever I have mistaken, my mind is open to conviction'.[2]

28. Salvation begins with what is usually termed (and very properly) *Preventing Grace*; including the first wish to please God, the first dawn of light concerning his will, and the first slight transient conviction of having sinned against him. All these imply some tendency towards life; some degree of salvation; the beginning of deliverance from a blind, unfeeling heart, quite insensible of God and the things of God. Salvation is carried on by *Convincing Grace*, usually in Scripture termed *Repentance*; which brings a larger measure of self-knowledge, and a farther deliverance from the heart of stone. Afterwards we experience the proper Christian salvation; whereby, *through grace*, we *are saved by faith*; consisting of these two grand branches, Justification and Sanctification. By Justification we are saved from the guilt of sin, and restored to the favour of God; by Sanctifcation we are saved from the power and root of sin, and restored to the image of God. All experience, as well as Scripture, shows this salvation to be both instantaneous and gradual. It begins the moment we are justified, in the holy, humble, gentle, patient love of God and man. It gradually increases from that moment, as a *grain of mustard-seed, which at first, is the least of all seeds, but,* afterwards *puts forth large branches,* and becomes a great tree; till, in another instant, the heart is cleansed from all sin, and filled with the pure love to God and man. But even that love increases more and more, till we 'grow up in all things into Him that is our Head'; till we all attain 'the measure of the stature of the fullness of Christ'.

Source: J. Wesley, *Sermons*, Vol. 5, pp. 106–7.

However, Wesley did provide a beautifully worded

summary of the 'Order of Salvation' in his sermon *On Working Out Your Own Salvation*, which is set out on the previous page [28].

We shall refer to this useful guide as we examine each stage of the salvation process.

Everything in the 'Order of Salvation' depends on the 'grace' made available through the ministry of Jesus, which is God's free gift to all. Charles Wesley expresses this fundamental truth in a hymn which has always been beloved by Methodists [29].

The fact that the word 'all' occurs in every single verse, and that the hymn is full of inclusive terms such as 'unconfined', 'general', 'undistinguishing' and 'universal', points to the Wesleys' conviction that salvation was possible for *all people*. In this sense, John and Charles Wesley were Arminian, rather than Calvinist, in their belief.[3]

The human condition

Fain would we cease from sinning
  In thought, and word, and deed;
From sin in its beginning
  We languish to be freed;
From every base desire,
  Our fallen nature's shame,
Jesus, we dare require
  Deliverance in thy name.

The whole history of the human race has, in Wesley's eyes, been characterized by self-will and sin. We have been created in God's image, but are all fallen creatures, and therefore, as Paul wrote, we are all 'in Adam'.[4] Wesley wrote of the 'total depravity' of man's nature before God, but he saw that, taken literally, such a view created two difficulties. First, it conflicted with the evidence of his own eyes and his experience of people. Secondly, it denied human freedom and made God responsible for both salvation and damnation. Wesley, in his search for a more convincing formula, dealt with both problems.

29.

Father, whose everlasting love
Thy only Son for sinners gave,
Whose grace to all did freely move,
And sent him down the world to save;

Help us thy mercy to extol,
Immense, unfathomed, unconfined;
To praise the Lamb who died for all,
The general Saviour of mankind.

Thy undistinguishing regard
Was cast on Adam's fallen race;
For all thou hast in Christ prepared
Sufficient, sovereign, saving grace.

The world he suffered to redeem;
For all he hath the atonement made;
For those that will not come to him
The ransom of his life was paid.

Why then, thou universal Love,
Should any of thy grace despair?
To all, to all, thy bowels move,
But straitened in our own we are.

Arise, O God, maintain thy cause!
The fullness of the Gentiles call;
Lift up the standard of thy cross,
And all shall own thy diedst for all.

Source: *A Collection of Hymns for the Use of the People Called Methodists*, No. 39, 1877 Edition.

In the first case, Wesley took great care to define what it meant to be 'fallen'. In our natural state we may well be socially responsible and even 'moral', judged by the world's standards. It is only in relation to God that we are 'totally depraved'. Before him, even our best actions are sinful, because they are not, in Wesley's words, 'done as God hath willed and commanded them to be done'.[5]

The second problem, the apparent denial of human freedom reflected in the Calvinist doctrine of predestination, was dealt with by Wesley's appeal to reason, experience, and what he called 'the clearest ideas we have of the divine nature and perfection'. This is illustrated by the next extract [30], part of an early letter which Wesley wrote to his mother Susanna.

30. What, then, shall I say of Predestination? An everlasting purpose of God to deliver some from damnation does, I suppose, exclude all from that deliverance who are not chosen. And if it was inevitably decreed from eternity that such a determinate part of mankind should be saved, and none beside them, a vast majority of the world were only born to eternal death, without so much as a possibility of avoiding it. How is this consistent with either the Divine Justice or Mercy? Is it merciful to ordain a creature to everlasting misery? Is it just to punish man for crimes which he could not but commit? How is man, if necessarily determined to one way of acting, a free agent? To lie under either a physical or a moral necessity is entirely repugnant to human liberty. But that God should be the author of sin and injustice (which must, I think, be the consequence of maintaining this opinion) is a contradiction to the clearest ideas we have of the divine nature and perfection.

Source: J. Wesley, Letters, Vol. 1, pp. 22–23, 29 July 1725.

We should note here that Wesley took great care not to oversimplify the way in which he defined 'sin'. He saw it as a condition, not merely a series of actions, because he believed that even our best deeds are tainted. Of course, not *all* our actions are sinful in quite the same sense, for we may be affected by illness or some other indisposition which can make us behave in a regrettable manner. Ignorance may also cause us to make mistakes in our genuine love and service of God. For instance, picture a very young child presenting her mother with a bunch of flowers which have been picked with loving care from the garden. The mother looks past her little daughter's smiling face to a trail of muddy footprints on the carpet. The child's blissful ignorance of the extra work she has made for her mother might not, in some people's eyes, be an excuse for her thoughtlessness. We are, however, thinking of a *very* young child, and her action, motivated by good intentions, can hardly be put in the same category as, for example, the sin of anger or pride.

Wesley accepted the biblical view of the Fall, in that though humanity is created in the image of God, the image has become distorted by our self-will. The image has not been shattered beyond repair, however, and no one is damned because of Adam's sin alone.

Otherwise, what hope would there be for any of us? Rather, the image of God in humanity has been distorted, and the Fall has damaged our relationship with God. Wesley held that salvation had to restore both the image *and* the relationship, and be a process in which we can take an active part. He believed neither that the Fall is completely the result of Adam's sin nor that original sin is completely our responsibility. This may be difficult for us to grasp, but Wesley was striking a balance between extremes, and the middle ground is often more difficult to define and defend.

While accepting and preaching the doctrine of the Fall and Original Sin, therefore, Wesley introduced an important modification – that of the prevenient grace of God.

Prevenient grace

Thy undistinguishing regard
Was cast on Adam's fallen race;
For all thou hast in Christ prepared
Sufficient, sovereign, saving grace.

Wesley's teaching on this subject was one of his most important contributions to the Protestant theology. We have already remarked upon his acute perception of the implications of certain theological positions and his desire to avoid extremes of doctrine. The same approach can be seen at this point. He modified the accepted notions of Original Sin and The Fall by the prominence he gave to the *prevenient* grace of God. It was unreasonable, he held, to saddle the whole of humanity with Adam's guilt. No one was finally damned unless he or she elected to be so.[6] The Swedish theologian, Harald Lindström, has summed up Wesley's stress on prevenient grace by saying that he 'is trying to combine the idea of personal responsibility and personal co-operation, where man's eternal destiny is at stake, with a conception of the situation of natural man which emphasizes the idea of saving grace.'[7]

There are two classic ways of viewing the human situation which have been termed, after their respective advocates, 'Augustinian pessimism' and 'Pelagian optimism'.[8] Wesley could accept neither as it stood.

'Augustinian pessimism' maintained, in essence, that we are all doomed to sin. Whatever we do is tainted, because we can do nothing right of ourselves. God therefore has to do *everything* for us. This view led inevitably to a doctrine of election – that some are predestined to be saved and some to be damned – and came to be connected with Antinomian teaching. Antinomianism (literally: 'against the law') regarded salvation as something that could only be achieved by faith. 'Works' or good behaviour, therefore, were not of primary importance. Indeed, placing the emphasis entirely upon God could have the effect of playing down the social aspects of the gospel and minimizing the importance of obedient service.

'Pelagian optimism', on the other hand, while acknowledging that there is a tendency within each of us to sin and that we need help, affirmed that each person has free will. At best, it could be interpreted as co-operation with God. At its worst, it saw humanity as being capable of saving itself by its own efforts. Taken to its extreme but logical conclusion, this doctrine could make the need for a Saviour redundant. This view came to be connected with Latitudinarian-ism,[9] which could lead to the danger of 'salvation by works' or of Christianity becoming really no more than a system of ethics.

A useful illustration of the need to preserve a balanced approach can be found in the parable of the Prodigal Son. On the one hand, we have the father running out to meet his son before he actually reaches home; on the other, we have the son himself coming to his senses and making up his mind to go back to his father. There need not be an unresolved tension here. There will always be a close relationship between divine and human initiative, and both are important. Yet there remains an essential paradox, salvation coming ultimately from God's grace, yet intimately involving us as individuals.

Wesley was very much aware of the dangers that the two extreme positions outlined above might create, and instead offered a third option – *prevenient grace*. In his sermon *What is Man?*, Wesley insists that we

have 'not only a house of clay, but an immortal spirit; a spirit made in the image of God'.[10] In such a spirit God has implanted 'prevenient grace'. This term describes the way in which God anticipates any move which we might make towards him, by giving of himself to us first. Another way of explaining it is to say that there has been given to every human being a capacity for entering into a relationship of love with God. It is therefore intrinsic to human nature. Wesley sometimes referred to it as 'preventing grace' ('preventing' having the original meaning of 'going before', not in the quite different sense in which we would use the word today) or 'natural conscience'. No person is totally depraved, he asserted, because God bestows grace to every human being at birth – hence the word 'prevenient' which, like 'preventing', literally means 'going before'. In his sermon 'On Working out our own Salvation' he affirmed that 'no man living is entirely destitute of . . . Preventing Grace', and added that 'every man has a greater or less measure of this'.[11] The next document [31] is a passage from this sermon, in which Wesley explains his thinking.

---

31. . . . it is only God that must quicken us; for we cannot quicken our own souls. For allowing that all the souls of men are dead in sin by *nature*, this excuses none, seeing there is no man that is in a state of mere nature: there is no man, unless he has quenched the Spirit, that is wholly void of the grace of God. No man living is entirely destitute of what is vulgarly called *Natural Conscience*. But this is not natural: it is more properly termed, *Preventing Grace*. Every man has a greater or less measure of this, which waiteth not for the call of man. Everyone has, sooner or later, good desires, although the generality of men stifle them before they can strike deep root, or produce any considerable fruit. Every one has some measure of that light, some faint glimmering ray, which, sooner or later, more or less, enlightens every man that cometh into the world. And every one unless he be one of the small number, whose conscience is seared as with a hot iron, feels more or less uneasy when he acts contrary to the light of his own conscience. So that no man sins because he has not grace, but because he does not use the grace which he hath.

Therefore, in as much as God works in you, you are now able to work out your own salvation . . . It is possible for you, to *love God, because he has first loved us*, and to *walk in love*, after the pattern of our great Master.

Source: J. Wesley, *Sermons*, Vol. 5, pp. 110–111.

Therefore, Wesley showed, we are able to co-operate with God *responsively*. The individual shares responsively in his or her own salvation, but the response is in the form of non-resistance to the working of prevenient grace initiated by God. We cannot be said to respond *responsibly*, as this would place too great an emphasis on our own efforts. Wesley thus preserved a middle course between human and divine initiative in the work of salvation.

One might ask, however, how Wesley could reconcile this free offer of salvation with the fact that many people have never had the gospel preached to them. In a letter to Thomas Whitehead in February 1748 he went some way to answering this point:

> The benefit of the death of Christ is not only extended to such as have the distinct knowledge of his death and sufferings, but even unto those who are inevitably excluded from this knowledge. Even these may be partakers of the benefit of his death . . .[12]

Wesley thus implies that those in this position will be judged by their response to the grace with which God works within them in a hidden and mysterious way. It is not a complete answer, of course, but an honest one, and shows Wesley's readiness to deal with the searching questions which were inevitably put to him.

Justification

> *Plenteous he is in truth and grace;*
> *He wills that all the fallen race*
>   *Should turn, repent, and live;*
> *His pardoning grace for all is free;*
> *Transgression, sin, iniquity,*
>   *He freely doth forgive.*

Prevenient Grace brings people to an awareness of their true condition, to a feeling of remorse and to a realization of the need to repent. This is the condition which is necessary before justification can take place.

For Wesley, repentance was far more than mere remorse. Indeed, in his sermon 'The Repentance of Believers' he describes it as 'the death of our working' and as 'a conviction of our utter sinfulness, and guiltiness, and helplessness'.[13] Moreover, he considered that believers needed to repent even after their conversion experience and, as he grew older, paid increasing attention to repentance as the 'necessary condition' of faith.[14] The reason for this is clear — stress on faith apart from repentance could appear to cheapen grace — but it led to a certain ambiguity in Wesley's statements on the issue.[15]

Justification, which is the next major stage in Wesley's 'Order of Salvation', is in some ways the doctrine that he expounded with the greatest clarity. Having accomplished the 'death of our working' which God has initiated by his prevenient grace, the climax is reached with our justification. In his sermon 'Justification by Faith', Wesley summed this up in a nutshell as 'pardon, the forgiveness of sins',[16] and in another sermon entitled 'Salvation by Faith', he described it as 'a deliverance from guilt and punishment, by the atonement of Christ . . . and a deliverance from the power of sin, through Christ formed in his heart'.[17] For Wesley, justification is totally a gift from God, and therefore can never be earned, still less deserved. It is by faith and faith alone that the sinner is justified. The relationship with God, previously broken by sin, is thus restored.

Whether the conversion was instantaneous or gradual, Wesley insisted that the convert was aware of the change in his or her heart. He was, however, surprised to find that instantaneous conversion was not only very common, but also more than adequately supported by scripture! This can be seen from our next extract [32], which is part of a conversation which Wesley had with Peter Böhler just prior to his Aldersgate experience.

This 'sure trust and confidence that Christ died for *my* sins, that He loved *me*, and gave himself for *me*', was Wesley's own joyful testimony to the prelude to what he termed 'New Birth', to which we shall now turn.

32. Sat. 22. – I met Peter Böhler once more. I had now no objection to what he said of the nature of faith: namely, that it is (to use the words of our Church) 'a sure trust and confidence which a man hath in God, that through the merits of Christ his sins are forgiven, and he reconciled to the favour of God.' Neither could I deny either the happiness or holiness which he described, as fruits of this living faith. 'The Spirit itself beareth witness with our spirit that we are the children of God;' and, 'He that believeth hath the witness in himself,' fully convinced me of the former: as 'Whatsoever is born of God, doth not commit sin;' and, 'Whosoever believeth is born of God,' did of the latter. But I could not comprehend what he spoke of an instantaneous work. I could not understand how this faith should be given in a moment; how a man could at once be thus turned from darkness to light, from sin and misery to righteousness and joy in the Holy Ghost. I searched the Scriptures again, touching this very thing, particularly the Acts of the Apostles; but, to my utter astonishment, found scarce any instances there of other than instantaneous conversions; scarce any so slow as that of St Paul, who was three days in the pangs of the new birth. I had but one retreat left; namely, 'Thus I grant, God wrought in the first ages of Christianity; but the times are changed. What reason have I to believe He works in the same manner now?'

But on Sunday, 23, I was beat out of this retreat too, by the concurring evidence of several living witnesses ... Here ended my disputing.

Source: J. Wesley, *Journal*, 22 April 1738.

The new birth

All things are possible to God,
  To Christ, the power of God in man,
To me, when I am all renewed,
  When I in Christ am formed again,
And witness, from all sin set free,
  All things are possible to me.

Whereas justification can be seen as the action of God through Christ on our behalf, the 'New Birth' is the beginning of the individual's new life in Christ. As we have seen, Wesley believed that in the Fall, sin has broken our relationship with God and distorted his image within us. Therefore salvation must involve the restoration of both relationship and image. Justification brings about a *relative* change in us because God treats us as though we were righteous and so restores our relationship with him. The 'New Birth' sees the beginning of a *real* change in the believer.

In one of his sermons that is not often quoted, 'The Great Privilege of Those that are Born of God', Wesley wrote that:

> Justification implies only a relative, the new birth a real, change. God in justifying us does something *for* us; in begetting us again, He does the work *in* us! [18]

In other words, the 'faith of a servant' has been replaced by the 'faith of a son', as Wesley himself described in his sermon on 'The New Birth' [33]. In it he uses the analogy of a baby's development to illustrate the change that occurs in the heart of a new convert.

33. A man may be 'born from above, born of God, born of the Spirit:' in a manner which bears a very near analogy to the natural birth.

Before a child is born into the world ... he has no knowledge of any of the things of the world, or any natural understanding ... It is only when a man is born, that we say, he begins to live. For as soon as he is born, he begins to see the light, and the various objects with which he is encompassed. His ears are then opened, and he hears the sounds which successively strike upon them. At the same time, all the other organs of sense begin to be exercised upon their proper objects. He likewise breathes and lives in a manner wholly different from what he did before. How exactly doth the parallel hold, in all these instances? While a man is in a mere natural state, before he is born of God, he has, in a spiritual sense, eyes and sees not ... ears, but hears not ... His other spiritual senses are all locked up; he is in the same condition as if he had them not. Hence he has no knowledge of God ... Therefore, though he is a living man, he is a dead Christian. But as soon as he is born of God, there is a total change in all these particulars. The 'eyes' of his understanding are opened' ... and 'he sees the light of the glory of God' ... His ears being opened, he is now capable of hearing the inward voice of God, saying, 'Be of good cheer, thy sins are forgiven thee: go and sin no more.' ... He 'feels in his heart ... the mighty working of the Spirit of God' ... He feels, he is conscious of a 'peace which passeth all understanding' ... and all his spiritual senses are then exercised to discern spiritual good and evil ... And now he may be properly said to *live*: God having quickened him by his Spirit, he is alive to God through Jesus Christ.

Source: J. Wesley, *Sermons*, Vol. 1, pp. 332–334.

In this experience of new birth, Wesley believed, the image of God which was lost in the Fall, now began to be restored. The process of this restoration is essentially a mystery, but its decisive beginning is important in two respects: it is necessary for growth in holiness and the key to present happiness. Inward renewal leads to spiritual peace and fulfilment. Furthermore, Wesley saw three characteristic marks of the new birth: faith, hope and love. Having being freed from the power of sin by faith, the Christian is given hope for the future and displays an ever-increasing love for both God and neighbour.

But what if a person sins *after* experiencing new birth? On this issue, Wesley shifted his position over the years. In his sermon 'The Marks of the New Birth', he seemed to be denying the possibility, claiming that 'ye are now dead to trespasses and sins', and that the new Christian 'cannot commit sin because he is born of God'.[19] However, as time went on he did admit that

it was possible for a person still to sin after being reborn, but maintained that sin no longer had the same power over him as before the new birth. In a later sermon entitled 'On Sin in Believers', Wesley explains that the Christian, though freed from the power of sin, still has to wrestle with a natural tendency to err from God's ways [34].

Sanctification

> *Thy sanctifying Spirit pour*
> *To quench my thirst and make me clean;*
> *Now, Father, let the gracious shower*
> *Descend, and make me pure from sin.*

Put briefly, sanctification may be said to be the gradual maturing of the believer following his or her new birth. In a Christian's pilgrimage of faith, Wesley saw that 'it is by slow degrees that he . . . grows to the full measure of the stature of Christ'.[20] This came to be expressed in his doctrine of 'sanctification', which depicted a *real* change in the life of the convert – not merely a relative one – and a continual growth in grace. Wesley wrote that 'Faith is a means in order to love, just as love is in order to goodness, just as goodness is in order to happiness', which illustrates the highly optimistic and dynamic picture of the future that he saw open to every human being.

What Wesley was doing was to take the teaching of Martin Luther further. Luther had reacted to the old attitudes, which seemed to suggest that salvation was obtainable by 'works', by laying an inordinate stress upon justification, almost making it an end in itself. Wesley, on the other hand, saw that justification was only part of a longer process in which God's image in the individual could be restored. For Wesley, faith was indeed the key to unlock the door to salvation. We have noted that it produced a new relationship with God – a relative change – within which a growth in grace – a real change – could occur. Sanctification was thus part of a true pilgrimage, the goal being Christian Perfection, which Wesley sometimes termed 'entire sanctification', or 'perfect love'.

---

34. The sum of all is this. There are in every person, even after he is justified, two contrary principles, nature and grace, termed by St Paul, the *flesh* and the *spirit*. Hence altho' even babes in Christ are *sanctified*, yet it is only in part. In a degree, according to the measure of their faith, they are spiritual: yet in a degree they are carnal. Accordingly, believers are continually exhorted to watch against the flesh, as well as the world and the devil. And to this agrees the constant experience of the children of God. While they feel this witness in themselves, they feel a will not wholly resigned to the will of God. They know they are in him, and yet find a heart ready to depart from him . . . The contrary doctrine is wholly new: never heard of in the church of Christ, from the time of his coming into the world, till the time of Count Zinzendorf.

Let us therefore, hold fast the sound doctrine 'once delivered to the saints', and delivered down by them with the written word to all succeeding generations: that altho' we are renewed, cleansed, purified, sanctified, the moment we truly believe in Christ, yet we are not then renewed, cleansed, purified altogether: but the flesh, the evil nature still *remains* (tho' subdued) and wars *against* the Spirit. So much the more, let us use all diligence in 'fighting the good fight of faith'. So much the more earnestly let us *watch and pray*, against the enemy within . . .

Source: J. Wesley, *Sermons*, Vol. 1, pp. 205–6.

Christian perfection

Finish then thy new creation,
  Pure and spotless let us be;
Let us see they great salvation,
  Perfectly restored in thee;
Changed from glory into glory,
  Till in heaven we take our place,
Till we cast our crowns before thee,
  Lost in wonder, love, and praise.

Perfection was the 'goal' of Wesley's 'Order of Salvation', but it could easily be misunderstood, and was! If he had encountered problems with the doctrines so far outlined, in this area he entered a veritable minefield. Christ's words in his Sermon on the Mount – 'You must therefore be perfect . . .' – have caused much heart-searching for Christians from that day to this. Is it actually possible for the ordinary Christian man or woman to attain such a state?

When Wesley was writing, difficulties generally arose from confusion over definitions, which he strove to clarify. An individual cannot be free from sin in its absolute sense, yet can be free from sin if it is defined as 'conscious separation from God'. Similarly, Christian perfection in terms of perfect conformity to the will of God is clearly inconceivable, but it is within the bounds of possibility for a person to live in a perfect relationship with God – or, as St Paul so frequently put it, to be 'in Christ'. Wesley never said that anyone could reach a state of 'sinless perfection'. 'Perfection', in the sense in which Wesley used it, meant 'an unbroken relationship with God'.[21] In the extract from his *An Earnest Appeal to Men of Reason and Religion* [35], Wesley explains how he understands the term 'Christian Perfection'.

One can see why Wesley's opponents accused him of abandoning the cherished tenets of the Reformation tradition,[22] but this was unfair. What Wesley was doing was removing an over-emphasis upon justification alone, and putting it into the context of the whole process of salvation. It was not, therefore, perfection in knowledge or complete freedom from human

---

35. Have you not another objection nearly allied to this, namely, that we preach perfection? True, but what perfection? The term you cannot object to, because it is scriptural. All the difficulty is to fix the meaning of it according to the Word of God. And this we have done again and again, declaring to all the world that Christian perfection does not imply an exemption from ignorance, or mistake, or infirmities, or temptations, but that it does imply the being so crucified with Christ as to be able to testify, '*I live not, but Christ liveth in me,*' and '*hath purified my heart by faith.*' It does imply '*the casting down of every high thing that exalted itself against the knowledge of God and bringing into captivity every thought to the obedience of Christ*' [cf. 2 Cor. 10:5]. It does imply '*the being holy as he that hath called us is holy, in all manner of conversation*' [I Peter 1:15], and, in a word, '*the loving the Lord our God with all our heart and serving him with all our strength*' [cf. Mark 12.33].

Now, is it possible for any who believe the Scripture to deny one tittle of this? You cannot. You dare not. You would not for the world. You know it is the pure Word of God. And this is the whole of what we preach. This is the height and depth of what we (with St Paul) call perfection: a state of soul devoutly to be wished by all who have tasted of the love of God . . .

Source: J. Wesley, *An Earnest Appeal to Men of Reason and Religion*, pp. 21–22.

---

mistakes, infirmities or temptation – 'involuntary sins'. Rather, it was perfect conformity to God's will and fellowship with him. The doctrine did cause some confusion, nonetheless. One of Wesley's lay preachers, Thomas Maxfield, took perfection too literally and had to be sharply reminded what it was *not*.[23] The fact that Wesley produced no less than three treatises on the subject of perfection bears witness both to its importance in his thinking, and to the many misunderstandings that it caused.

Wesley admitted that a person could fall from grace, but he also asserted that this blissful state could be recovered. In this, he parted company with Luther and even more with Calvin, who saw justification as a 'once and for all' event. These are fine but important distinctions which Wesley took great care to make clear, as we can see from the extract on the opposite page [36], which is taken from his sermon on 'Christian Perfection'.

36. In the first place, I shall endeavour to show, in what sense Christians are *not perfect*. And both from experience and Scripture it appears, first, that they are not perfect in knowledge: they are not *so* perfect in this life as to be free from ignorance ... Nor, secondly, from mistake; which indeed is almost an unavoidable consequence of it, seeing those who 'know but in part' are ever liable to err touching the things which they know not ... Hence, even the children of God are not agreed as to the interpretation of many places in holy writ, nor is their difference of opinion any proof that they are not the children of God ... We may, thirdly, add, nor from infirmities ... I mean hereby, not only those which are properly termed *bodily infirmities*, but all those inward or outward imperfections which are not of a moral nature ... Nor can we expect till then to be wholly free from temptation. Such perfection belongeth not to this life ...

Christian perfection, therefore does not imply ... an exemption either from ignorance, or mistake, or infirmities, or temptations. Indeed, it is only another term for holiness ...

In what sense, then, are Christians perfect? ... The very least which can be implied in these words, is, that the persons spoken of therein, namely real Christians, or believers in Christ, are made free from outward sin ... Indeed it is said, this means only, He sinneth not *wilfully*; or he doth not commit sin *habitually* ... secondly, to be freed from evil thoughts and evil tempers ...

Every one of these can say with St Paul, 'I am crucified with Christ: nevertheless I live; yet not I, but Christ liveth in me.' – words that manifestly describe a deliverance from inward as well as outward sin ... It remains, then, that Christians are saved in this world from all sin, from all unrighteousness; that they are now in such a sense perfect, as not to commit sin, and to be freed from evil thoughts and evil tempers ...'

Source: J. Wesley, *Sermons*, Vol. 3, pp. 4–27.

We can thus summarize Wesley's teaching in the following way.

Christian Perfection can be experienced in this life, in a Christian's relationship with God and with other people. It was necessarily a 'limited' perfection, as we have noted above. Wesley never gave up the ideal of sinlessness, though he *never* used the term 'sinless perfection'. He never claimed it for himself, but did cite others – for instance, John Fletcher – as examples. It could be lost, but equally it could be regained. It could be both instantaneous and gradual, in that the initial experience of a perfect relationship with God

always had to be sustained and built upon as part of a continual process. The essence of Christian Perfection, for Wesley, was perfect love. Holiness of heart must necessarily be accompanied by holiness of *life*.

In this respect, Wesley was guarding against spiritual introspection. He never wavered from his belief that inward holiness is inextricably bound up with service to others. A verse from one of his hymns illustrates this concern:

> Inflame our hearts with perfect love,
>   In us the work of faith fulfil;
> So not heaven's host shall swifter move
>   Than we on earth, to do thy will.

Assurance

> *Wherefore, in never ceasing prayer,*
> *My soul to thy continual care*
>   *I faithfully commend;*
> *Assured that thou through life shalt save,*
> *And show thyself beyond the grave*
>   *My everlasting friend.*

We come finally to the doctrine of Assurance, which forms a natural conclusion to Wesley's 'Order of Salvation'. It brings together three basic themes: God's word to us; Christ's work for us on the cross; the Spirit's witness within us. Wesley saw the first two as objective, gifts of God which do not depend on our response. The third, however, depends on our experience – on our response to the first two.

Wesley firmly believed that a Christian could have an assurance of present salvation. This was something very different from the Calvinist conviction of 'once saved, always saved'. It was rather a continual awareness of our present spiritual condition, and avoided the dangers of 'quietism' into which he felt many of the Moravians had slipped. 'Quietism' – or 'stillness', as it was sometimes termed – was a kind of spirituality which minimized human effort and responsibility, placing the emphasis upon the complete self-abandonment of the individual to God. Wesley would have nothing to do with this passive style of religious life.

The origins of Wesley's emphasis upon assurance

are not, as we might imagine, to be found in the Aldersgate Street experience. He was aware of the question of assurance long before. We find him writing on the subject, for example, in an early letter to his mother, in which he was very critical of the views which Dr Jeremy Taylor had put forward in his book *Of Living and Dying*. Taylor was trying to guard against any form of 'easy' salvation, but Wesley thought that he had gone too far in his argument [37].

---

37. In the ninth section of the fourth chapter he says:

'. . . A true penitent must all the days of his life pray for pardon and never think the work completed till he dies. Whether God has forgiven us or no we know not, therefore still be sorrowful for ever having sinned.'

I take the more notice of this last sentence, because it seems to contradict his own words in the next section, where he says that by the Lord's Supper all the members are united to one another and to Christ the head: The Holy Ghost confers on us the graces we pray for, and our souls receive into them the seeds of an immortal nature. Now, surely these graces are not of so little force, as that we can't perceive whether we have them or no; and if we dwell in Christ, and Christ in us, which he will not do till we are regenerate, certainly we must be sensible of it. If his opinion be true, I must own I have always been in great error; for I imagined that when I communicated worthily, i.e. with faith, humility, and thankfulness, my preceding sins were *ipso facto* forgiven me. I mean, so forgiven that, unless I fell into them again, I might be secure of their ever rising in judgement against me at least in the other world. But if we can never have any certainty of our being in a state of salvation, good reason it is that every moment should be spent not in joy but fear and trembling; and then undoubtedly in this life WE ARE of all men most miserable!

Source: J. Wesley, *Letters*, Vol. 1, pp. 19–20, 18 June 1725.

Wesley was steering a careful course between the two extremes of constant doubt and complacency. He also showed that it was possible for a Christian to have a *present* assurance and a *future* hope. 'The holiest men still need Christ,' he argued,[24] since perfection invariably was a gradual process, and it 'is a long time, even many years, before sin is destroyed'.[25] This future hope will always be present by virtue of the dynamic way in which Wesley saw the Christian faith.

In other words, we may be assured of true forgiveness in this life, yet hope that our growth in grace will be consummated in heaven. Wesley, therefore, was being quite consistent when he wrote that the believer could share in 'not barely a future happy state in heaven, but a state to be enjoyed on earth'.[26]

Summary

Careful study of Wesley's 'Order of Salvation' reveals certain tensions and ambiguities. They include that between divine initiative (of the Good Shepherd) and human response (for example, in the Prodigal Son); between 'Augustinian pessimism' and 'Pelagian optimism', faith and works, personal salvation and social righteousness, present assurance and future hope. Wesley struck a balance between the Reformer's preoccupation with faith alone, and the Roman Catholic perceived tendency to give undue weight to merit and works. In this, he was very much a child of the Enlightenment, reconciling reason and revelation.

We may note finally that throughout his writings, Wesley made remarkably few references to Hell, despite acknowledging the desperate need to take sin seriously. This was because his theology was essentially optimistic, founded on the grace of God. We must remember, furthermore, that Wesley's doctrines were meant to be understood, believed, and above all, *lived*. The ultimate testimony to their validity is that they were recognizable, and capable of being followed by those who became his fellow believers.

For Discussion

1. How would you define 'sin'?
2. In what ways, in your experience, can men and women co-operate with God in their salvation?
3. What is the difference between remorse and repentance?
4. Do you think that Christ's words in his Sermon on the Mount, 'Be perfect, therefore, as your heavenly Father is perfect', are a command, or a promise?
5. How can a Christian display a sense of assurance without appearing to be arrogant?

6

The Growth of Methodism to Wesley's Death

By Thine unerring Spirit led,
We shall not in the desert stray;
We shall not full direction need,
Nor miss our providential way;
As far from danger as from fear,
While love, almighty love, is near.

In 1738 John Wesley was thirty-five years of age. He was quite short in stature, being about five foot six inches tall, but had a striking presence. This was due partly to his prominent nose, firm jawline and rather piercing blue eyes, and partly to his general bearing. Leadership, as we have seen already, came naturally to him, but the streak of authoritarianism within him was tempered by a kindly benevolence and a degree of tolerance with which he has not always been credited. Portraits show him to be a neat, tidy man, who wore his hair long in contrast to the prevailing fashion for wigs. His appearance confirmed what was true of his life-style in general. He was indeed a methodical man, frugal, industrious, and possessed of seemingly limitless stamina. He could be a formidable opponent in debate, but his greatest gift lay perhaps in his ability to inspire and organize.

Charles Wesley's portraits reveal a very different character. Like his brother, he was not a tall man, but had rounder facial features that hinted at a softer personality. His more emotional nature has already been commented upon. However, though he lacked John's extraordinary energy, he had great courage and enjoyed considerable success as a preacher, even under difficult circumstances. In his private life he was spared his brother's matrimonial anguish. Whereas John's marriage to Molly Vazeille was little short of disastrous,[1] Charles enjoyed a happy and settled life with Sarah Gwynne, whom he married in 1749. Thereafter he spent less time travelling than John, being content to live first in Bristol and from 1771 in London.

The Wesley brothers now became the centre of what has been called 'the Methodist Revival', the story of which can be divided roughly into three phases. The years 1739 to 1749 saw the initial spread of the revival, which was characterized by opposition of varying kinds. The next thirty years was a period of country-wide expansion. Finally, the decade from 1781 to 1791 witnessed certain key developments which accelerated the process by which Methodism became a separate denomination. In this chapter we shall focus our attention on some of the main features of early Methodism, and conclude with a rather more detailed look at the way in which the break with the Church of England came about.

Shortly after his experience at Aldersgate Street, John Wesley visited the Moravian communities at Marienborn and Herrnhut[2] in Germany. He had long wished to do so, and though critical of the Moravians in some respects,[3] was deeply impressed by those he met. 'I would gladly have spent my life here,' he wrote on 12 August. Wesley learned a great deal, and he was later to adapt some of the Moravian patterns of organization for his own purposes. He returned to England on 17 September 1738 much invigorated, and wrote in his journal, 'I began again to declare in my own country the glad tidings of salvation.'

Perhaps at this stage we should say something about George Whitefield, who has been referred to earlier in connection with the Holy Club. It was Whitefield who really initiated the Methodist revival. Deeply influenced by his contact with the Wesleys, Whitefield had an experience in 1735 which he described as 'a new birth'. After his ordination he went to Georgia, spending most of the time putting his natural talent as a preacher to good use. After his return to England, he began large open-air meetings which attracted the same degree of support (and opposition) as John Wesley's were to do, though his greatest successes came probably in Scotland and South Wales. Although there are stories of people collapsing in tears during his sermons, and on one occasion even being reduced to convulsions, most such accounts are grossly exaggerated. Whitefield was no mere demagogue, and criticisms of him as a 'hit and run' preacher are unfair. In 1741 he set up a chapel at Moorfields in Bristol and later, through the patronage of Selina, Countess of Huntingdon, opened a Tabernacle in Tottenham Court Road in London. In the end he virtually burned himself out, and died in 1770 at the relatively early age of fifty-six.

Undoubtedly Whitefield was the most striking orator of the revival, but his long-term impact was less than that of the Wesleys for two basic reasons. First, he lacked John Wesley's powers of organization and administration. Secondly, his over-rigid theology with its emphasis on the doctrine of predestination had less lasting appeal than the Wesleys' Arminianism with its message of universal salvation.[4] Whitefield remained a firm friend of the Wesleys notwithstanding their theological differences, and it was Whitefield's example and encouragement that led John to embark on open-air preaching.

Preaching and preachers

Give the pure word of general grace,
And great shall be the preachers' crowd;
Preachers, who all the sinful race
Point to the all-atoning blood.

Open their mouth, and utterance give;
Give them a trumpet-voice, to call
On all mankind to turn and live,
Through faith in Him who died for all.

In 1739 George Whitefield invited John Wesley to join him in Bristol, where his open-air preaching had had a marked impact on the brutalized miners at the colliery at Kingswood. We may be surprised to learn that Wesley, despite all that happened later, was at first very reluctant to preach in the open air, as is shown by his own comments at the time [38].

> 38. In the evening I reached Bristol, and met Mr Whitefield there. I could scarce reconcile myself at first to this strange way of preaching in the fields, of which he set me an example on Sunday; having been all my life (till very lately) so tenacious of every point relating to decency and order, that I should have thought the saving of souls almost a sin, if it had not been done in a church.
>
> Sun. April 1. – In the evening (Mr Whitefield being gone) I begun expounding our Lord's Sermon on the Mount (one pretty remarkable precedent of field-preaching, though I suppose there were churches at that time also), to a little society which was accustomed to meet once or twice a week in Nicholas Street.
>
> Mon. 2. – At four in the afternoon, I submitted to be more vile, and proclaimed in the highways the glad tidings of salvation, speaking from a little eminence in a ground adjoining to the city, to about three thousand people . . .
>
> *Source*: J. Wesley, *Journal*, 31 March – 2 April 1739.

Indeed, he remained uneasy about engaging in it for the rest of his life. Although this may seem surprising, it is not so difficult to appreciate if we remember Wesley's background. He was an Oxford don who had had very mixed experiences in Georgia. Both his brothers expressed concern about his open-air preaching. As a high churchman, John himself had a built-in reverence for consecrated places of worship. In his view, they were the proper places to preach. It was not that open-air preaching was anything entirely new but in this case it was without invitation or permission from other Anglican clergy. We should also remember that anything contrary to the established nature of the Church of England at this time tended to be classified as 'dissent'. Therefore, Wesley's reluctance was quite understandable and his comment 'I submitted to be more vile', was an accurate summary of his feelings about the matter.

Wesley was no peddler of 'hellfire and damnation'. Rather, the impact of his sermons owed itself to the emphasis he placed on personal acceptance of God's forgiveness and love. This, of course, laid Wesley open to the charge of preaching what eighteenth-century ecclesiastics called 'experimental religion', or 'enthusiasm'. Whilst the second charge was unfounded, the first was undoubtedly true. Wesley's congregations, like Whitefield's, were often hearing for the first time in their lives a gospel which was for them personally, and his message came like a blast of fresh air.

The terms 'preachers', 'helpers' and 'assistants' may appear a little confusing at first. The first two terms initially meant virtually the same thing. John Wesley's 'helpers' could be either laymen or Anglican priests. Some laymen remained in their own locality to become what they are today – Local (lay) Preachers. Others travelled the country preaching, and in the process of time became identical with the full-time ministers, though they were only ordained at a much later date, as we shall see. The senior ordained 'helpers' came to be called 'assistants to Mr Wesley', and these were the forerunners of the present day Superintendents. All, however, came under the umbrella title of 'preachers'.

Wesley himself travelled between four and five thousand miles a year, initially on horseback and then, as he grew older, in a specially adapted coach. During his life he probably travelled a quarter of a million miles on horseback, and can lay fair claim to hold the world's record. Wesley's early helpers were notable characters, and fairly early on it became apparent that the work could not continue to expand if it were entrusted only to ordained clergymen. There had to be some control and discipline. The *Twelves Rules of a*

Helper [39] were therefore designed to maintain a balance and avoid the danger of preachers becoming either 'gentlemen' or undisciplined fanatics. The document is so interesting that it is quoted in full.

39. Q.3. What are the Rules of an Assistant?
A.1. Be diligent. Never be unemployed a moment, never be triflingly employed, never while away time; spend no more time at any place than is strictly necessary.
  2. Be serious. Let your motto be, 'holiness unto the Lord'. Avoid all lightness as you would avoid hell-fire, and laughing as you would cursing and swearing.
  3. Touch no woman. Be as loving as you will but hold your hands off 'em. Custom is nothing to us.
  4. Believe evil of no one. If you see it done, well. Else take heed how you credit it. Put the best construction on every thing. You know the judge is always supposed to be on the prisoner's side.
  5. Speak evil of no one, else your word especially would eat as doth a canker. Keep your thoughts within your own breast till you come to the person concerned.
  6. Tell everyone what you think wrong in him and that plainly and as soon as may be; else it will fester in your heart. Make all haste, therefore, to cast the fire out of your bosom.
  7. Do nothing 'as a gentleman'. You have no more to do with this character than with that of a dancing-master. You are the servant of all; therefore,
  8. Be ashamed of nothing but sin; not of fetching wood or drawing water, if time permits; not of cleaning your own shoes or your neighbour's.
  9. Take no money of any one. If they give you food when you are hungry or clothes when you need them, it is good. But not silver or gold. Let there be no pretence to say we grow rich by the gospel.
 10. Contract no debt without my knowledge.
 11. Be punctual: do everything exactly at the time. And, in general, do not mend our rules but keep them, not for wrath but for conscience' sake.
 12. Act in all things not according to your own will but as a son in the gospel. As such, it is your part to employ your time in the manner which we direct: partly in visiting the flock from house to house (the sick in particular); partly, in such a course of reading, meditation and prayer as we advise from time to time. Above all, if you labour with us in the Lord's vineyard, it is needful you should do that part of the work which we direct, at those times and places which we judge most for his glory.

Source: Minutes of First Annual Conference, Friday 29 June 1744.

These 'Rules' tell us much about the ethos of early Methodist preaching, and clearly bear Wesley's stamp. When they were published in 1753, the words were slightly amended, the most marked addition being the following instructions added as part of Rule 11:

> You have nothing to do but save souls. Therefore, spend and be spent in the work. Observe. It is not your business to preach so many times ... but to save as many souls as you can. Therefore, you will need all the sense you have, and to have your wits about you.

Wesley himself generally preached extempore, often for over an hour. His voice was clear and he could speak quite loudly when the occasion demanded – at one time to 12,000 people gathered in Gwennap Pit in Cornwall – and he used little of the flowery terminology that characterized Anglican preaching in the eighteenth century. Wesley's sermons started appearing in print from 1746 onwards. Reading them today requires a little more concentration than one would give twentieth-century devotional literature, but patience will be amply rewarded. We have to bear in mind that they were not always preached as they were written, and so have to imagine the effect that his spoken words had at the time. For the most part, the sermons we have in print are 'sermonic essays' written up after the event. Always, however, his clarity of thinking is as evident as his zeal to win others for Christ.

The story of Wesley's preachers is a fascinating one. John Fletcher, the closest of Wesley's friends, was perhaps the nearest to what Wesley considered to be an 'ideal Methodist preacher'. He spent most of his life as priest of the parish of Madeley in Shropshire, preaching and caring for his congregation in a devout and saintly manner. Others, like Howell Harris from Brecon, earned their reputations as accomplished lay preachers. The careers of such men as John Berridge, who began a startling revival at Everton in Bedfordshire, Vincent Perronet who exercised a scholarly pastoral ministry at Shoreham in Kent, William Grimshaw, who was the vicar of Haworth in Yorkshire, and many others, make absorbing reading. Some of the more detailed studies of Methodism to be found in the bibliography will give a much fuller picture than space allows here. We should also note that Wesley had many women helpers, including members of his own family. Their story is one which has only fairly recently received much attention from historians.[5] There were few women preachers at this stage, however, and whether women should preach or not, as we shall see in chapter 8, was to be one of the bones of contention in Methodism in the years following Wesley's death.

Opposition

> *What tho' a thousand hosts engage,*
>   *A thousand worlds, my soul to shake?*
> *I have a shield shall quell their rage,*
>   *And drive the alien armies back;*
> *Portrayed it bears a bleeding Lamb:*
> *I dare believe in Jesu's name.*

It was inevitable that Wesley and his followers should meet with opposition. Many Anglican clergy, especially the hierarchy, saw the early Methodist preachers as a threat. The Bishop of Bristol, Joseph Butler, was an early critic, and a rather disagreeable interview with Wesley served only to confirm Wesley's fears that Methodist meetings could not be accommodated within the Church of England's set up. Some Anglicans attacked Wesley simply because they were jealous of his success, though many had genuine, if misplaced, fears concerning the revival. Methodists seemed to be encouraging wild emotionalism amongst the common people; their doctrines appeared unsound; field-preaching and the growth of Methodist groups (or societies) were a challenge to church order and the authority of the regular clergy. Wesley, in other words, was 'rocking the boat'.

The story of Methodism in these early years was thus by no means a peaceful one. In addition to the hostile reactions of groups within the Church of

England, there were internal disagreements, notably the sharp theological differences with Whitefield. Wesley and his followers had to face a certain amount of popular opposition as well.

Much has been made of the violent reaction to Wesley and his preachers from unruly crowds. There were certainly frequent examples of mob violence. The early Methodists often went into areas where the civil authorities could exercise only minimal control. In the context of the eighteenth century, rioting was sometimes the only way in which popular feeling could be expressed, and in a land consisting mainly of isolated villages, outsiders tended to be viewed with great suspicion. At times, Methodist preachers even became the scapegoats for other causes of local grievance, and the Wesley brothers both experienced life-threatening moments. John's journal entry for 4 July 1745 [40] should not be regarded as a piece of exaggerated or sensational journalism, for incidents such as his brush with the mob in Falmouth were not uncommon.

---

40. *Thur.* 4. − I rode to Falmouth. About three in the afternoon I went to see a gentlewoman who had been long indisposed. Almost as soon as I was set down, the house was beset on all sides by an innumerable multitude of people. A louder or more confused noise could hardly be at the taking of a city by storm. At first Mrs B and her daughter endeavoured to quiet them. But it was labour lost. They might as well have attempted to still the raging of the sea . . . The rabble roared with all their throats, 'Bring out the Canorum! Where is the Canorum?' (an unmeaning word which the Cornish generally use instead of Methodist). No answer being given, they quickly forced open the outer door, and filled the passage . . .

Among those without, were the crews of some privateers, which were lately come into the harbour. Some of these, being angry at the slowness of the rest, thrust them away, and, coming up all together, set their shoulders to the inner door, and cried out, 'Avast, lads, avast!' Away went all the hinges at once, and the door fell back into the room. I stepped forward at once into the midst of them, and said, 'Here I am. Which of you has anything to say to me? To which of you have I done anything wrong?'

Source: J. Wesley, *Journal*, 4 July 1745.

At Falmouth, as in numerous other places where he was threatened, Wesley displayed great calm and courage. On that particular occasion he was able to speak to the crowd without interruption, and was permitted to go on his travels in peace. Even so, physical attacks, varying in extent from place to place, continued sporadically. But by the early 1750s violent opposition had virtually ceased.[6]

Societies, classes and connexion

> See, Jesu, thy disciples see,
>   The promised blessing give;
> Met in thy name, we look to thee,
>   Expecting to receive.
>
> Thee we expect, our faithful Lord,
>   Who in thy name are joined;
> We wait, according to thy word,
>   Thee in the midst to find.

Societies

In addition to organizing his preachers, Wesley built up a structure that would sustain Methodism's preaching ministry. It was here, perhaps, that his genius for invention and improvization can be most clearly seen. He was never afraid to borrow from others what might prove useful for his own purposes. At one of the Methodist Conferences recently, a speaker aptly summed up the picture by saying that, 'Methodism was handed down by God bit by bit as it was needed.' True indeed!

As we might expect, the first societies developed in Bristol. They were, initially, small groups who met weekly for worship and fellowship, prayer and instruction. They were never intended, of course, to be separate churches, and the meetings were carefully timed to avoid parish services. The word 'Society' was not new, having its origin in the previous century, and the early ones in Baldwin Street and Nicholas Street in Bristol were not originally Methodist Societies. The very first societies met in people's homes, but that soon changed. In a recent study, Rupert Davies has written that:

In the summer of 1739, Wesley purchased a piece of

land in the Horsefair in Bristol, and built the first 'New Room' there. This was to provide accommodation for both the Baldwin Street and the Nicholas Street societies, as well as for those who had been converted or strongly influenced by Whitefield and Wesley's preaching . . . It was on 11 July 1739, in the presence of Whitefield and Wesley, that the first distinctively Methodist Society was born . . .[7]

The New Room, standing in the heart of Bristol's shopping centre, has long been a 'Mecca' for Methodists worldwide. It has been preserved in its original state, complete with Wesley's own study and the small bedchambers used by the itinerant preachers. In fact, time spent at the New Room can give a better flavour of early Methodism than a visit even to Epworth, which has also become something of a tourist attraction over the years.

We should note that Wesley became increasingly unhappy with the Fetter Lane community in London, which had been established shortly after the Bristol societies. He felt that the members were straying towards 'quietism' – the kind of passive spirituality to which Moravian influence could lead. This was too much for Wesley, who, as we have seen, always tried to maintain a balance between theological extremes.

The classes

Interestingly, the classes had their origin in finance! Wesley had been wondering how best to care for the society members, since apart from a select few who met in 'Bands' (see below), they only met together in the weekly society meeting. It was actually a Captain Foy who suggested a system whereby members should contribute to the cost of the New Room, and from this, the practice began of the twelve 'class members' meeting together. However, raising money was not the primary purpose, as Wesley himself made clear – see the following two extracts from his journal – when he was in Bristol and London on 15 February and 25 March 1742 [41].

---

41. Mon. 15. – Many met together to consult on a proper method for discharging the public debt; and it was at length agreed: 1. That every member of the society, who was able, should contribute a penny a week. 2. That the whole society should be divided into little companies or classes, – about twelve in each class. And, 3. That one person in each class should receive the contribution of the rest, and bring it to the stewards, weekly . . .

Thurs. 25. – I appointed several earnest and sensible men to meet me, to whom I showed the great difficulty I had long found of knowing the people who desired to be under my care. After much discourse, they all agreed, there could be no better way to come to a sure, thorough knowledge of each person, than to divide them into classes, like those at Bristol, under the inspection of those in whom I could most confide. This was the origin of our classes in London, for which I can never sufficiently praise God; the unspeakable usefulness of the institution having ever since been more and more manifest.

Source: J. Wesley, *Journal*, 15 February and 25 March 1742.

The classes swiftly became a means whereby small groups could meet for Bible study, prayer and religious conversation. Their purpose was never seen as being merely administrative; rather, their most important function was pastoral and devotional. Wesley himself was quite ruthless at times when he visited local societies, and members who failed to take advantage of the worship and fellowship of the early Methodist groups were removed from the lists as 'ceased to meet'. However, the classes, with their informal and intimate style of functioning, were ideal for recruiting new members. And new members there were in plenty during Wesley's lifetime.

We earlier referred to the 'Bands'. These were smaller units, less widespread and much more elitist in terms of their membership and discipline. It may well have been here, in the detailed questions concerning sin and perfection which were regularly asked, that the structured questions originated which even today form the basis of so many of the agendas of Methodist meetings, especially the Local Preachers' Meeting. There was little that was fundamentally new in what he introduced, and with some justification he has been called the 'arch ecclesiastical extemporizer'.

The Connexion

As the revival spread across the country, Wesley saw the need to organize Methodists on a national as well as a local level. It was decided that the itinerant lay preachers should meet with the ordained ministers to consider 'what to teach, how to teach and what to do, i.e. how to regulate our doctrine, discipline and practice'.[8] The aim of the Conferences, as they were called, was to enable Wesley's assistants to advise him, though since he chaired the meetings, put the questions and took the minutes, it was clear who was in control! The remark made by Pawson, one of his most faithful supporters, that 'even the Pope himself never acted a part such as this' was an exaggeration, but even Wesley himself admitted to being somewhat autocratic. Over the years the number of laymen present at Conference increased from the original four in 1744 to forty-one by 1753. It was not until 1878 that a lay person was admitted who was not a preacher.

There were originally seven Circuits – London, Bristol, Cornwall, Evesham, Yorkshire (which included six other counties!), Newcastle and Wales – though the number grew as the eighteenth century wore on. Their task was to administer the spiritual feeding, teaching and guidance of the Methodist people. The first Quarterly Meeting, which resembled Conference at circuit level, dates from October 1748 and was held at Todmorden Edge. By the middle of the eighteenth century, therefore, much of the apparatus of what was to become the Methodist Church was in place.

Before we examine Methodism's relationship with the Church of England in Wesley's later years, we should note one area with which Wesley became involved and in which Methodism has retained a strong interest. This was education.

George Whitefield had founded a school for miners' sons at Kingswood in Bristol, and on his return to Georgia, it came under Wesley's care and control. The site was developed and a new school opened in 1748 for the sons of Methodists, particularly the itinerant preachers. Its traditions owed much to Wesley's own family upbringing and educational experiences, and as we might expect, the regime there placed heavy emphasis upon religious instruction, discipline and correction. Wesley's *A Plain Account of the People Called Methodists*, contained in a letter written in 1748 to Vincent Perronet, the vicar of Shoreham in Kent, is the most detailed description we possess of early Methodism. In the letter he expresses his concern for the educational welfare of children [42].

---

42. Another thing which had given me frequent concern was the case of abundance of children. Some their parents could not afford to put to school; so they remained like 'a wild ass's colt'. Others were sent to school, and learned at least to read and write; but they learned all kind of vice at the same time: so that it had been better for them to have been without their knowledge than to have bought it at so dear a price.

At length I determined to have them taught in my own house, that they might have the opportunity of learning to read, write, and cast accounts (if no more), without being under almost a necessity of learning Heathenism at the same time: And after several unsuccessful trials, I found two such Schoolmasters as I wanted; men of honesty and of sufficient knowledge, who had talents for, and their hearts in, the work.

They have now under their care near sixty children . . . A happy change was soon observed in the children, both with regard to their tempers and their behaviour . . . they were diligently instructed in the sound principles of religion, and earnestly exhorted to fear God and work out their own salvation.

Source: J. Wesley, *Letters*, Vol. II, pp. 308–309.

Wesley was not solely concerned with children's education. He saw the need for his preachers to be educated in all aspects of life, so that their work might be all the more effective. This partly accounts for the huge amount of material which Wesley himself had published, including his famous *Christian Library* which contained distillations of what Wesley considered to be important works of theological and devotional literature. It included writings from the Early Fathers, Roman Catholic theologians, English and European scholars. Needless to say, the extracts were carefully edited by Wesley himself. It appeared between 1749 and 1755, and provided his preachers with an invaluable resource.

Wesley's own books were designed to be small enough to carry, short enough to read, and cheap enough to buy – and they covered a wide range of topics, not merely those relating to theology or the Bible. He wrote on a huge number of issues. In his *Primitive Physic*,[9] probably the best known of his non-theological books, he supported the use of the new electrical machines for curing certain ailments. He wrote about politics, slavery, marriage, music and education – to name but a few areas – with a clarity and breadth of knowledge that seems remarkable to our specialized society today.

We now move on to look briefly at Methodism's relationship with its 'elder brother' – one might even say, 'foster parent' – the Anglican Church.

Relations with the Church of England

> *What mighty troubles hast Thou shown*
> *Thy feeble, tempted followers here!*
> *We have through fire and water gone,*
> *But saw Thee on the floods appear,*
> *But felt Thee present in the flame,*
> *And shouted our Deliverer's name.*

In 1784 Wesley said, 'I believe I shall not separate from the Church of England until my soul separates from my body', and three years later he stated that 'when the Methodists leave the Church, God will leave them'. To his life's end he affirmed his loyalty to the Church of England. However, Anglican criticism of Methodists – that, like all 'enthusiasts', they were disloyal, schismatic, and even encouraged heresy – only served to create among Methodists a sense of

being different. These feelings were perhaps heightened by the very inaccuracy of such indictments.

With the benefit of hindsight, we can see that it was becoming almost impossible for Methodism to continue as a kind of 'ginger group' within the Church of England. Wesley himself probably acknowledged in his heart that separation would come one day. It has been said that he was 'like a skilful rower who keeps his eyes on the shore whilst every stroke of his oars takes him farther away'.[10] However, neither side actively shunned the other. In 1766 Wesley warned his preachers not to absent themselves from Anglican worship more than twice a month, and *not* to end Methodist services with the Lord's Supper. He also insisted that Methodist services should not be held at the same time as Anglican ones, as can be seen by his Journal entry of 24 October 1787 [43].

---

43. Tues. 24. – I met the classes at Deptford, and was vehemently importuned to order the Sunday service in our room at the same time with that of the church. It is easy to see that this would be a formal separation from the Church. We fixed both our morning and evening service, all over England, at such hours as not to interfere with the Church; with this very design, – that those of the Church, if they chose it, might attend both the one and the other. But to fix it at the same hour, is obliging them to separate either from the Church or us; and this I judge to be not only inexpedient, but totally unlawful for me to do.

Source: J. Wesley, *Journal*, Tuesday 24 October 1787.

That was in 1787. But it was clear that, from the earliest days, relations with the Church of England would pose a problem. The Conference of 1747 had wrestled with these difficulties, as is shown in extract [44].

However, the law was being broken in a technical sense by the building of Methodist chapels. By and large Wesley had always sought to avoid the stigma of being dubbed a Dissenter, and the registration of preaching houses was delayed until 1787. In April 1777, when the foundation stone of New Chapel in City Road was laid, Wesley denied any break with the

44.

Q.2. Are not Methodists guilty of making such a schism?

A.   No more than rebellion or murder. They do not divide themselves at all from the living body of Christ. Let any prove it if they can.

Q.3. But do not they divide themselves from the Church of England?

A.   No. They hold communion therewith now in the same manner as they did twenty years ago, and hope to do so until their lives' end.

Q.4. You profess to obey both the governors and rules of the Church; yet in many instances you do not obey them. How is this consistent? Upon what principles do you act while you sometimes obey and sometimes not?

A.   It is entirely consistent. We act at all times on one plain, uniform principle: 'We will obey the rules and governors of the Church whenever we can, consistently with our duty to God. Whenever we cannot, we will quietly obey God rather than men.

Q.5. But why do you say you are thrust out of the Church? Has not every minister a right to dispose of his own church?

A.   He ought to have, but in fact he has not. A minister desires I should preach in his church, but the bishop forbids him. That bishop then injures him and thrusts me out of that church.

Source: Minutes of the Fourth Annual Conference, Wednesday 17 June 1747.

Church of England. Yet it was a place of worship with provision for a communion area, together with a burial ground. One cannot help feeling that many present on that occasion were aware of an inevitable trend.[11]

Three events in 1784 hastened the separation.

The first was the signing of the Deed of Declaration 28 February 1784. Wesley had originally hoped that Fletcher of Madeley would succeed him, but the latter was gravely ill, and died the following August. Charles Wesley was too old, and there was no single individual whom Wesley considered able to take on the mantle of leadership. It had to be the Conference itself. The Deed, to quote Maldwyn Edwards,

gave Methodism an independent legal status. The vital step had been taken to change a Society into a Church with its own executive body, its own doctrinal standards, its own connexional organization and discipline, its own ministry, and its own liturgical forms.[12]

The constitution of the 'Legal Hundred', as the appointed Conference was termed, virtually ensured the legal separation of Methodism after Wesley's death. By the Deed, subsequent Conferences had the legal authority to replace its members when they died, thus guaranteeing its continued existence.

The second major event in 1784 was the ordinations for America on 1 and 2 September. In 1783 the thirteen American colonies, who had declared their independence in 1776, were now finally free from British control. In common with many of his countrymen, Wesley saw the loss of the American colonies as a tragedy. He also realized that the disruption which the War of Independence caused had exacerbated problems which already faced Methodists in the New World. The first Methodist Society had been formed in 1766, and three years later three preachers were sent from Britain to help in the growing work. In 1771 they were joined by the most famous of all, Francis Asbury. By the time war ended in November 1782, there were over fifteen thousand American Methodists, most of whom sought a religious independence that would match their political freedom. Almost as soon as peace was declared, Wesley received a letter from one of the American Methodist preachers pleading for help.

What was Wesley to do? The Anglican clergy in America had, for the most part, been hopelessly compromised by the war, and many simply left the country. There had already been an acknowledged shortage of ordained ministers to administer the sacraments. The War of Independence merely made the need more acute. Wesley's appeal to the Bishop of London in 1780 to ordain ministers for America had been met with a blank refusal. The Bishop's response that there were 'three ministers in that country already', provoked an impassioned reaction. 'I mourn for poor America', Wesley concluded in his letter of reply.[13]

By 1784 Wesley's mind was made up. On 10 September his letter to 'Our brethren in America' explained the reasons for his decision [45]. It is interesting to note that the second paragraph of this excerpt reveals that, in addition to the obvious need that existed, Wesley's own reading helped his change of mind concerning the question of ordination.

---

45.   1. By a very uncommon train of providences many of the Provinces of North America are totally disjoined from their Mother Country and erected into Independent States. The English Government has no authority over them, either civil or ecclesiastical, any more than over the States of Holland. A civil authority is exercised over them, partly by the Congress, partly by the Provincial Assembles. But no one either exercises or claims any ecclesiastical authority at all. In this peculiar situation some thousands of the inhabitants of these States desire my advice; and in compliance with their desire I have drawn up a little sketch.

2. Lord King's *Account of the Primitive Church* convinced me many years ago that bishops and presbyters are the same order, and consequently have the same right to ordain. For many years I have been importuned from time to time to exercise this right by ordaining part of our travelling preachers. But I have still refused, not only for peace's sake, but because I was determined as little as possible to violate the established order of the National Church to which I belonged.

3. But the case is widely different between England and North America. Here there are bishops who have a legal jurisdiction: in America there are none, neither any parish ministers. So that for some hundred miles together there is none either to baptize or to administer the Lord's Supper . . .

4. I have accordingly appointed Dr Coke and Mr Francis Asbury to be Joint Superintendents over our brethren in North America; as also Richard Whatcoat and Thomas Vesey to act as elders among them . . .

Source: J. Wesley, *Letters*, Vol. 7, pp. 238–239.

The ordinations were duly carried out. Wesley had neither welcomed the decision nor avoided it. He concluded his letter by saying that 'if any one will point out a more rational and scriptural way of feeding and guiding these poor sheep in the wilderness, I will gladly embrace it. At present I cannot see any better method than that I have taken.'[14] It is somewhat ironic that when the American Methodists took episcopacy into their system, Wesley himself disapproved in no uncertain terms!

The third thing that accelerated the process of separation from the Church of England, was Wesley's revision of the Book of Common Prayer in 1784. It was published under the title *The Sunday Service of the Methodists in North America, with other occasional services*. Wesley had been approached in previous years by some of his own followers who wished to alter some aspects of Anglican liturgy. How far-reaching were the changes that Wesley eventually made has been the source of some debate.[15] However, it was a very important step, and one which Wesley carried out with the American situation in mind.

There were subsequent revisions of the book, though only in 1784 was there a reference to 'North America' in the title. This is interesting, because it is by no means clear how far Wesley intended it to be used in England. He certainly never planned that it should replace the Book of Common Prayer, but one has the feeling that he was fighting a losing battle. From 1788 the *Sunday Service* was permitted in Methodist preaching houses on Sunday mornings.

These three factors – the Deed of Declaration, the ordinations for America and the revision of the Prayer Book – simply accelerated a process that, by the 1780s had become inevitable. By 1791, the year of Wesley's death, separation was only a matter of time. Wesley himself had always maintained that he had only done what had to be done, as can be seen by his comments on the Conference of 1788 [46].

---

46. One of the most important points considered at this Conference, was that of leaving the Church. The sum of a long conversation was: 1. That, in a course of fifty years, we had neither premeditatedly nor willingly varied from it in one article either of doctrine or discipline. 2. That we were not yet conscious of varying from it in any point of doctrine. 3. That we have in a course of years, out of necessity, not choice, slowly and warily varied in some points of discipline, by preaching in the fields, by extempore prayer, by employing lay preachers, by forming and regulating societies, and by holding yearly Conferences. But we did none of these things till we were convinced we could no longer omit them, but at the peril of our souls.

Source: J. Wesley, *Journal*, 19 July 1788.

Whereas John Wesley saw separation as regrettable but ultimately unavoidable, Charles viewed the above events with great dismay. As early as 1755 he had expressed grave concern lest his brother be swayed by those who wished to leave the Church of England. He remained an evangelical high churchman to the end of his life, and any thoughts of separation from the church he loved filled him with dread. In August 1785 he wrote to his brother saying, 'When once you began ordaining in America, I knew, and you knew, that your preachers here would never rest till you ordained them.'[16] John replied by reaffirming his fidelity to the Church of England, 'from which I have no more desire to separate than I had fifty years ago'. The rest of his letter to Charles was somewhat equivocal.[17] It was not that John was being economical with the truth. Rather, he knew in his heart that the Church of England could now no longer contain Methodism. Its development had gone too far. As the end of his days approached, John could claim with all honesty, 'I live and die in the Church of England,' but he admitted that his own personal loyalty was not shared by all of his followers.

Within a very few years the break was formalized. In 1791, the year of Wesley's death, the Conference elected William Thompson as President and Thomas Coke as Secretary. Two years later, Conference attempted to leave the door open for those who wished to remain part of the Church of England. Methodist ministers were to be ordained by being 'received into full connexion', rather than by the more controversial method of the laying on of hands. However, this ruling did no more than offer a temporary sop, and was withdrawn in 1836. That same Conference of 1793 gave permission for Methodist preachers to administer the sacrament wherever societies were unanimously in favour of them doing so. Opinions were still divided, and the 'Plan of Pacification' of 1795 attempted a further compromise. It allowed Methodist societies to have the sacraments, provided that their local leaders (or 'trustees', as they were known) were in favour and Conference gave its permission.

The truth of the matter was that such pronounce-ments were simply an acknowledgment that the process of separation, however piecemeal and drawn out, could no longer be avoided.

Postscript

> I'll praise my Maker while I've breath;
> And when my voice is lost in death,
>   Praise shall employ my nobler powers:
> My days of praise shall ne'er be past,
> While life, and thought, and being last,
>   Or immortality endures.[18]

Wesley died in 1791. Popular tradition has it that he passed away with the affirmation, 'Best of all, God is with us,' on his lips. Actually, his last words were the first line of one of Isaac Watts' most famous hymns: 'I'll praise my Maker, while I've breath', though he could only manage the first two words. His funeral was simple, according to his instructions. His body was wrapped in a coarse shroud and placed in a cheap coffin, carried by poor men – and the service was held at 5.00 am to avoid a crowd. The substitution, in the funeral liturgy, of the word 'father' in the phrase '. . . the soul of our dear brother here departed . . .', was perhaps a small indication of the tremendous sense of loss felt by the thousands present.

Time Line of Events

1738 (Sept)	John Wesley returns from his visit to Germany
1739	John Wesley preaches in the open air at Bristol First Methodist Society meets in Bristol
1742	Classes begin to be formed
1744	First meeting of Conference
1748	First Quarterly Meeting Kingswood School opens
1749	The *Christian Library* begins to appear
1766	First Methodist Society in the New World
1770	Death of George Whitefield
1776	American Declaration of Independence
1777	Foundation stone of New Chapel in City Road laid
1783	End of the war with the American colonies
1784 (Feb) (Sept)	Deed of Declaration The ordinations for America John Wesley's revision of the Prayer Book
1787	Registration of preaching houses
1788	Death of Charles Wesley
1791 (Feb)	Death of John Wesley

For Discussion

1. John Wesley was a reluctant convert to open-air preaching. How effective do you think it is today?

2. Which of the 'Twelve Rules of a Helper' do you feel were the most helpful? Are there any of which you disapprove?

3. Why are small groups so important to the spiritual life of a church?

4. What devotional books have helped you most as a Christian, and why?

5. Which of the various factors mentioned in the chapter were the most important, in your opinion, in leading to Methodism's separation from the Church of England?

7

Wesley's Theology 3: The Means of Grace

The gift which He on one bestows,
We all delight to prove;
The grace through every vessel flows,
In purest streams of love.

We now turn to some of the central elements in early Methodism's devotional life. In particular, we shall see how the Wesleys' ideas concerning the 'means of grace' were applied to worship and the sacraments. Bearing in mind the theological emphases of the preaching and writing of both the Wesleys, it is hardly surprising that, to this day, the sustaining and building up of the believer has been seen as an important, and even crucial, aspect of the church's work and that great stress has been laid upon the 'means of grace'.

For a definition of what John Wesley meant by the term, we can do no better than to turn to his sermon on the same subject. He begins:

> By *means of grace* I understand, outward signs, words or actions, ordained of God, and appointed for this end, to be the ordinary channels whereby he might convey to men, preventing, justifying, or sanctifying grace.[1]

He continues by adding some important comments on the nature of sacraments and the way in which the grace of God operates. These remarks can be found in the next document [47], which follows the words just quoted.

47. I use this expression 'Means of grace', because I know none better, and because it has been generally used in the Christian Church for many ages: in particular, by our own Church, which directs us to bless God, both for the 'Means of grace', and hopes of glory; and teaches us that a Sacrament is, 'An outward sign of inward *grace*, and a *means* whereby we receive the same.'

The chief of these means are prayer, whether in secret or with the great congregation; searching the scriptures, (which implies reading, hearing, and meditating thereon); and receiving the Lord's Supper, eating bread and drinking wine in remembrance of Him: and these we believe to be ordained of God, as the ordinary channels of conveying his grace to the souls of men . . .

As to the *manner* of using them . . . it behoves us, first, always to retain a lively sense, that God is above all means. Have a care therefore of limiting the Almighty. He doeth whatsoever and whensoever it pleaseth him . . . Secondly, Before you use any means, let it be deeply impressed on your soul, 'There is no *power* in this.' . . . Neither is there any *merit* in my using this . . . But because God bids, therefore I do; because he directs me to wait in this way; therefore, here I wait for his free mercy, whereof cometh my salvation . . . Thirdly, In using all means, seek God alone. In and thro' every outward thing, look singly to the *power* of his Spirit, and the *merits* of his Son. Beware you do not stick in the *work* itself; if you do, it is all lost labour. Nothing short of God can satisfy your soul. Therefore, eye him in all, thro' all, and above all.

Source: J. Wesley, *Sermons*, Vol. 1, pp. 247, 264–5.

It can be seen that Wesley was concerned to avoid the twin dangers of 'quietism' and salvation by works. To use these means of grace is important but simply turning up for communion on a Sunday does not guarantee that we are saved! Even so, because the means of grace both bring men and women to faith and confirm committed believers in it, they are to be used by both seekers and believers at every stage of their spiritual journey.

Before we consider the 'means of grace' in turn, we should note two things.

First, Wesley had been brought up within the tradition of high church sacramentalism, and his evangelical conversion in 1738 did not change his view of the importance of the sacraments. Raymond George summarizes this by saying that 'he retained to the end of his life such a regard for the sacraments as entitles him to be regarded as both a sacramentalist and an evangelical,' and rightly asserts that there was no inherent contradiction in this.[2] What Wesley did was to maintain a balance between Christian worship and Christian living. It was only much later that some Methodists tended to reduce the emphasis on the sacraments.

Secondly, Wesley was careful not to teach that the means of grace had any intrinsic power by themselves. They were outward signs of God's grace which could only be received by faith. Thus, for example, in affirming Christ's real presence at the Lord's Supper, Wesley maintained that Christ encountered the believer in the Sacrament, not in the elements alone. However, he could not embrace the low view of the Lord's Supper held by some, who felt it to be of subsidiary importance to the preached word. By stressing, however, that God chooses to use both means of grace, Wesley preserved an objective element in his teaching. In short, he was careful once more to steer a middle course between extreme positions. In some ways, present-day Methodism still adheres to the ideas which Wesley expounded and the practices which early Methodists followed, but in other respects it has evolved different approaches. Methodist churches, for example, vary considerably from place to place in the frequency with which the sacrament of

Holy Communion is celebrated.

We now turn to 'the means of grace' themselves.

The Lord's Supper

Author of life divine,
Who hast a table spread,
Furnished with mystic wine
And everlasting bread,
Preserve the life Thyself hast given,
And feed and train us up for heaven.

In the eighteenth century the Lord's Supper was 'for the most part neither highly valued nor frequently celebrated in the Church of England'.[3] The religious conflicts of the previous century, the shortage of clergy, and the influence of rationalism with its suspicion of anything which resembled 'superstition', all contributed to this state of affairs.

The Holy Club, therefore, immediately attracted attention by its stress upon the regular reception of communion. Wesley himself at one time received it daily, though on average he communicated once every four days throughout his lifetime. While in Georgia, he had administered the Lord's Supper according to very strict rules, even refusing communion to those who had not been baptized by an episcopally ordained minister. After 1738, very little changed in Wesley's sacramentalism, as has been already pointed out. In the *Rules of the Bands* which he drew up in 1744, there was the injunction: 'constantly to attend on all the ordinances of God; in particular . . . to be at Church and at the Lord's Table every week . . .'[4] The importance which Wesley attached to the Lord's Supper may be seen by the extract from one of his sermons entitled 'The Duty of Constant Communion', which he first wrote in the early 1730s [48]. In 1788 Wesley himself wrote about the sermon in retrospect: 'I have added very little, but retrenched much; as I then used more words than I do now. But I thank God, I have not yet seen cause to alter my sentiments, in any point which is therein delivered.'[5]

48. I am to show, that it is the duty of every Christian to receive the Lord's Supper as often as he can.

The first reason why it is the duty of every Christian so to do, is because it is a plain command of Christ . . . A second reason why every Christian should do this, as often as he can, is because the benefits of doing it are so great, to all that do it in faith and in obedience to him . . . As our bodies are strengthened by bread and wine, so are our souls by these tokens of the body and blood of Christ. This is the food of our souls: this gives strength to perform our duty, and leads us on to perfection. If, therefore, we have any regard for the plain command of Christ, if we desire the pardon of our sins, if we wish for strength to believe, to love and obey God, then we should neglect no opportunity of receiving the Lord's Supper . . .

It is highly expedient for those who purpose to receive this, whenever their time will permit, to prepare themselves for this solemn ordinance, by self-examination and prayer. But this is not absolutely necessary. And when we have not time for it, we should see that we have the habitual preparation which is absolutely necessary, and can never be dispensed with on any account, or any occasion whatever. This is, first, a full *purpose* of heart, to keep all the commandments of God. And, secondly, a sincere *desire*, to receive all his promises.

Source: J. Wesley, *Sermons*, Vol. 5, pp. 335–337.

Wesley also administered the sacraments to the sick and saw no conflict with established Anglican practice in doing so. Early Methodists received communion at their own parish churches, but gradually they began to receive it in Methodist rooms and chapels. This probably began in Bristol, and by 1745 the practice had spread to London, though the custom did not become widespread until the 1770s and 1780s. Initially, Wesley did not approve of this, but he modified his views in the light of the changes that occurred over the years. As we saw in the last chapter, from ordaining preachers for America in 1784 it was but a short step to ordaining men for the work in Scotland, and in 1788 and 1789 he ordained a number of preachers for work in parts of England where the Methodist societies were not able to receive the Holy Communion on a regular basis.

What had changed, then, in Wesley's attitude to Holy Communion? Very little, in terms of his view of its importance – but we can discern a significant shift in his response to the question of who should be admitted. It is clear that he came to believe very strongly that the Lord's Supper could be a converting as well as a confirming ordinance. People could be brought to faith as well as be built up in it. This is shown in the brief extract from his journal dated 27 June 1740 [49].

49. In the ancient Church, every one who was baptized communicated daily . . . But in latter times many have affirmed that the Lord's Supper is not a converting, but a confirming ordinance. And among us it has been diligently taught that none but those who are converted, who have received the Holy Ghost, who are believers in the full sense, ought to communicate. But experience shows the gross falsehood of that assertion that the Lord's Supper is not a converting ordinance . . . Our Lord commanded those very men who were then unconverted, who had not yet received the Holy Ghost, who (in the full sense of the word) were not believers, to do this 'in remembrance of' Him.

Source: J. Wesley, *Journal*, Friday 27 June 1740.

Should everyone be admitted, then? The cherished belief that Methodism has always had an 'open table' needs some qualification in this respect. Though Wesley came to see that anyone with a degree of faith and a sincere desire for God's grace – even though not yet a full believer – should be allowed to partake, he also was aware of the need for some safeguards. Even as early as 1747 notes of admission were distributed, later to be replaced by class tickets. However, the prime conditions were a desire to receive communion, and a recognition of the individual's utter sinfulness and helplessness.

We can, therefore, summarize Wesley's theology of the Lord's Supper as follows.

He believed that it was a memorial of the death of Christ, and therefore an occasion for people to be reminded of Christ's work on the cross, and for them to re-examine their faith. By their participation, communicants could be spiritually nurtured. It was also a re-presentation or a setting forth – not a repeat – of the sacrifice which Christ once offered, making it a reality for those present.[6] He held that the Lord's Supper was an occasion at which Christ is really present (though not solely in the elements), and can be

50.

Jesu, at whose supreme command
    We now approach to God,
Before us in thy vesture stand,
    Thy vesture dipped in blood!
Obedient to thy gracious word,
    We break the hallowed bread,
Commemorate thee, our dying Lord,
    And trust on thee to feed.

Now, Saviour, now thyself reveal,
    And make thy nature known;
Affix thy blessed Spirit's seal,
    And stamp us for thine own:
The tokens of thy dying love
    O let us all receive;
And feel the quickening Spirit move,
    And sensibly believe!

The cup of blessing, blessed by thee,
    Let it thy blood impart;
The bread thy mystic body be,
    And cheer each languid heart.
The grace which sure salvation brings
    Let us herewith receive;
Satiate the hungry with good things,
    The hidden manna give.

The living bread, sent down from heaven,
    In us vouchsafe to be:
Thy flesh for all the world is given,
    And all may live by thee.
Now, Lord, on us thy flesh bestow,
    And let us drink thy blood,
Till all our souls are filled below
    With all the life of God.

Source: A Collection of Hymns for the Use of the People Called Methodists, 1780 edition, No. 901.

influence was most strong. One of the Wesleys' lesser known hymns on the Lord's Supper, which first appeared in *A Collection of Hymns for the Use of the People Called Methodists* in 1779, is reproduced here [50]. In all probability both brothers collaborated in its writing. The second and third verses show quite clearly how John and Charles saw communion both as an agent of conversion and a means whereby the faith of established believers can be strengthened.

Baptism

Eternal Spirit! descend from high,
    Baptizer of our spirits thou!
The sacramental seal apply,
    And witness with the water now.

As with the Lord's Supper, Wesley's writings on baptism were more concerned with the practical issues of churchmanship than with its theological foundations. Because his theology was influenced by his experience of widely different human situations, it was inevitable that his ideas should change during his long ministry. In Wesley's view, the purpose of baptism was to start an individual on the road to faith – to begin what the Lord's Supper was intended to preserve and develop. It was a gift from God, an ordinance to be accepted.

There were three things he regarded as essential for a baptism to be valid, and these he maintained throughout his life: it must be conducted by an episcopally ordained minister, with the application of water and in the name of the Trinity. Wesley was widely criticized in Georgia for re-baptizing those who had been baptized by non-episcopally ordained men. At that point in his life, however, his zeal for correctness had not yet been tempered by a sensitivity which that very difficult pastoral situation required!

Wesley also believed in infant baptism, on the grounds that the benefits of this sacrament – i.e. the gifts of God's grace – should be made available to children as much as to adults. He was confirmed in this view by the fact that scripture provided authority for it.[8] He set out his beliefs quite fully in a long essay

received by faith into believers' hearts. Finally, he saw it as a link between the past and the future, 'a foretaste of the heavenly banquet prepared for all mankind,' thus joining the sacrifice of those sharing in the communion with 'all the company of heaven'.[7]

Charles Wesley shared his brother's views on the sacrament of Holy Communion, and wrote many hymns on the subject. John encouraged Charles to publish them so that their use could be more widespread, and the early years of the Methodist Revival saw a marked increase in the number of people taking communion in those parishes where Methodist entitled *A Preservative Against Unsettled Notions in Religion*, which was published in 1758. This discourse included some of his own father's writings on the subject, and its intention was to remind the Methodist people of the validity and importance of infant baptism. Before discussing children's baptism, Wesley made a number of statements about baptism in general. An extract from the first section of this essay shows how his thinking had developed [51].

---

51. 1. What are the *benefits* we receive by baptism is the next point to be considered. And the first of these is the washing away the guilt of original sin by the application of the merits of Christ's death . . . that the person to be baptized may be 'washed and sanctified by the Holy Ghost, and, being delivered from God's wrath, receive remission of sins and enjoy the everlasting benediction of his heavenly washing' . . .

2. By baptism we enter into covenant with God, into that 'everlasting covenant' which 'he hath commanded for ever': that new covenant which he promised to make with the spiritual Israel, even to 'give them a new heart and a new spirit, to sprinkle clean water upon them' (cf. Ezek. 36.26, 25) . . .

3. By baptism we are admitted into the Church and consequently made members of Christ its head. As the Jews were admitted into the Church by circumcision, so are the Christians by baptism . . .

4. By baptism, we who were 'by nature children of wrath' are made the children of God. And this regeneration which our Church in so many places ascribes to baptism is more than barely being admitted into the Church, though commonly connected therewith. Being 'grafted into the body of Christ's Church, we are made the children of God by adoption and grace' . . .

Source: J. Wesley, 'Treatise on Baptism', *Works*, Vol. X, p. 191.

Wesley's use of the term 'regeneration' needs a little explanation. It is not an easy subject to grasp. However, we may take comfort from the fact that Wesley found it difficult too, and of all his writings, those on baptism are perhaps the least lucid. It has also been an area of considerable (and often confused) debate within Methodism in recent years.

Most of Wesley's high church contemporaries believed that when a child – or an adult – was baptized, the person actually received a degree of spiritual renewal, whether or not he or she was old enough to be conscious of it. In their opinion there was an objective reality to baptism. In other words, by baptism the regenerated individual experienced a 'new birth'. In the 'Treatise', Wesley himself seems to be suggesting that a *real* change occurs even in infants. The principle behind this is sometimes described as being *ex opere operato*, which simply means that the grace of God operates irrespective of the individual's awareness or attitude.

However, Wesley could see from his own experience that this was not entirely true. He hinted at this later in the 'Treatise' by saying that 'herein a principle of grace is infused which will not be wholly taken away unless we quench the Holy Spirit of God by long-continued wickedness.'[9] In his sermon 'The New Birth' which was written in 1760, Wesley discussed the relationship between baptism and New Birth in believers [52].

---

52. 1. And first, it follows, that baptism is not the New Birth: they are not one and the same thing . . . it is manifest, baptism the sign, is spoken of as distinct from regeneration, the thing signified.

In the Church Catechism likewise the judgment of our Church is declared with the utmost clearness: 'What meanest thou by this word, sacrament? I mean an outward and visible sign of an inward and spiritual grace. What is the outward part, or form in baptism? Water, wherein the person is baptized, in the name of the Father, Son and Holy Ghost. What is the inward part, or thing signified? A death unto sin, and a new-birth unto righteousness.' Nothing therefore is plainer, than that, according to the Church of England, baptism is not the New Birth.

2. From the preceding reflections, we may, secondly observe, that as the New-Birth is not the same thing with baptism, so it does not always accompany baptism: they do not constantly go together. A man may possibly be *born of water*, and yet not be *born of the Spirit*. There may sometimes be the outward sign, where there is not the inward grace . . . 'The tree is known by its fruit:' and hereby it appears too plain to be denied, that divers of those, who were children of the devil before they were baptized, continue the same after baptism; 'for the works of their father they do;' they continue servants of sin, without any pretence either to inward or outward holiness.

Source: J. Wesley, *Sermons*, Vol. 1, pp. 337–339.

This extract shows Wesley giving regeneration a slightly different emphasis, in that he denies that baptism automatically leads to a life of faith and commitment to Christ.

Does a sacrament achieve what it signifies by itself, or is it merely a sign? Wesley felt that a way could be found between these two extremes. He believed that with children, baptism was an initiation. Though they were too young to show faith and repentance, infants still needed to be washed from the guilt of original sin. By baptism they were regenerated. But as they grew up they were very liable to 'sin away their baptism' – Wesley said that he had done this himself. In adults, however, there had to be some evidence of faith and repentance, and Wesley did not believe that baptism guaranteed that regeneration had taken place. Not all baptized adults, he felt, were born again. Thus Wesley appeared to think of infant and adult baptism in two slightly different senses.

It may be helpful here for us to remember what Wesley taught about prevenient grace, and to think in terms of baptism as a beginning. First and foremost, the sacrament is a celebration of what God, not man, is doing. God bestows his grace before a person (if an infant) is aware of it, but the benefits of God's grace need to be consciously appropriated in order for the baptized individual to obtain full salvation.

Incidentally, Wesley did not believe that baptism was absolutely necessary for a person to be saved. In May 1750 he wrote a letter to a Baptist Minister named Gilbert Boyce, in which he declared:

> You think the mode of baptism is 'necessary to salvation': I deny that even baptism itself is so; if it were, every Quaker must be damned, which I can in no wise believe. I hold nothing to be (strictly speaking) necessary to salvation but the mind which was in Christ.[10]

In the final analysis, Wesley admitted that the sacrament of baptism was a mystery of God – a sentiment echoed many times in his brother's hymns, such as the one given here [53].

53.

Come, Father, Son, and Holy Ghost,
   Honour the means ordained by thee!
Make good our apostolic boast,
   And own thy glorious ministry.

We now thy promised presence claim.
   Sent to disciple all mankind,
Sent to baptize into thy name;
   We now thy promised presence find.

Father! in these reveal thy Son:
   In these, for whom we seek thy face,
The hidden mystery make known,
   The inward, pure, baptizing grace.

Jesus! with us thou always art:
   Effectuate now the sacred sign,
The gift unspeakable impart,
   And bless the ordinance divine.

Eternal Spirit! descend from high,
   Baptizer of our spirits thou!
The sacramental seal apply,
   And witness with the water now.

O that the souls baptized therein
   May now thy truth and mercy feel;
May rise and wash away their sin!
   Come, Holy Ghost, their pardon seal!

Source: *A Collection of Hymns for the Use of the People Called Methodists*, 1780 edition, No. 476.

Other Methodist services

Come, let us use the grace divine,
And all, with one accord,
In a perpetual covenant join,
Ourselves to Christ the Lord.

Apart from the two sacraments there were other services which, as 'means of grace', were necessary for a healthy spiritual life. Originally, Methodist services were looked on merely as supplementing the liturgy and sacraments of the Church of England. Therefore the distinctive characteristics of Methodist worship came into being in rather a piece-meal way, with the express purpose of deepening fellowship and enriching personal faith. When Societies met together, ιt was usually for what we would call a 'preaching service', since it was assumed that Methodists were also attending their local parish churches.

For a brief idea of how Wesley saw these services, we can look at his comments to the 1766 Conference [54]. Wesley's pronouncements are quite understandable if we remember the sensitive relationship which existed between Methodism and the Church of England. He had no intention of provoking needless censure. Methodist services were generally held during the evening, simply because Anglican liturgical services were held in the mornings and afternoons, and when gas lighting became widespread, the custom became firmly established. Prayer meetings tended to be held mid-week – for example, at the Foundery they were held on Wednesdays and Fridays at 5.00 am!

---

54. But some may say, 'Our own service is public worship.' Yes, *in a sense*: but not such as supersedes the Church Service. We never designed it should. We have a hundred times professed the contrary. It presupposes public prayer, like the sermons at the University. Therefore I have over and over advised, Use no *long prayer*, either before or after sermon. Therefore I myself frequently use only a collect, and never enlarge in prayer, unless at intercession, or on a watch-night, or on some extra-ordinary occasion.

If it were designed to be instead of Church Service, it would be essentially defective. For it seldom has the four grand parts of public prayer; deprecation, petition, intercession, and thanksgiving. Neither is it, even on the Lord's day, concluded with the Lord's Supper.

The hour for it on that day, unless there is some peculiar reason for a variation, should be five in the morning, as well as five in the evening. Why should we make God's day the shortest of the seven?

But if the people put ours in the place of the Church Service, we hurt them that stay with us, and ruin them that leave us. For then they will go nowhere, but lounge the Sabbath away, without any public worship at all. I advise, therefore, all the Methodists in England and Ireland, who have been brought up in the Church, constantly to attend the Service of the Church, at least, every Lord's day.

Source: *Minutes* of Conference of 1766.

There were other forms of worship peculiar to Methodism. The best known were the Love-feast, the Watch-night and the Covenant services.

The Love-feast

This dated from the days of the early church, and had long fallen into disuse. It was revived by the Moravians, and became a general feature of the Evangelical Revival in England. Love-feasts were held quarterly, or even monthly in some areas, usually on Sunday evenings. Bread was broken and water drunk from a common cup, or the 'Loving Cup', as it was called. Money was collected for the poor and hymns were sung, some of them specially composed for the purpose. Apart from prayers and hymn singing, the most prominent feature of these services was the sharing of personal testimonies. In *A Plain Account of the People Called Methodists*, Wesley gives a statement concerning the institution of the Love-feast among the societies [55].

---

55. In order to increase in them a grateful sense of all God's mercies, I desired that, one evening in a quarter, all the men in Band, on a second, all the women, would meet; and on a third, both men and women together; that we might together 'eat bread', as the ancient Christians did, 'with gladness and singleness of heart'. At these Love-feasts (so we termed them, retaining the name, as well as the thing, which was in use from the beginning) our food is only a little plain cake and water. But we seldom return from them without being fed, not only with the 'meat which perisheth', but with 'that which endureth to everlasting life'.

Source: J. Wesley, *Works*, Vol. VIII, pp. 258–9.

The first Conference of 1744 opened with a Love-feast, and until 1748 only members of the Bands were admitted. But in 1759 Wesley records in his Journal that he held a Love-feast for 'the whole society' – members being required to produce their quarterly class ticket of membership. Eventually the Love-feast declined, but the surprising thing is that it never seems to have been confused with the Lord's Supper.[11]

The Watch-night service

This too had its origins in the early centuries of the Christian Church, and nocturnal vigils were held by Moravian communities. Wesley himself attended some of these when he visited them in Germany in

1738, and saw their potential value. The first Methodist Watch-night service probably dates from 12 March 1742, and this extract from *A Plain Account* gives a good impression of its character and origin [56].

---

56. About this time I was informed that several persons in Kingswood frequently met together at the school; and, when they could spare the time, spent the greater part of the night in prayer, praise and thanksgiving. Some advised me to put an end to this; but, upon weighing the thing thoroughly, and comparing it with the practice of the ancient Christians, I could see no cause to forbid it. Rather, I believed it might be made of more general use. So I sent them word, I designed to watch with them on the Friday nearest the full moon, that we might have light thither and back again. I gave public notice of this the Sunday before, and withal that I intended to preach; desiring they, and they only, would meet me there, who could do it without prejudice to their business or families. On Friday abundance of people came. I began preaching between eight and nine; and we continued a little beyond the noon of night, singing, praying, and praising God. They we have continued to do once a month ever since, in Bristol, London, and Newcastle, as well as Kingswood; and exceeding great are the blessings we have found therein. It has generally been an extreme solemn season; when the Word of God sunk deep into the heart (even of those who till then knew Him not).

Source: J. Wesley, *Works*, Vol. VIII, pp. 246–7.

The Covenant service

There were no connections with the Moravians here, and scholars are agreed that the Covenant service grew out of English Puritanism after the Restoration of 1662. It provides yet another example of how Wesley took an existing pattern or idea, and re-shaped it. He has left us an account of its institution in his Journal [57]. Wesley's authority for this lay, not surprisingly, in the Bible, in which the practice of renewing one's covenant with God is a prominent feature. He saw it as a glorious opportunity for the Methodist people corporately to reaffirm their commitment to God. From 1762 it was held on New Year's Day, and from 1778 on the first Sunday in the New Year.

---

57. *Wed.* Aug. 6. – I mentioned to the congregation another means of increasing serious religion, which had been frequently practised by our forefathers, and attended with eminent blessing; namely, the joining in a covenant to serve God with all our heart and with all our soul. I explained this for several mornings following; and on *Friday* many of us kept a fast unto the Lord, beseeching Him to give us wisdom and strength, to promise unto the Lord our God and keep it.

Mon. 11. – I explained once more the nature of such an engagement, and the manner of doing it acceptably to God. At six in the evening we met for that purpose, at the French church in Spitalfields. After I had recited the tenor of the covenant proposed, in the words of that blessed man, Richard Alleine, all the people stood up, in testimony of assent, to the number of about eighteen hundred persons. Such a night I scarce ever saw before. Surely the fruit of it shall remain for ever.

Source: John Wesley, *Journal*, 6/11 August 1755.

The Richard Alleine referred to in the entry was a Presbyterian minister ejected from his church following the Act of Uniformity of 1662. In 1663 he wrote a defence of Puritanism, and in his conclusion urged his people to make a formal covenant with God. To this day, the Covenant service has remained a distinctive part of the Methodist worship. For many it is one of the high points of the year. The words of the actual covenant prayer, repeated by all present, are breathtaking – provided that they are taken as seriously as they are intended! [58]

---

58. I am no longer my own, but yours. Put me to what you will, rank me with whom you will; put me to doing, put me to suffering; let me be employed for you or laid aside for you, exalted for you or brought low for you; let me be full, let me be empty; let me have all things, let me have nothing; I freely and wholeheartedly yield all things to your pleasure and disposal. And now, glorious and blessed God, Father, Son, and Holy Spirit, you are mine and I am yours. So be it. And the covenant now made on earth, let it be ratified in heaven. Amen.

Source: *The Methodist Service Book*, Methodist Publishing House 1975, p. D10.

The hymns of Charles Wesley

My heart is full of Christ, and longs
Its glorious matter to declare!
Of Him I make my loftier songs,
I cannot from his praise forbear;
My ready tongue makes haste to sing
The glories of my heavenly King.

John Wesley's hymns are comparatively few in contrast to the enormous number penned by his brother. Perhaps his greatest contribution was as a linguist, and his translation of hymns from the German have provided us with lasting treasures. One of the best known is 'What shall we offer our good Lord', which was originally written by August Spangenberg. Undoubtedly many of Charles' hymns bear the mark of his brother's influence. John often edited verses where he thought they could be improved, either in rhyme or in theology. The unassuming Charles never worried about hymns in which John had made changes occasionally appearing under common authorship, and in a number of instances it is difficult to tell which of the brothers is actually the main composer.

For many, however, Charles Wesley is *the* hymn writer of Methodism. His hymns run into thousands, though it is sometimes forgotten that he also wrote a great deal of poetry.[12] From the verses quoted at the beginnings of chapters and sections in this book, it will have already become clear that Charles' hymns covered a wide range of theology as well as human emotion. Dr Frank Baker has written that, 'the "sweet singer" of Methodism provided in his robust scriptural song both spiritual education and an inspiring means of giving expression to the richly varying experiences of those pressing along the highway of personal religion'.[13]

We may not find all Charles' language appealing today. One criticism of his hymns is that many of them display what some (perhaps unkindly) have called his 'worm theology'. Lines such as

If so poor a worm as I,
May to Thy great glory live . . .

and

If now thou talkest by the way
With such an abject worm as me . . .

may seem very strange to us now. Our credulity may be stretched even further by,

That only name to sinners given,
Which lifts poor dying worms to heaven.[14]

Charles used the term 'worm' on many occasions in his hymns because his intense belief in the unworthiness of the individual. Moreover, he was not afraid to write about sin and death – and joy and heaven, too. He was a man of his time who expressed himself strongly. 'Whether we are attracted or repelled by Charles Wesley's heightened spiritual temperature,' writes Frank Baker, 'one thing cannot be questioned – his utter sincerity'.[15] If in today's somewhat lower spiritual temperature we find his words over-emotional, we should recall that they were simply a reflection of his intense desire to see salvation obtained by all.

Charles' hymns are littered with biblical allusions. 'And can it be', so popular with revivalists, contains no fewer than eleven from the New Testament alone – but the accusation of obscurity can only be true for those who do not know their Bibles well! Nor was he afraid to adapt secular music and lyrics if they suited his purpose. His great hymn, 'Love divine, all loves excelling', for example, is thought to have been inspired by Purcell's song 'Fairest isle, all isles excelling'. It has been suggested that there are just as many allusions in Charles' hymns to Milton's *Paradise Lost* as there are to the Bible, though since the former itself draws so heavily upon scripture, it is difficult to know what exactly this proves.

The first substantial hymn book by the brothers was published in 1780 under the title *A Collection of Hymns for the Use of the People called Methodists*.[16] These hymns were intended for personal devotion, as well for general congregational use, as John's comments in the Preface show [59].

59. Such a Hymn-Book you have now before you. It is not so large as to be either cumbersome or expensive; and it is large enough to contain such a variety of hymns as will not soon be worn threadbare. It is large enough to contain all the important truths of our most holy religion, whether speculative or practical; yea, to illustrate them all, and to prove them both by Scripture and reason; and this is done in a regular order. The hymns are not carelessly jumbled together, but carefully ranged under proper heads, according to the experience of real Christians. So that this book is, in effect, a little body of experimental and practical divinity.

. . . I would commend it to every truly pious reader, as a means of raising or quickening the spirit of devotion; of confirming his faith; of enlivening his hope; and of kindling and increasing his love to God and man.

Source: *A Collection of Hymns for the Use of the People Called Methodists*, 1780 edition.

It is therefore with some justification that Methodists have tended to regard their hymn books as being second only to the Bible as a theological and devotional resource. Charles Wesley died in 1788, and was buried, according to his last wishes, in the cemetery of his own parish church. His hymns remain his greatest legacy, for no other writer or composer has so perfectly captured the spirit of early Methodism.

For Discussion

1. What is the importance of the sacrament of Holy Communion for you?

2. Why has the subject of infant baptism been the cause of so much controversy in recent years?

3. Is it really necessary for Christians to go to church? If so, why?

4. What are your feelings on reading the Covenant prayer?

5. Which of Charles Wesley's hymns are your favourites?

8

Controversies and Divisions

Shepherd divine, our wants relieve
In this our evil day,
To all thy tempted followers give
The power to watch and pray.

Long as our fiery trials last,
Long as the cross we bear,
O let our souls on thee be cast
In never-ceasing prayer!

John Wesley's legacy

For all his achievements, John Wesley failed in one respect. He was unable to leave Methodism to develop trouble-free along the lines he had envisaged. Far from reviving the Church of England, it gradually became a distinct and separate denomination. Furthermore, although Methodist churches were successfully planted all over the world in the nineteenth century, the fifty or so years after Wesley's death were not happy ones at home, even though they saw an overall growth in the number of members. This chapter traces the story of Methodism during this difficult period, during which Wesley's successors faced problems of internal order and discipline as well as those arising from the social and political factors which became increasingly important in Britain after 1791.

An idea of the seriousness of the situation can be gained from reading the resolutions passed by the Conference of 1820, some of which are reproduced here [60]. In that year Methodist membership, which by then numbered over 200,000, showed a decrease

60. 1. We, on this solemn occasion, devote ourselves afresh to God; and resolve, in humble dependence on His grace, to be more than ever attentive to personal religion, and to the Christian instruction and government of our families . . .

3. Let us consecrate ourselves fully and entirely to our proper work as servants of Christ in His Church, giving ourselves 'wholly' to it, both in public and in private, and guarding against all occupations of our time and thoughts which have no direct connexion with our great calling and which would injuriously divert our attention from the momentous task of saving souls, and taking care of the flock of Christ . . .

12. Let us ourselves remember, and endeavour to impress on our people, that we as a Body do not exist for the purpose of party; and that we are especially bound by the example of our Founder, and by our constant professions before the world, to avoid a narrow, bigoted, and sectarian spirit . . . Let us therefore maintain towards all denominations of Christians, who 'hold the Head', the kind and catholic spirit of primitive Methodism

Source: Minutes of the Liverpool Conference of 1820.

for the first time in living memory. The resolutions were intended to be read annually to the preachers at each Conference.

How far Wesley's successors managed to maintain a 'kind and catholic spirit' to members of their own spiritual family during the troubled years of the first half of the nineteenth century is a matter of some debate.

On his death, Wesley had left a large number of societies comprising 72,476 members (as calculated by the 1791 Conference); a connexional organization headed by the annual Conference; an itinerant ministry; a reasonably fixed standard of doctrine, and at least three major areas of uncertainty. How were the Methodist people to be led and guided into the future? Could the growing tensions between preachers and laity be resolved? What would happen to Methodism's relationship with the Church of England?

1. Leadership

The leadership question was in some ways the least serious of these three problems. Wesley's death created something of a vacuum. This was understandable, because of his immense stature and his style of leadership. His 'benevolent autocracy' was, as we have seen, characterized by close personal contact with and attachment to his followers, especially the preachers, and it kept the Methodist people together during his long life. At different times Wesley himself thought that either Fletcher of Madeley or his brother Charles might succeed him. However, he outlived them both, and in 1791 there was no single person who could take his place.

However, if – as some people had rather unfairly thought – Methodism had ever been 'Mr Wesley's private army', it had already ceased to be so for some time. The Deed of Declaration of 1784[1] made sure that Methodism's leadership would be conciliar, in that power and decision-making would be shared among the preachers. The Conference was now firmly in the driving seat, and proposals in 1794 and 1795 to introduce a form of episcopate were firmly quashed. The Connexion, moreover, was divided into geog-

raphical districts under presidents, who were later renamed 'Chairmen'. In short, the pattern for the future development of Methodism had been set.

2. Preachers and laity

The relationship of the preachers (that is, those appointed by Wesley, who included a few ordained clergy) to the Methodist lay people was to be a source of recurrent crises for many years. We can think of the problem in terms of 'centre' and 'circumference'. A definite tension existed between the Conference of preachers at the centre with the privilege and responsibility for order and government, and the trustees, stewards, class leaders, local preachers and so on, who exercised a certain degree of power at the local level.

For example, in 1791 a suggestion was put to the Conference by fifty Cornish laymen that the Legal Hundred be abolished and the circuits and societies be put much more under the control of lay people. Conference's reaction, not surprisingly, was lacking in enthusiasm. This pattern of resistance to change was to be repeated again and again, and forms an interesting parallel to the national scene. The unreformed House of Commons was to give an equally negative response to demands for change prior to the Great Reform Act of 1832. The Deed of Declaration, as we have seen, had made sure that the government of the Connexion would be fairly and squarely in the hands of the preachers,[2] and this enactment was to be a continual source of debate for generations to come.

3. Methodists and Anglicans

This third area of difficulty was also one that underlay much of the history of Methodism in the nineteenth century. It was a problem simply because Methodists were divided about what their relationship with the Church of England should be. Different groups emerged.

There were those – they have been described as 'Church Methodists' – who accepted the Church of England as an institution as Wesley had done but who were also aware of the inconsistencies in Methodism's position, especially after 1784. Nevertheless they clung to a belief that Methodism was something of a 'half-way house' between Anglicanism and Dissent proper, and some at least hoped for a reunion. Others – termed 'Methodist Dissenters'[3] – viewed the break with the Church of England with reluctance but realized that Methodism was a growing, developing and changing movement, with its own distinct future. What united Methodists of all opinions was the doctrine of 'evangelical Arminianism' – the free gift of God's grace for all – and a passionate desire to save souls for Christ. Therefore, though in the first half of the nineteenth century many splits occurred within the Connexion, they tended to be caused by disagreements over church *order* rather than doctrine.

The Church of England was not without its factions, either. The Oxford Movement of the 1830s and 1840s was an attempt by certain high churchmen to stem what they saw as a decline in the religious life of the country by recalling the Church of England to its former devotion and spirituality. Its leaders – John Henry Newman, Edward Pusey, John Keble, Hurrell Froude and others – sought by means of preaching and writing to recapture the ancient traditions of that Church. They wished to re-emphasize dignity, ritual and ceremony in worship and restore a 'high' view of the ministry, while not neglecting the importance of experience in the individual's faith. It was, therefore, in what it sought to affirm, as much a movement of the heart as of the head. The Oxford Movement caused splits within the Church of England itself, but did not produce widespread defections to Methodism. Undoubtedly a shiver of horror went down some Methodist spines when Newman was received into the Roman Catholic Church in 1845, but Methodism was by then well established and had little to fear. The most significant result was that, until the next century, Anglicans and Methodists were to be even further apart.

Splits within Methodism

What troubles have we seen,
What conflicts have we passed,
Fightings without, and fears within,
Since we assembled last!

But out of all the Lord
Hath brought us by his love;
And still he doth his help afford,
And hides our life above.

Conflicts indeed! It is true that the first half of the nineteenth century saw other issues, apart from internal ones, which were not unconnected with the problem of order and unity. The fear of revolution in Britain at the turn of the century, the attitude of the government towards Methodists in these troubled years, relations with the Church of England – all these were potential sources of difficulty. In spite of this, the overall picture one has of Methodism during this period is of a denomination struggling to hold itself together. Lest this seem a prelude to a depressing account of non-stop schism, however, some positive aspects can be identified.

Methodist leaders were used to coping with the problem of secession. There had been divisions long before Wesley's death. As we saw in chapter 6, the disagreement over the doctrine of predestination had caused Whitefield and Wesley to part company before the middle of the eighteenth century. A steady trickle of Methodists also left to join either the Church of England or one of the Dissenting Churches because they were unhappy with what was happening within Methodism itself during Wesley's lifetime. There was, therefore, nothing new or remarkable about this.

Secondly, the divisions were not so much about fundamental differences in theology or doctrine. Rather, they were often caused by personal differences, misunderstandings or tactlessness on the part of individuals and groups, and while separations are always tragic, it was easier than it might have been for the separate groups to come back together in the future.

Methodism also suffered from the inevitable tendency that radical movements have to run further and faster than their leaders intend. This was no bad thing, perhaps. Furthermore, the first half of the nineteenth century saw a widespread re-awakening of a more democratic spirit, which in Methodism could be seen in the way that the grass roots became increasingly at odds with the more conservative hierarchy. Indeed, it could be said that the seeds of division were already present in the eighteenth century revival, in that what happened in the nineteenth century was merely an expression of the radical energy that characterized early Methodism. There was, therefore, a kind of inevitability in the emergence of breakaway groups.

The story is nevertheless an unhappy one because both splinter and parent groups were 'right in what they affirmed, and wrong in what they denied'.[4] There was a place for both order and freedom, central control and local initiative, as Methodists have since come to realize. Most of the reforms which the breakaway groups were asking for eventually became an accepted part of Methodism, in the same way that all but one of the Chartists' demands in 1848 were to become recognized features of British political life.[5] All the main groups which seceded formed their own connexions, with conferences, circuits, superintendents and local preachers, and all remained Methodist at heart. Perhaps the greatest source of regret was that for so long, energy was wasted in internal dissension when there was a crying need for outreach.

We now examine them briefly in turn.[6]

The Methodist New Connexion (1797)

The founder of the first Methodist offshoot was Alexander Kilham, who was born in Epworth, of all places! In 1785 he became a preacher for Mr Wesley and was ordained in 1792. The 'Plan of Pacification'

of 1795 left him bitterly disappointed, as it seemed to rule out any further extension of lay participation and power in church government. Kilham's reply took the form of a booklet entitled *The Progress of Liberty* written in 1795. Bearing in mind what has been said already concerning the demands made by those who were to form separate groups, it is interesting to compare his requests with current Methodist practice. All of them seem quite reasonable to us today. Kilham proposed that the consent of members be obtained before individuals were admitted or expelled and class leaders appointed; that lay preachers should be examined and approved by leaders' and circuit meetings; that any proposed itinerant minister should be approved by the circuit meeting, and that lay delegates should be appointed by circuits to district meetings and by district meetings to Conference. All of these demands, though opposed by the Conferences at the time, were eventually to be adopted.

Kilham was expelled in July 1796 under acrimonious circumstances,[7] and soon a group of like-minded preachers gathered to form 'The New Itinerancy', as it was first known. The Methodist New Connexion was never very large – in 1822 it had 10,856 members in 26 circuits – but it remained a progressive group throughout the nineteenth century, becoming part of the United Methodist Church in 1907.

The Independent Methodists (1806)

This group grew out of a series of 'cottage meetings' in Warrington in 1796, originally being known as 'Quaker Methodists' because they adopted many Quaker customs. It was at their first Conference at Macclesfield in 1806 that they adopted the name 'Independent Methodists'. Their emphasis, as suggested by their title, lay on the freedom and independence of the local church, authority being vested in the members themselves. They were in conseqence 'congregational' in structure. Thus the annual meeting of their Connexion could not – nor can it still, as they remain separate from the main body of Methodism – make any laws binding on the churches, or intervene in the affairs of any church without its consent. The Independent Methodists, with their unpaid ministers and loyal followers, were never very widespread but still survive in the Bristol area and the northwest of England.

The Primitive Methodists (1811)

Founded jointly by Hugh Bourne and William Clowes, from Stoke and Burslem respectively, this offshoot grew out of 'camp meetings' – outdoor gatherings which harked back to the days of field-preaching and were enjoying a spate of popularity in America. The first was held in May 1807, though the best known was the second meeting at Mow Cop (a fairly unremarkable hill in Cheshire) in July of the same year. Neither Bourne nor Clowes wished to leave the Methodist Connexion, but they were both expelled on the grounds that camp meetings were contrary to its order and discipline. Considering it was the beginning of a time of general social unrest in this country, when conservative forces in both government and churches were wary of the dangers of sedition, it is not surprising that the activities of Bourne and Clowes were regarded with such disfavour by the Methodist hierarchy. In 1807 the Liverpool Conference referred to the camp meetings as 'highly improper and likely to be of considerable mischief'.

The Primitives were the largest of the offshoots (the main body of Methodists had by this time come to be known as Wesleyans), and therefore of considerable importance and interest. They represented a desire not only to be free from the constraining influence of Conference but to be free to experiment in worship. The nickname 'Ranters' by which they were sometimes known originated in Belper because of their habit of singing in the streets there. Their singing in church could be remarkable, as we can see in this account of one of their services [61].

---

61. It is to the chapel we are going – the gathering place for worship, the house of God. It is a plain, unpretentious building, commodious enough, but lacking both in beauty and comfort. In the pulpit is a tall, spare man, with a face in which mysticism and intelligence are strangely blended. We learn that he is a miner from a neighbouring colliery . . . Never shall I forget the singing of that service. There was a little scraping and twanging of fiddle-strings before all the stringed instruments – of which there were a dozen – were brought into accord with the organ, but then such a glorious outburst of music as could not fail to help the spirit of devotion. How these North folks could sing . . .

After the first hymn came the prayer. Prayer is not for criticism. When a man is talking with his Maker, he should be safe from the attacks of fault finders. But there are men who have what the old Methodists called the 'gift of prayer', and the preacher had that gift . . . The pitman preacher talked with God with the familiarity which comes of frequent communion, and yet, withal, with a reverence that moved even the restless youths sitting near the pulpit . . . And the preacher carried his congregation along on the strong pinions of his own faith, until a low rumbling of murmured responses broke forth in loud 'Amens'. Suddenly one man sprang to his feet, and, with a loud shout of 'Praise the Lord', jumped into the air . . .

The reading of the Scriptures was interspersed with a few remarks here and there more or less appropriate – generally less – and the service would not have suffered by their omission. But the Sermon – who shall describe it? It was a Sermon to be heard, not to be reported. What a mixture of humour, passionate appeal, thrilling exhortations and apposite illustrations it was . . . Laughter and tears this preacher commanded at will, and when he closed with heart-searching appeals to the unconverted to fly to the Cross for pardon, one almost wondered that men and women did not spring to their feet and rush somewhere – anywhere, exclaiming with Bunyan's Pilgrim, 'Life, Life, Eternal Life!'

The service was over, and, with the remembrance of that sermon as a life-long legacy, we retraced our steps homeward, stronger for having sat at the feet of this rugged Elijah of the coalpit, a hewer of coals for six days down in the deep dark mine, and a very flame of fire on the seventh.

Source: *Primitive Methodist Magazine* (1896), pp. 830–1.

As with the other breakaway groups, the Primitive Methodists placed great emphasis upon the role of lay people, women as well as men. Their first Conference in 1820 was attended by two laymen and one travelling preacher from each circuit. A higher proportion of Primitives tended to be drawn from the lower social groupings than were the Wesleyans. However, the commonly held belief that most of their members came from the ranks of unskilled workers is a mistaken one.

The table [62] shows the occupational structure of Methodism in the early part of the nineteenth century. If we examine the various social groups from which the Wesleyan and Primitive Methodists were drawn, it becomes clear that skilled workers formed the largest percentage. The first figure is the number in the sample, the second is the percentage of the whole which each grouping formed, the sample being taken from a number of non-parochial registers dating from 1830 to 1837.

62. Occupations	Wesleyans		Primitives	
	Total	%	Total	%
Merchants and manufacturers	76	1.7	13	0.5
Shopkeepers	253	5.8	93	3.9
Farmers	239	5.5	135	5.6
Artisans	2750	62.7	1149	47.7
Labourers	415	9.5	387	16.1
Colliers, miners etc.	334	7.6	301	12.5
Other occupations	318	7.2	329	13.7
TOTALS	4385	100.0	2407	100.0

Note: 'Artisans' include all skilled workers, whether employed in factories or domestic industry. 'Labourers' include industrial workers in unskilled occupations, and agricultural workers.

Source: A. D. Gilbert, Religion and Society in Industrial England, Longman 1976, p. 63.

The Bible Christians (1815)

This next offshoot also grew out of a desire for freedom. Unlike the Primitives, who spread from the Stafford and Cheshire borders throughout Britain, the Bible Christians were mainly to be found in the West Country. The name derived from their belief that all problems should be solved by recourse to the Bible. Their founder, William O'Bryan, was born in Luxulyan in Cornwall and was twice an unsuccessful candidate for the Methodist ministry. Nonetheless, he developed an independent preaching ministry that was to result in the founding of small groups in Cornwall and Devon.

His followers – who often came from areas where Methodism had little or no influence – were not actually Methodists themselves and therefore could not be really described as being schismatic. Indeed, they took great care not to compete with Methodists and often worked alongside them. The Bible Christians can be regarded as being part of the Methodist tradition since they were organized on similar lines and their theological emphases and style of worship differed little from that of the Primitives, with whom they had surprisingly little contact. They were notable for a number of reasons: the prominent part that lay people took in administering their organization; the admission – for the first time in Methodism – of women itinerant preachers by their Conference in 1819; missionary enterprises which were remarkable considering the size of their movement,[8] and their leading role in the rise of the Temperance Movement.

The United Methodist Free Churches (1857)

In the middle of the century a number of smaller associations who had seceded from the main Wesleyan body came together to form the United Methodist Free Churches. Since the story is a complicated one, we simply note some of the more interesting details.

The first of these splinter groups, the Protestant Methodists, broke away as a result of a dispute in 1827 in Leeds. This became known as the 'Leeds Organ Controversy'. The wealthy and influential trustees in Leeds installed an organ in Brunswick Chapel against the wishes of the local congregation and the preachers of the surrounding area, who voted to ban what they considered to be a 'godless instrument'. An appeal by the trustees was upheld by Conference, much to the dismay of the church members. It was, therefore, far more than a parochial issue concerning the style of worship at Brunswick Chapel. It was about 'unscriptural domination' by the hierarchy of Wesleyan ministers. The Secretary of Conference, Jabez Bunting – about whom more is said later in this chapter – was in no doubt himself about the real issues. This can be seen in his remarks in a letter to Joseph Entwistle, the superintendent of the Bristol circuit, in December 1827 [63].

---

63. . . . Now about Leeds . . . The organ is the *mere pretext* among the *heads* of the schism; and would, I believe, be cheerfully abandoned, if there were any ground whatever to believe that such a concession would cure the evil. But the root of it lies much deeper. There was a *radical* faction there, whose meetings had assumed all the fearful characters of a *Methodistical Luddism*[9] (*secret vows or bonds*, etc., included) and of whom it was indispensable to the *permanent peace* of the Society that it should be forthwith purged . . . The case was the most awful and perplexing I ever saw. We at one time had no hope but in dissolving the Society, and nearly all our more respectable friends were right, the *poor Leaders, and younger Leaders and Local Preachers* were largely infected with the spirit of revolt against the first principles of our existing Church Government. At last things brightened . . . *Nine tenths* of the Brunswick Congregation and Society are on one side; and the work in that Chapel prospers amidst all this horrible bustle.

Source: W. R. Ward (ed), *The Early Correspondence of Jabez Bunting 1820–1829*, Royal Historical Society 1972, p. 164.

In 1837 the Protestant Methodists were united with two other groups: the Arminian Methodists under Henry Breedon who had been expelled in 1831, and Dr Samuel Warren's Wesley Methodist Association which had been formed in 1835. Warren, the superintendent of the Manchester circuit, vehemently opposed Jabez Bunting's proposal that a Methodist theological institute be set up, being convinced that such an institution 'would increase power in the hands of a few individuals' – including, in particular, Bunting! Along with a number of other preachers, he was expelled at the Conference of 1835 and became the first President of the Wesleyan Methodist Association in August of the same year. In 1849 this body was to be joined by yet another offshoot – the Wesleyan Reform Society – in the course of a dispute so serious that it is estimated to have cost the parent Wesleyan Methodists 100,000 members.

The 'Fly Sheets' controversy of the 1840s, as this dispute was called, had its origins in the same debate concerning Conference's authority and what was perceived to be ministerial domination. One of the leading opponents of the theological institute had been a gifted, sincere but unstable preacher by the name of James Everett. His fondness for writing anonymous diatribes against the Methodist hierarchy was to lead to his eventual expulsion in 1849. He now became the centre of widespread discontent with the leadership of Wesleyan Methodism, by writing a series of very critical articles entitled *Fly Sheets from the Private Correspondent*. No name appeared against these tracts and Everett never admitted authorship, though it was clear who had penned them. Witty and eloquent they certainly were. The Wesleyan Conference, however, could not ignore their caustic and sometimes abusive attacks, especially against the Secretary, Jabez Bunting.

How far-reaching this conflict became is revealed by the letter written by William Clarkson, the superinten-

---

64. I will endeavour briefly to lay before you the present state of the Derby Circuit and would feel greatly obliged for any suggestion you could make to me . . .

. . . The Local Preachers have kept to law and rule, and given me no trouble. Indeed, the great increase of members of society, the excellence of the congregations and the flourishing state of the finances left them no room to complain.

But no sooner did they learn that Messrs Everett, Dunn and Griffith were expelled from connection with the Conference, than they called a public meeting at which resolutions simply expressive of sympathy for them were moved, but the movers and seconders of these resolutions made remarks condemnatory of the proceedings of Conference, and sufficient, we think, to make out a good case of charge against 3 at least of the parties . . .

Many feel great indignation against me and several radical families have absented themselves from my ministry since Conference, because I brought charges against Mr Dunn at the last District Meeting, and he and Mr Griffith have been expelled; nevertheless, in despite of all odium, I am determined, the Lord being my helper, to do calmly and firmly whatever I believe to be right and fitting in the present exigency . . .

Source: W. R. Ward (ed), *Early Victorian Methodism: The Correspondence of Jabez Bunting 1830–1858*, OUP 1976, pp. 380–2.

dent of the Derby circuit, to Jabez Bunting in September 1849, in which the writer describes some of the problems he faced in his circuit following the crisis [64]. Samuel Dunn and William Griffith who are mentioned in the text, were associates of Everett and expelled along with him.

The Wesleyan Reform Society – or the Wesleyan Reformers as they were more commonly known – became a separate connexion in 1849. Although approaches to the Primitive Methodists, the Bible Christians and the Methodist New Connexion all came to nothing, the Wesleyan Reformers found sufficient common ground with the Wesleyan Methodist Association which now contained the Protestant and Arminian Methodists to form the United Methodist Free Church in 1857. Not all joined. Those with reservations formed themselves into a separate body in 1859, somewhat confusingly called the Wesleyan Reform Union. However, these small steps were anticipating the much greater achievements of 1907 and 1932.

The story of these divisions is, indeed, a complicated one. An overall picture can be gained by referring to the accompanying diagram, (Fig.1) which shows the steady progression towards union. The groups which remained separate in 1907 are in italic; those marked with an asterisk still exist separately today.

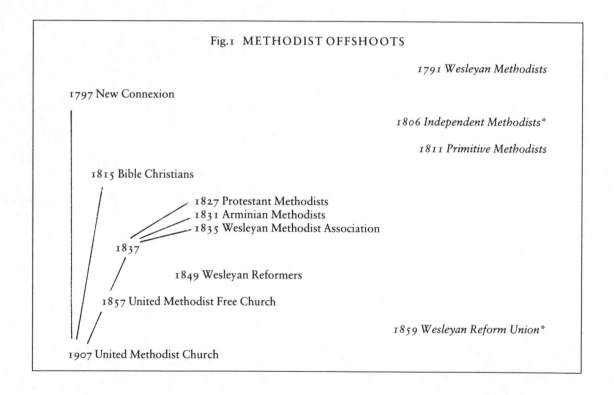

Fig.1 METHODIST OFFSHOOTS

1791 Wesleyan Methodists

1797 New Connexion

1806 Independent Methodists*

1811 Primitive Methodists

1815 Bible Christians

1827 Protestant Methodists
1831 Arminian Methodists
1835 Wesleyan Methodist Association

1837

1849 Wesleyan Reformers

1857 United Methodist Free Church

1859 Wesleyan Reform Union*

1907 United Methodist Church

Jabez Bunting

Lord, in the strength of grace,
With a glad heart and free,
Myself, my residue of days,
I consecrate to thee.

Thy ransomed servant, I
Restore to thee thy own;
And, from this moment, live or die,
To serve my God alone.

In our brief discussion of the major offshoots the name of the Revd Dr Jabez Bunting has been mentioned several times. He above all people symbolized the Wesleyan hierarchy, for the breakaway groups at least. During these troubled years, Bunting was the most important figure involved in the process of working out in practical terms what the Methodist Connexion was in theory. Born in Manchester, he entered the Wesleyan ministry in 1803. It was soon apparent that here was a man of immense gifts, whose ability as a preacher, writer and administrator quickly marked him out for leadership.

Since he was elected President of Conference in 1820, 1828, 1836 and 1844, served as Secretary of Conference from 1814–1820, and held numerous other high offices, Bunting was in an ideal position to influence the Methodist leadership. Today we might call him the ideal 'committee man'. He had many opponents and was disliked for his apparent lack of interest in the spiritual welfare of the Methodist people. This was unfair. However, his strongest critics were justified in attacking his reluctance to accommodate other people's views when his own were challenged. One historian has referred to Bunting as the 'Pope of Methodism'.[10] An exaggeration, no doubt, but certainly the way in which some saw him.

Nevertheless, he stood head and shoulders above his contemporaries. The Methodist historian John Kent has led recent moves to rehabilitate Bunting by showing that what he was trying to achieve, in effect, was the preservation of Wesley's 'system' of administering the Connexion. He alone grasped the fact that Methodism's most appropriate role was to be 'an ecclesiastical bridge between Dissent and the Establishment'.[11] In some ways Bunting most truly represented what could be said to be the 'Wesleyan ideal', in the sense that – in the eyes of his supporters, of course – he fulfilled the role which it was believed was John Wesley's own view of the way in which the Methodist leadership should develop.

An idea of the strength of Bunting's beliefs may be gained from the following extract from a speech to the Leeds Methodists at a Public Breakfast given in his honour in June 1850 [65]. Since this was given towards the end of his life, it represents a fair summary of his views on the authority and responsibility of the ordained ministry. In formal Methodist parlance, of course, they were still referred to as the 'preachers'.

---

65. The Christian Church, though it may not be a perfect body, yet, in a very high and important sense, as far as human regulation and human vigilance can keep it, ought to be a pure body. We must not have unholy men – men notoriously and undeniably such – within the pale of our Methodism. We must not allow such men, from any fear of Christian discipline, administered affectionately and kindly, to deprive us of our Purity . . . There must be persons invested with some degree of responsibility and some degree of power. Where there is duty, there must be power to carry that duty into effect; and those should not receive the power who have not the responsibility. I think that this consideration has, in great measure, been lost sight of . . . Talk of the power of the preachers! Why, they would be a very odd set of preachers if they had no power. They would not be the preachers of the New Testament. They would not be the order of preachers which the Scriptures recognize, men especially called of God, and then especially set apart by the concurrence of the church – the ministry and the people together – to take charge, as its pastors, of the Purity of the body. If we are to have that charge, we must have power. We may exercise it erroneously in many instances, but that is no argument for abolishing the power. What is there that may not be abused, if men are not so wise and holy as they should be?

Source: Dr Bunting's Visit to Leeds, June 19th, 1850 (Leeds 1850), pp. 25–26.

We now turn to Methodism's relationship with the secular world in the first half of the nineteenth century.

Methodism, society and government

Forth in thy name, O Lord, I go,
My daily labour to pursue,
Thee, only thee, resolved to know
In all I think, or speak, or do.

In this age of revolution, Methodism was viewed with considerable disfavour in government circles in the 1790s. The events in France were fresh in people's minds and further revolutions would occur in many parts of Europe in 1820, 1830 and 1848. It was, therefore, understandable that – however unjustly – Methodists found themselves under suspicion of having revolutionary tendencies. In retrospect we can sympathize with the Tory governments of the day in their fear that the revolution in France might infect Britain, even though historians are now agreed that this fear was misplaced.

Nonetheless, it was a cause of deep concern within Methodism. This can be seen in the following excerpt from a letter from Robert Pilter to Jabez Bunting dated 23 October 1819 [66]. Robert Pilter was superintendent minister of the North Shields circuit and was greatly concerned by the way in which one of his local preachers had opposed the action of the Manchester magistrates in dealing with the 'Peterloo Massacre' of that same year.[12] In his letter Pilter mentions that he has written to the President of Conference, Jonathan Crowther, and relates to Bunting part of the latter's answer to his plea for advice. The expression 'put him off the plan' meant that the young man referred to in the extract would have his name removed from the circuit preaching plan and therefore be forbidden to conduct services.

66. On Monday the 11th instant a meeting of reformers was held at Newcastle for the purpose of expressing their opinion on the Manchester Murders as they call them. 50 or 60,000 people attended, amongst whom were a great number of our own people, several of our Leaders and some of our Local Preachers. One of the latter William H. Stephenson, a young man who teaches a school at Burton Colliery in this Circuit went upon the hustings and made a speech, condemning in strong terms the conduct of the Manchester magistrates: this has given very great offence to most of the Travelling Preachers and respectable friends in this neighbourhood and to none more than myself, and I have been advised at all events to *put him off the plan*.

. . . I wrote to the President for his advice . . . The substance of Mr President's reply is as follows. 'I do not believe that we are called either to pull down Governments or to prop them up. We are called to promote the salvation of souls . . . It was Mr Wesley's opinion and advice, that the Methodists should never appear in politics as a body . . . My opinion and advice is this, that you give him a serious admonition, including in this your thoughts on his recent conduct, and your advice that he keep out of such matters in future. I verily believe that this will be the best line of conduct that you can pursue. If you expel such men, the Kilhamites and Ranters will greedily gather them up. In politics I think our present duty is neutrality . . .' My writing to the President was a profound secret . . .

Now my dear Brother what must I do? . . . no personal considerations shall deter me from the performance of my duty. But amidst so many conflicting considerations and interests, I am at a loss how to act . . .

Source: W. R. Ward (ed), *The Early Correspondence of Jabez Bunting 1820–1829*, Royal Historical Society 1972, pp. 21–24.

An interesting paradox is that, while Methodism was considered by some at the time as being potentially dangerous, certain historians have tried to show that it actually saved England from revolution in the early years of the nineteenth century. In particular, the French historian Elie Halévy came to the conclusion that Methodism, primarily among the nonconformist sects, was a conservative influence.[13] In what has become known as 'the Halévy thesis', he argued that

Methodism encouraged the lower classes to work without complaining, to live thrifty, sober lives and to practice submission to their superiors as well as to the will of God. This rather naïve judgment was attacked by other historians who pointed to the disruptive impact of the various schismatic Methodist groups such as the 'Ranters'. Halévy neatly sidestepped this criticism by saying that, on the contrary, the existence of so many breakaway groups resulted in Methodism's moderating influence being spread even more widely. He concluded that 'everywhere it was a spirit of reaction against the rationalism and republicanism of the old Nonconformity'.[14]

Some Methodists, it is true, might have unusual ways of worshipping and behaving in the eyes of staid Anglicans but they were far from being politically subversive. In particular, the Wesleyans were concerned to impress upon the public at large and the governments of the day that they were honest, respectable, law-abiding, loyal citizens. The 1792 Conference, for example, exhorted its preachers in the following declaration:

> None of us, shall either in writing or in conversation speak lightly or irreverently of the Government. We are to observe that the oracles of God command us to be subject to the higher powers; and that honour to the King is there connected with the fear of God.

Some ministers even removed powder from their wigs in order not to be accused of wasting precious flour in wartime!

Consider the letter from John Stephens, the superintendent of the Manchester circuit to Jabez Bunting, written on 1 February 1821, part of which is reproduced here [67]. It is a good example of the basic conservatism of many Wesleyan Methodists. Stephens had stood out as a champion of order and loyalty to the government during the Peterloo crisis, expelling large numbers of radicals from membership and preventing Methodists from taking part in further political demonstrations. While many of his contemporaries suffered great mental agony during this crisis-filled period, he did not!

67.

My Dear Sir,

. . . I should be happy to give you an account of our affairs since the last Conference; but I have been so much personally concerned in them, that such a history from me would savour too much of egotism . . .

The objects we have kept in view are, 1st., to give the sound part of this society a decided ascendency. 2. So to put down the opposition as to disable them from doing mischief. 3. To cure those of them who are worth saving. 4. To take the rest one by one, and crush them when they notoriously commit themselves. The plan is likely to succeed. They are completely at our mercy. We have no long speeches; no moving and seconding wild and absurd resolutions; not a soul of them ventures to propose anything without first consulting me and obtaining my consent. A few of the ringleaders have taken the sulks, and seldom attend our meetings; but for this we are not sorry. We have peace; we meet and do our business; and part like men of God. They are down and we intend to keep them down. That they are not annihilated is rather for want of will than power; we wish to be careful in rooting up the tares, lest we should root up the wheat also. The poor people are getting better wages. Provisions are cheap. Their leaders have deceived them in their promises of revolution. They are growing tired of radicalism, and as that dies religion will revive.

Our congregations are good. Methodism stands high among the respectable people . . .

Source: W. R. Ward (ed), *The Early Correspondence of Jabez Bunting 1820–1829*, Royal Historical Society 1972, pp. 61–2.

It is correct to see Methodism as a stabilizing influence in the areas where it was strong – in its encouragement of thrift, obedience, and high moral standards. However, it would be a gross exaggeration to say that Methodism actually had sufficient political impact to prevent revolution from breaking out in this country. In this respect, Halévy was wrong. The forces of order were too strong, the forces of change too weak, for this to have been the case. The truth was that Methodism, in effect, looked both ways. It contained radical and conservative elements, the result being that Bunting and his colleagues had to tread a very careful path indeed during these years.

Time Line of Events

1797	Methodist New Connexion formed
1806	Independent Methodists break away
1807	Camp meeting at Mow Cop
1811	Primitive Methodists become a separation connexion
1815	End of the Napoleonic wars Bible Christians formed
1819	'Peterloo' massacre
1827	The Leeds organ dispute
1832	First Parliamentary Reform Act
1835	Wesleyan Methodist Association founded
1845	Newman is received into the Roman Catholic Church
1846–9	The 'Fly Sheets' controversy
1848	The third and final outbreak of Chartism
1849	Wesleyan Reform Association comes into being
1857	United Methodist Free Church formed Death of Jabez Bunting

For Discussion

1. What qualities of leadership should an ordained minister display?

2. How far do your sympathies lie with the breakaway groups, and how far with the Methodist hierarchy?

3. Which aspects of the service described in Document 60 did you find appealing, and which unattractive? Why?

4. What practical advice would you give to a church whose members disagree over fundamental issues yet who want to live together in harmony?

9

Towards Union

Joined in one spirit to our Head
Where he appoints we go;
And still in Jesu's footsteps tread,
And show his praise below.

From about the middle of the nineteenth century Methodism[1] entered a somewhat happier period that reflected the more settled political and economic climate of the country as a whole. The mid-Victorian era was relatively prosperous, since the fruits of industrialization began at last to be seen in the slow improvement of overall living standards. Moreover, the fifty years before the outbreak of the First World War saw an enormous number of changes brought about by a succession of progressive governments. The great reforms introduced by Gladstone and Disraeli from the 1860s to the 1880s were equalled by the achievements of the Liberal governments of Asquith and Lloyd George from 1906 to 1914. Almost every sphere of life was affected. By 1914, many of the political, economic and social foundations of modern Britain had been laid.

The 'age of imperialism', as this period has been called, undoubtedly secured even greater wealth for Britain, but it had many unattractive features. A severe depression, for example, blighted the late 1870s and the poor, inevitably, were the worst affected. Moreover, even the prolonged struggle of the working classes to assert themselves in the late nineteenth century – a struggle which saw the rise of trade unionism and the eventual founding of the Parliamentary Labour Party – produced casualties, among them the Liberal Party itself, and Christians found their loyalties divided. Again, although secularism was in its infancy and working-class people were only converted to its doctrines in very small numbers, Beatrice Webb observed, shrewdly, that 'it was during the middle decades of the nineteenth century that, in England, the impulse of self-subordinating service was transferred, consciously and overtly, from God to man'.[2] In such a climate, it is hardly surprising that many felt that the churches were composed of middle-class, narrow-minded moralizers whose biblical literalism and over-enthusiastic tactics in evangelism were alienating the common people.

As the century wore on, Methodism had to grapple with these issues, and one gets the impression that it did so with growing confidence and renewed optimism. We have already noted the limited progress towards Methodist unity as early as the 1850s, and further steps were taken in 1907, the last stage being reached in 1932. Before tracing these events in more detail, however, we shall examine the impact of the main social and political concerns of the period. We shall, therefore, adopt a thematic approach, dealing with poverty, various moral issues and education, as well as the rise of labour movements, and beginning with some general comments concerning religion and society in Victorian England.

Religion and the working classes

Outcasts of men, to you I call,
 Harlots, and publicans, and thieves!
He spreads his arms to embrace you all;
 Sinners alone his grace receives;
No need of him the righteous have;
He came the lost to seek and save.

The popular belief that Victorian people of all classes were ardent and regular church attenders is, in fact, mistaken. For all the efforts of Methodists and their fellow Christians in the eighteenth and nineteenth centuries, the working classes were never, to any great degree, won over to church attendance and membership. The first half of the nineteenth century was certainly a time of general religious expansion, but the churches were painfully aware that they were not attracting many members of the working classes. Indeed, since the beginning of the Industrial Revolution in the mid-eighteenth century, working-class people were less affected by traditional religion than any other social group.

An indication of this can be provided by a brief examination of the Religious Census of 1851 – the only one of its kind. The total attendance at churches on 30 March 1851 was: Church of England 5,292,551; Roman Catholics 383,630, and the main Protestant dissenting Churches (Presbyterian, Methodist, Congregationalist, Baptist) 4,536,264. Horace Mann, the agent of the registrar-general, estimated that, allowing for people attending two or three times on that Sunday, the total number of persons attending worship once or more on census Sunday was 7,261,032. In his calculations, Mann assumed that 30% of the total population could not be expected to attend. These included infants, the very elderly and infirm, and those who were compelled to work on Sunday. Since the Census gave the total population of England and Wales as 17,927,609, roughly 12.5 million were potential churchgoers.

It is difficult, of course, to draw hard and fast conclusions from one set of figures. However, even placing the most optimistic construction on the above numbers, we can estimate that no more than about 58% of the people attended a Christian service of any kind. The churches had indeed failed to gain the allegiance of a substantial proportion of the population. This extract from the official report which accompanied the results shows that Horace Mann was in no doubt about this [68].

68. The most important fact which this investigation as to attendance brings before us is, unquestionably, the alarming number of non-attendants. Even in the least unfavourable aspect of the figures just presented, and assuming (as no doubt is right) that the 5,288,294 absent every Sunday are not always the same individuals, it must be apparent that a sadly formidable portion of the English people are habitual neglecters of the public ordinances of religion. Nor is it difficult to indicate to what particular class of community this portion in the main belongs. The middle classes have augmented rather than diminished that devotional sentiment and strictness of attention to religious services by which, for several centuries, they have so been eminently distinguished. With the upper classes, too, the subject of religion has obtained of late a marked degree of notice, and a regular church-attendance is now ranked among the recognized proprieties of life. It is to satisfy the wants of these two classes that the number of religious structures has of late years so increased. But while the *labouring* myriads of our country have been multiplying with our material prosperity, it cannot, it is feared, be stated that a corresponding increase has occurred in the attendance of this class in our religious edifices. More especially in cities and large towns it is observable how absolutely insignificant a portion of the congregations is composed of artizans . . .'

Source: Horace Mann, *Census of Great Britain, 1851. Religious Worship in England and Wales* (abridged from the official report, Routledge 1854).

Mann made it quite clear that working-class people were the main non-attenders and suggested a number of reasons for their absence. He believed that the poor saw religion as a middle-class luxury, felt that the churches had an unfeeling attitude towards working-class poverty and were acutely aware of the way in which Sunday worship emphasized social divisions. These divisions could be seen in the obvious disparities in dress of the worshippers and in the way that 'respectable' pews paid for by the wealthy contrasted with the free seating for the poor. Even today, one can occasionally see displayed outside older church buildings the notice proclaiming that 'All seats in this church are free'. An insufficiency of church buildings – especially in the newer urban areas – together with a corresponding shortage of ministers, also affected the low numbers of working-class attenders. Probably the single most important reason for their absence, however, was simply that huge numbers had no contact with any Christian body.

Some attempts were made to reach the unchurched. One notable Anglican historian has defended the churches against accusations that they paid little attention to the plight of the labouring masses, by asserting that, 'much of what was done to relieve the poor was done by religious men and women, and a lot of it by men and women who represented a church in doing it'.[3] A great deal of good work was indeed done by individuals, but the overall picture of failure is inescapable.

Methodism and social issues

Thy mind throughout my life be shown,
  While, listening to the sufferer's cry;
The widow's and the orphan's groan,
  On mercy's wings I swiftly fly,
The poor and helpless to relieve,
My life, my all, for them I give.

The various Methodist connexions – the Primitive Methodists, Bible Christians and smaller offshoots rather more than the Wesleyans – did include some working-class people. Those local churches with a high proportion of working-class members were invariably to be found in the newer industrial areas, and their life and worship had a flavour that was quite distinct from middle-class Wesleyan bodies in other parts of the country.

Some impressions of working-class Methodism can be gained from the diary of an unnamed traveller who visited a United Methodist Free Church chapel in downtown Manchester in 1871 [**69**]. It is difficult to say how far the situation in question was typical of the country as a whole. The description which the writer gives of both the building and the service he attended is certainly characteristic of Methodism in the poorer urban areas. His comments on the sermons make interesting reading, and one wonders what kind of worship *he* was accustomed to!

---

69. The Lever Street Chapel stands a few yards from the corner of Ancoats Lane. We dismiss its external architecture with the remark that it belongs to the early order of Methodism, being simply an ugly black building, with a number of rectangular doors . . . The outside looks so dirty that it is a relief to gain the interior which is as remarkable for its cleanly appearance, being painted throughout a light grey – gallery, pulpit, walls, and all except the pews. One would imagine it would be a relief to many a soul to escape from the close courts and dirty hovels in the neighbourhood of the chapel into its interior, where there is at least light and space. Doubtless it is so to some; but the congregation is not large, and as is the case with most city churches and chapels of all denominations, a considerable number of its members come from the suburbs to the place or worship in connection with which they have been brought up . . .

The sermons of the Manchester Free Methodists cannot be described as intensely spiritual; they are rather familiar exhortations relating to the common circumstances of life. They abound in warnings against many specially-named places of amusement, and deal largely in the temptations to which young people, particularly apprentices and servant girls, are subjected. As the bulk of the congregation is composed of the working classes, there is doubtless a special applicability about much of this preaching.

Source: 'A Wanderer', *Sketches of Methodism in Manchester*, 1871, pp. 15f.

Generally speaking, however, the lower strata of society – particularly those engaged in unskilled labour – were not well represented within Methodism as a whole.[4] In this respect, the composition of Methodism mirrored that of other denominations. This did not mean, however, that there were not Methodists everywhere who were concerned with social issues in the latter half of the nineteenth and early part of the twentieth centuries.

Hugh Price Hughes (1847–1902) was one of the most prominent figures involved in tackling social problems. Born in Carmarthen and the son of a doctor, Hughes entered the Wesleyan ministry at an early age and rapidly acquired a reputation for being a brilliant preacher. His main gift lay in his ability to combine theory and practice – a high degree of theological expertise with a passionate concern for the physical welfare of his fellow men and women. It was Hughes who, perhaps more than any of his contemporaries, expressed the nonconformist element in Wesleyan Methodism, which up to that time had always occupied the somewhat uncertain ground between the Church of England and Dissent. As the founder and editor of the *Methodist Times*,[5] he was able to publicize his views on both social issues and the need for more co-operation between nonconformists. In the 1880s and 1890s, under his influence, Methodism leaned more positively towards the Free Churches.[6]

Hugh Price Hughes' importance can be seen in two areas. The first was the National Council of Free Churches, whose formation in 1896 owed much to his drive and leadership. This movement was intended to be an association of Free Church representatives who would consult together on matters of common concern, such as mission to the unchurched, education and questions of public morality. An idea of the kind of views which Hughes held may be gained by studying an extract from his presidential address to this body at its first meeting in 1896, in which he outlined its purpose [70].

70. In the first place and emphatically, it is not a 'political' movement in the sense in which that greatly abused word is usually employed . . . The Church of Rome and the Church of England have been almost wrecked again and again by the folly of their ecclesiastical rulers in identifying them with the interests of a particular political party. God forbid that we should ever imitate their suicidal example . . . But there are great causes, such as the Temperance Movement, the Purity Movement, the Anti-Gambling Movement and the Peace Movement which, although they have their political sides are essentially moral and Christian, and which, without fear of internal discord, we must promote with all our might . . .

I come now to consider the specific objects of this organized ecclesiastical Movement . . . The first is 'to facilitate and promote fraternal intercourse among the Evangelical Free Churches' . . .

And so I pass naturally to the second great object that we set before ourselves – the deepening of our own spiritual life . . . We are confronted in every part of this country by a vast Unreached Majority of the people. In every city, town and village, the great majority are outside all the Churches . . . No aggressive attempt to bring men to Christian decision has in it a rational or scriptural guarantee of permanence unless it is based upon the organized fellowship of the Christian Church . . .

I come now to the most novel, the most characteristic and the most necessary part of our appointed work. The Constitution, which you will consider tomorrow, suggests that one essential object of this Movement should be 'to advocate the New Testament doctrine of the Church'.

It is high time we made a more positive statement of our Faith . . . Our vocation, in real and happy association with one another, is to 'seek first the kingdom of God and his righteousness' – the reconstruction both of human society and of personal life on a Christian basis . . .

Source: *Proceedings of the First National Council of the Evangelical Free Churches*, 1896, pp. 24–38.

While Hughes, therefore, was concerned with doctrinal questions, he also placed great emphasis upon practical matters. In his preaching and writing he constantly stressed the need for personal commitment to Christ, accompanied by an involvement in social and political issues.[7] Unless social responsibility was harnessed to evangelical zeal, the churches would fail in their mission to the people of Britain. This leads us to the second, more general area with which he was concerned.

Hugh Price Hughes has been associated with what became known as the 'Nonconformist Conscience'. In the *Methodist Times* Hughes had attacked the Irish leader Charles Stuart Parnell for not resigning from politics following his involvement with a married woman, Mrs Kitty O'Shea. Hughes and his supporters were branded as pious interferers, and the expression 'Nonconformist Conscience' was first used by their critics in *The Times* newspaper in 1890. Hughes was happy to adopt the label, however, and it quickly came into general use. The precise meaning of the phrase is very difficult to spell out. In some ways it was simply used to indicate a growing awareness that social evils needed combating. The nonconformists were not the only members of late nineteenth-century British society to have a conscience! Indeed, some of its greatest advocates were guilty of serious inconsistency. Hughes, for example, while quick to condemn such evils as gambling and drunkenness, was one of the chief supporters of imperialism – which inevitably had an unpleasant racist aspect. John Kent has argued that 'the exponents of the Conscience . . . often gave the impression that they were more concerned about power than morality . . . and that their moral judgments were at the mercy of their political needs'.[8] For its supporters, the Nonconformist Conscience was a rallying cry. For its opponents, it represented a new form of narrow-minded religious disapproval.

Within Methodism, the Conscience found its practical expression in the 'Forward Movement', which has been described as 'the last great attempt to reach those alienated from all the churches'.[9] If the gospel was seen to have a social dimension, then church organization and structure had to change and Hughes challenged Methodism to adapt its itinerant system of ministry to cope with what were perceived to be the special social and spiritual needs of the working classes. The building of Central Halls, still a special feature of Methodism in our big cities, was an attempt to meet this need and show that Christians could combine 'the sacrament with the soup-ladle'.

One venture deserves particular mention. This was the famous 'Bermondsey Settlement' in London founded in 1891 by John Scott Lidgett (1854–1953),

who in some ways was Hugh Price Hughes' natural successor. His breadth of vision and driving energy ensured that he occupied a central place in Wesleyan Methodism from the 1890s onwards, and it was fitting that he should become the President of the Uniting Conference of 1932. In his *Reminiscences*, written in retirement, Lidgett outlined the basic aims underlying the founding of the Settlement [71].

---

71. The Main object of the Settlement was to bring a force of educated workers to give help to all the highest interests of the neighbourhood, religious, educational, social, and administrative. Its aims were defined at the outset in the following terms:

1. To bring additional force and attractiveness to Christian work.
2. To become a centre of social life, where all classes may meet together on equal terms for healthful intercourse and recreation.
3. To give facilities for the study of Literature, History, Science, and Art.
4. To bring men together to discuss general and special social evils and to seek their remedy.
5. To take such part in local administration and philanthropy as may be possible.
6. And so to do all this that it shall be perfectly clear that no mere sectarian advantage is sought, but that it shall be possible for all good men to associate themselves with our work.

Source:. J. Scott Lidgett, *Reminiscences*, Epworth Press 1928, p. 31.

In the eyes of the general public Methodism has often been associated with particular issues. While this is an over-simplification, Methodism has always taken a stricter stance towards gambling than it has towards some other subjects, because this was – and still is – an evil to be found at every level of society. In Victorian times the affluent might regard it as a harmless diversion. For the poor, however, it could easily spell ruination. So, too, could alcohol, of which Methodism has traditionally been seen as the foe. Though times have changed, it is worth remembering the strength of people's feelings on this subject in the last century, as shown by the letter written by a Methodist minister to

Jabez Bunting in 1848 [72]. The writer, Richard Tabraham,[10] was the superintendent of the Clitheroe circuit and a leading champion of abstinence in his day.

---

72. The subject which has for years engaged my thought and prayers is the position of *Methodism* towards the extraordinary *moral movement*, abstinence from all intoxicating drink . . . This was increased by the awful instances I have witnessed of ministers, their families, officers, members etc. again and again falling under the power of liquor, the fact that many pleaded the example of ministers and others as an encouragement to drink, and this issued in inebriety, the souls we could not secure for Christ through this fell evil, the hundreds of thousands of pounds which our own ministers and people alienated from Methodism, especially from our *glorious missionary cause* every year to spend on drink . . .

Believe me dear Doctor, I have mourned for many years over what has really appeared to me *hostility* as well as apathy to *Abstinence* among many of our leading ministers and some of our official people . . .

God has given you the influence due to your talents, age, station, to his own gracious bestowments so long continued – your brethren justly love you, and would listen to your far-seeing suggestions. O has not the time come when temperance should be promoted *peaceably, connexionally*, by us, in our *schools, congregations*, societies – yea among the preachers? Who knows but you, Doctor, are God's ordained instrument to aid Methodism in the most permanent and effectual manner, in the suggestion of some great connexional scheme, which shall silence gainsayers, rejoice thousands of mourning hearts, save thousands of souls; help all our funds, do immense good, and little harm, and make Methodism an increasing wonder in the world? . . .

Source: W. R. Ward (ed), *Early Victorian Methodism: The Correspondence of Jabez Bunting 1830–1858*, OUP 1976, pp. 362–364.

Methodism and education

> *Happy the man who wisdom gains,*
> *Thrice happy who his guest retains;*
> *He owns, and shall forever own:*
> *Wisdom, and Christ, and heaven are one.*

From its earliest days, Methodism was involved in education. Kingswood School – which moved to its present site in Bath in 1852 – was not the only contribution that Wesley made to education. There were schools attached to the London Foundery and the Orphan House at Newcastle.

The nineteenth century also saw the proliferation of Sunday schools, which had been pioneered by Robert Raikes. The early ones were unquestionably set up with the intention of inculcating a sense of subordination and respect in children, and rather less with educational principles in mind.[11] Indeed, the teaching of basic literacy and numeracy skills was not considered worthwhile by governments until the nineteenth century. The old prejudices that education for the poor was mischievous and unnecessary lingered until the 1820s. For their part, Sunday schools were first seen as a way of countering the evils of vagrancy, depravity and delinquency – among adults as well as children – as much as a method of spreading the gospel.

Throughout the nineteenth century there was a running battle between the state, the Church of England, and the various Dissenting bodies over education. The story is complex but interesting. Controversy centred on the nature of what was taught in schools, on how education was to be controlled and by whom, and (inevitably) on the question of funding.[12] By the 1860s it had become obvious to governments that some kind of state-supported system was necessary. Indeed the powerful secularist lobby argued that free elementary education – without religious ties – was possible, provided it was financed through local rates. The 'voluntarists', as they were known, were divided. Some were determined that the state should not encroach further into the field of education and thus weaken the link between religious instruction and children's general educational development, a link which they saw as essential. Others, while affirming the importance of church schools, could see the value of using local rates.

In 1870 a national system of elementary (primary) education was introduced for children between the ages of five and twelve by Forster's Education Act. Schooling was not compulsory: locally-elected school boards which had the power to set up schools where there was insufficient provision had the discretion to compel attendance only where they saw fit. Neither was education made free by the 1870 Act. Clause 25 provided for board funds – met from local rates – to pay the fees of necessitous children in board and church schools of all types. This was seen by many Nonconformists as favouring Anglican children, since it was felt that the local school boards would inevitably be dominated by Church of England representatives.[13]

Until 1870, Methodism had stood somewhere between the two extremes of religious and secular control. Thereafter, Methodist leaders gave increasing support to state provision of schools, so long as religious instruction remained free from Anglican or denominational bias. This is clearly shown by the extract from the minutes of the Wesleyan Conference of 1891 [73]. The 'Conscience Clause' referred to in the last paragraph allowed children to absent themselves from doctrinal lessons if their parents wished.

In this respect, Methodists of all the denominations were probably the most realistic in their attitude. They realized that, in the long run, voluntary schools could not compete with the state, and that religious squabbles would serve only to hinder progress. For their part, successive governments accepted that the state could no longer merely supervise education, though they wisely consulted the churches when considering future legislation.[14] When the next major Education Bill was introduced in 1902, most Methodists opposed it only on the grounds that financial aid from the rates was given to *all* voluntary schools – which seemed to give undue favour to the Church of England. The general attitude of the Methodist Church was to support the extension of secondary education, provided that it did not become entirely secular in emphasis. By the turn of the century, therefore, 'Methodism by its very spirit and organization had become a reading, studying denomination.'[15]

Methodism and Labour movements

> *Thus may I show the Spirit within,*
> *Which purges me from every stain;*
> *Unspotted from the world and sin,*
> *My faith's integrity maintain;*
> *The truth of my religion prove*
> *By perfect purity and love.*

The relationship of Methodism to the British Labour movement at the turn of the century is an interesting subject about which much has been written and provides a continuing source of debate amongst secular and religious historians.

It was inevitable, given the nature of religious life in this country in the nineteenth century, that the Labour movement as a whole would be tinged with religion. Late nineteenth-century socialists even had their own Sunday schools. The appeals of Philip Snowden, one of the most prominent socialists of the time, for people to come to the front to sign up as members of the Independent Labour Party were popularly referred to as 'Philip's Come to Jesus'. In 1891 the first of the 'Labour Churches' was set up in Manchester by a

---

73. The Conference . . . directs that the following Resolutions be printed in the *Minutes*, viz.:–

1. That the primary object of Methodist policy in the matter of Elementary Education should be the establishment of School Boards everywhere . . . and the placing of a Christian unsectarian school within reasonable distance of every family . . .

2. That no National system of Education will meet the necessity of the country, which shall exclude from the Day Schools the Bible and religious instruction therefrom by the Teachers, suited to the capacities of the children.

5. That the Committee is prepared to accept any reasonable proposals for Free Education; but insists that all Schools freed by the aid of public grants must be so far placed under public management, as . . . to prevent their misuse for sectarian purposes.

9. That the experience of twenty years has shown that the Conscience Clause has, to a considerable extent, proved to be ineffectual and unreal as a protection for parents and children against religious intolerance and oppression . . .

Source: *Minutes* of the 1891 Conference, reprinted in Rupert Davies, A. R. George and Gordon Rupp (eds), *A History of the Methodist Church in Great Britain*, Vol. 4, Epworth Press 1988, pp. 590–591.

Unitarian minister named John Trevor. These curiously named groups were an attempt to bridge the gap between nonconformists and socialism, but the 'sermons' were basically political lectures, and the few religious characteristics they had soon disappeared. In any case, there were only ever around thirty Labour Churches, and most of these had closed by 1914.

There had been a long connection between Methodism and working-class groups. The famous Tolpuddle Martyrs were all Wesleyans,[16] and Primitive Methodists were prominent in the Trade Union movement from an early stage. It was a Primitive Methodist, Joseph Arch, who founded the National Agricultural Labourers' Union in 1872 which, at its peak, had 160,000 members. However, religion in general – and Methodism in particular – was only one of a number of factors which shaped Labour's development. Some historians, notably Robert Wearmouth,[17] have made a great deal of the part that Methodism played. The truth is less romantic. Churches and chapels were simply not organized for secular purposes, and the Labour movement did not have its origins in religion. Methodism and nonconformity as a whole might give a subtle colouring to British socialism, but we must beware of over-stressing the links.

The working-class groups which came together to form the parliamentary Labour Party in 1906 were a heterogeneous collection whose attitudes to religion ranged from outright rejection to various degrees of approval and warmth. It is worth noting that working-class groups who were sympathetic to the churches in principle often discovered, to their disappointment, that many nonconformists inclined towards the Liberals. Not surprisingly, the Wesleyans lacked any real commitment to the special interest of Labour as a separate political party. Many were losing their old allegiance to the Tories and increasingly identified with the Liberals. Further leftward moves, however, were beyond them. F. W. MacDonald, who succeeded Hugh Price Hughes as President of Conference in 1899, was probably expressing the feelings of the majority of the Methodist people towards politics, when he made these remarks in his inaugural address [74].

74. One of the possible dangers to which I have referred is that of seeking to use our compact and organized strength in the sphere of politics . . . But I trust we shall continue to maintain as a church our independence and neutrality, and preserve our civic freedom on public questions. There are indeed few political issues of such a nature that all good men must necessarily be on the same side . . . I believe that concerted action in the political sphere is about the last use we should make of our influence as a church, and that in the meantime the best political service we can render to our country is to bring the power of a living Christianity to bear upon the people at large, and so to assist in the formation of a public opinion hostile to wrongdoing of every kind, and favourable to truth and justice, to religion and virtue.

Source: F. W. MacDonald, As a tale that is told: Recollections of many years, Cassell & Co. 1919, p. 242.

Overseas missions

> O for a trumpet voice,
>   On all the world to call!
> To bid their hearts rejoice
>   In him who died for all;
> For all my Lord was crucified,
> For all, for all my Saviour died.

At this stage we should say something briefly about Methodist missions abroad. It was inevitable that the same zeal which inspired such remarkable growth during the eighteenth century revival in Britain should be directed overseas. Wesley himself had seen 'all the world as my parish', and his followers quickly took him at his word.

Beginning with Scotland, Ireland and the Shetlands,[18] and then moving further afield to America and the Caribbean, overseas missions had become a firmly established feature of Methodism by the 1780s. Lest too much be attempted too soon, it was decided that the main thrust of Methodist missionary activity should begin in the New World, followed by the West Coast of Africa. Undoubtedly, the central figure in these early years was Dr Thomas Coke, who had been appointed in 1784 superintendent minister for work in America.[19] It was his vision and energy, more than anyone else's, which acted as a catalyst for the steady expansion of missionary enterprises. Like Whitefield before him, Coke burned himself out by the age of sixty-six, but his death in 1814 en route to Ceylon helped spur initiatives in India.

The latter part of the nineteenth century saw the major European powers engaged in a race to establish colonies throughout Africa and Asia, and Christian missionaries became caught up in this process. It is undeniable that the missionary (and the doctor) followed closely on the heels of the explorer, the soldier and the diplomat. It would be an exaggeration, however, to say that missionaries were 'agents of imperialism'. Their progress was significantly slower in comparison with the speed with which the political 'scramble for Africa' took place. Methodists were not so naïve as to be unaware of the potential conflict of interest. This is shown by the remarks made by the chairman of the Wesleyan Methodist Missionary Society, John Hardy, as early as 1838 [75].

---

75. We all know, from experience, that colonization is too often followed by tyranny and oppression; and we, unlike the Jews with respect to the Canaanites, have no commission to extirpate any nation. To evangelize is one thing; to colonize another. The colonist goes 'with arms of mortal temper in his hands'; with the musket, the bayonet, and the gunpowder; but your Missionaries go with the 'sword of the Spirit, which is the word of God'. I trust they will be permitted to go unmolested. Nothing can be greater than their disinterestedness in that cause. They cannot be suspected of any objects of ambition: they go poor and defenceless, to make many rich; whereas colonists generally go to make many poor, in order to enrich a few. To Christianize countries like these is indeed a great object of ambition, and it deserves from Christians all the credit which I trust it receives.

Source: The annual meeting of The Wesleyan Methodist Missionary Society, reprinted in N. Allen Birtwhistle, 'Methodist Missions' in Rupert Davies, A. R. George and Gordon Rupp (eds), *A History of the Methodist Church in Great Britain*, Vol. 3, Epworth Press, 1983, p. 9.

The history of Methodist missions is one of courage and perseverance in the fact of opposition and, quite often, great hardship. Innumerable memorial plaques in churches and theological colleges in this country

which list the names of those who died prematurely – from malaria, cholera, or simply from exhaustion – are poignant testimonies to the cost of overseas missions. Leaders such as Coke, William Shaw, William Arthur and Thomas Freeman are deservedly remembered for their immense achievements, and their stories make fascinating reading.

Before leaving the area of overseas missions, however, three important points need to be made. First, the initiative did not belong solely to the missionaries who were sent out from Britain. The contribution of lay people who had either emigrated or who were indigenous to the areas was of immense significance, and has sometimes been underestimated. Secondly, although the paternalistic approach of these missionaries can be criticized from today's vantage point, they went with the highest of motives, as servants of God with his love in their hearts. Finally, we should remember the part played by the Methodist people at home. Huge sums of money, raised for and channelled through the missionary societies of the different Methodist connexions, bear witness to the enthusiasm, commitment and sacrifice of ordinary members.

We now conclude this chapter by examining the way in which the various branches of Methodism came together in 1932.

Methodist union

Let us join – 'tis God commands –
Let us join our hearts and hands;
Help to gain our calling's hope,
Build we each the other up.

The First World War left an indelible mark on all the churches in Britain. When, on a single day in July 1916, 60,000 British soldiers were killed, wounded or captured at the Battle of the Somme, it would not be an exaggeration to say that the twentieth century had truly arrived. Things could never be the same again. It was not that the Great War produced any radically different threats to religion. Rather, it acted as a catalyst of social change. 'War,' wrote Marx, 'is the locomotive of society'. The churches had failed to win the working classes. They now began to lose the middle classes as well. Methodism was no different in this respect from any of the other main denominations and, like them, faced declining attendances. Theological controversies contributed to a general feeling of uncertainty, but Methodist leaders often appeared complacent and out of touch with the times. No longer could they rely on the widespread deference of the people.

The union of 1932, which largely came about in response to these challenges, was prefaced by a smaller, but no less significant formation of the United Methodist Church in 1907 from the Methodist New Connexion, the Bible Christians and the United Methodist Free Churches, as can be seen by the accompanying diagram (Fig.2)

The 'union current' had begun to flow even earlier, as has been suggested in previous chapters. Some would see 1878 as the crucial date, for in that year the Wesleyan Conference finally admitted lay representatives, thereby removing at a stroke one of the main bones of contention with its fellow Methodists. There

were other factors which helped speed the process. Wesleyan Methodism had gradually moved away from exclusive control by the ordained ministry, and the social differences between the Wesleyans and others had diminished, thus blurring the distinction between the various groups.

The union itself was the scene of great celebrations all over the country. From the Methodist Central Hall in Westminster – now regarded as Methodism's headquarters – thousands joined in a march of witness to a rally in Hyde Park, which was followed by a great uniting Conference at the Albert Hall. The general sense of euphoria found its expression in the publication in 1933 of *The Methodist Hymn Book*, which by containing a balanced selection of hymns gave all three traditions an honoured place in the future.

Such a momentous agreement between the Wesleyans, Primitives and United Methodists was not achieved without difficulty. The Wesleyans, being the largest of the three connexions, felt less need to join than the others, and the required seventy-five per cent majority among their ordained ministers was only just achieved. Compromises had to be extracted from all

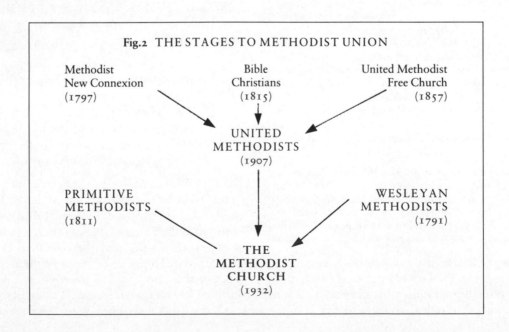

Fig.2   THE STAGES TO METHODIST UNION

Methodist New Connexion (1797)

Bible Christians (1815)

United Methodist Free Church (1857)

UNITED METHODISTS (1907)

PRIMITIVE METHODISTS (1811)

WESLEYAN METHODISTS (1791)

THE METHODIST CHURCH (1932)

participants. The Wesleyan practice of always having a ministerial President was retained but, out of deference to the Primitives whose President had sometimes been a layman, a new (lay) office of Vice-President was created. For their part, the Wesleyans conceded the dissolution of the Legal Hundred, while the other two groups accepted a Conference session for ministers only.

Not surprisingly, doctrinal issues prompted the greatest amount of discussion. What should be the doctrinal basis? The Wesleyans tended to favour John Wesley's Sermons and his Notes on the New Testament, since these contained, in their view, all the essential Evangelical and Protestant doctrines and were a reliable commentary on scripture. The other Methodist groups wished the greatest emphasis to be placed upon the Bible itself. The compromise which was achieved can be seen in the first part of the doctrinal clauses of the Deed of Union [76].

It was a masterpiece of diplomacy. The most important tenets of all three uniting bodies were preserved, yet there was sufficient open-endedness in the document to allow for latitude of interpretation. None of the groups was wholly satisfied but all were reasonably happy with the agreed formulae.

A great deal of hard bargaining also lay behind the statement about the ordained ministry. Disagreements over this had separated groups in the past. So too, had the issue of lay administration of Holy Communion.

---

76. The Methodist Church claims and cherishes its place in the Holy Catholic Church which is the Body of Christ. It rejoices in the inheritance of the Apostolic Faith and loyally accepts the fundamental principles of the historic creeds and of the Protestant Reformation. It ever remembers that in the Providence of God Methodism was raised up to spread Scriptural Holiness through the land by the proclamation of the Evangelical faith and declares its unfaltering resolve to be true to its Divinely appointed mission.

The Doctrines of the Evangelical Faith which Methodism has held from the beginning and still holds are based upon the Divine revelation recorded in the Holy Scriptures. The Methodist Church acknowledges this revelation as the supreme rule of faith and practice. These Evangelical Doctrines to which the Preachers of the Methodist Church both Ministers and Laymen are pledged are contained in Wesley's *Notes on the New Testament* and the first four volumes of his *Sermons*.

The *Notes on the New Testament* and *The 44 Sermons* are not intended to impose a system of formal or speculative theology on Methodist Preachers, but to set up standards of preaching and belief which should secure loyalty to the fundamental truths of the Gospel of Redemption and ensure the continued witness of the Church to the realities of the Christian experience of salvation.

Source: The Deed of Union: *The Constitutional Practice and Discipline of the Methodist Church*, Section 2: 4.

---

77. Christ's Ministers in the Church are Stewards in the household of God and Shepherds of His flock. Some are called and ordained to this sole occupation and have a principal and directing part in these great duties but they hold no priesthood differing in kind from that which is common to all the Lord's people and they have no exclusive title to the preaching of the gospel or the care of souls. These ministries are shared with them by others to whom also the Spirit divides His gifts severally as He wills.

It is the universal conviction of the Methodist people that the office of the Christian Ministry depends upon the call of God who bestows the gifts of the Spirit the grace and the fruit of which indicate those whom He has chosen.

Those whom the Methodist Church recognises as called of God and therefore receives into its Ministry shall be ordained by the imposition of hands as expressive of the Church's recognition of the Minister's personal call.

The Methodist Church holds the doctrine of the priesthood of all believers and consequently believes that no priesthood exists which belongs exclusively to a particular order or class of men but in the exercise of its corporate life and worship special qualifications for the discharge of special duties are required and thus the principle of representative selection is recognised.

The Preachers itinerant and lay are examined tested and approved before they are authorised to minister in holy things. For the sake of Church Order and not because of any priestly virtue inherent in the office the Ministers of the Methodist Church are set apart by ordination to the Ministry of the Word and Sacraments.

The Methodist Church recognises two sacraments namely Baptism and the Lord's Supper as of Divine Appointment and of perpetual obligation of which it is the privilege and duty of Members of the Methodist Church to avail themselves.

Source: The Deed of Union: *The Constitutional Practice and Discipline of the Methodist Church*, Section 2: 4.

Resistance to the latter came, as we might expect, from the Wesleyans and they won the day. The Primitive and United Methodists, however, were mollified by the statements in the doctrinal clauses which balanced 'high' and 'low' views of the ministry. The latter part of Section 2 of the Deed of Union which deals primarily with the role and function of ministers, illustrates how skilful the compromise was [77]. Since 1932, those not ordained have needed the special authorization of the Methodist Conference in order to preside at the Lord's Supper.

How would the decisions that were reached by the uniting Conference of September 1932 be received by members at the grass roots? Whilst the changes at national level came into effect immediately, local societies, it has to be said, were not as swift to embrace union, despite the record number of candidates offering for the ministry in that year. Regional variations make generalization difficult, but the overall pattern was of steady, if uneven, progress. Some circuits – and churches – were amalgamated at once. Others continued for many years as they were. Conference had no power to close churches or compel circuits to join together. Decades afterwards, ex-Wesleyan churches could be seen alongside ex-Primitive or ex-United societies in the same street.

In the end, the changes were accepted as a new generation grew up with no memory of, or loyalty to, the three former separate bodies. With the effects of another world war to contend with and fresh challenges to face, there was too much at stake for old rivalries to be allowed to persist.

Time Line of Events

1851   First religious census in Britain

1852   Kingswood School moves to Bath

1867   The franchise is extended to some working-class men

1868   Gladstone becomes Prime Minister for the first time

1870   Forster's Education Act

1872   Joseph Arch founds the National Agricultural Labourers' Union

1873   Onset of the 'Great Depression'

1882   Married Women's Property Act

1890   The phrase 'Nonconformist Conscience' first used

1906   Formation of the Labour Party

1907   Formation of the United Methodist Church

1914   Outbreak of World War I

1918   Universal suffrage for men over 21 and women over 30

1926   The General Strike

1932   Methodist Union

For Discussion

1. Can the churches *ever* hope to attract working-class people?

2. How middle class is your own church? Why is this?

3. What would you say to someone who claims that 'religion and politics should never be mixed'?

4. In what ways do you feel that the churches should be directly involved in primary and secondary school?

10

Methodism Since 1932

In this final chapter we shall take a brief look at the way in which Methodism has evolved since 1932. Some would say that it is impossible to write the history of a period that covers one's own lifetime, and it is certainly difficult to see very recent times in a proper perspective. The year 1989, for example, ushered in developments in Europe of such magnitude that their political, social and economic consequences will not be fully realized for a generation to come. Nevertheless, the task of appraising modern developments is worthwhile, and Christians should at least attempt to 'read the signs of the times' in order to equip themselves to meet future challenges. For this purpose we shall again use the 'camera' with a wide-angle lens which was employed in chapter 1, and continue with a thematic, rather than a chronological approach, to consider how Methodism has changed over the past fifty years.

The post-war challenge

> To serve the present age,
> My calling to fulfil:
> O may it all my powers engage
> To do my Master's will!

Although the Second World War did not perhaps have quite such a profound impact on the Methodist Church as the 1914–18 conflict, it nonetheless left its mark. The war years saw a further decline in membership. In 1932 the membership of the Methodist Church in England and Wales had been recorded at 838,019. Ten years later it was 762,300 and by 1952 it had shrunk to 738,962.[1] Whether or not the war actually accelerated the downward trend, there is no doubt that, comparatively speaking, the greatest losses occurred in the 1960s.[2]

Membership statistics do not tell the whole story, of course, and it would be unwise to use them as the sole basis for measuring the spiritual health of any church. There were gains as well as losses.

The immediate post-war years presented a huge challenge to the Methodist people which they accepted with renewed optimism. New church buildings gradually replaced the great numbers which had been destroyed by bombing. In the newer urban areas where large council estates were appearing, a great number of enterprising projects were put in hand. It is estimated that in the latter part of the 1950s the Methodist Church opened on average two new churches or church halls a week. Few could afford buildings that were used for little more than three or four hours on Sundays, and so many were designed with a flexibility that catered for both worship and community activities. Happily, this trend was in line with a growing emphasis in theology upon the 'servant church' – that a social gospel and personal salvation must go hand in hand. Cynics might see this in terms of 'necessity being the mother of invention'. Most Methodists would argue that they were simply responding to the needs of the age.

How far were the post-war years a story of renewal rather than decline? One Methodist historian has commented that 'in many ways the Church emerged from the ordeal strengthened rather than weakened'.[3] Weakened in *numbers* it might be, but there were signs that a greater sense of realism was beginning to replace the complacency of earlier years. The post-war climate was one in which organized religion could no longer assume the acquiescence and support of society as a whole. Such backing, indeed, had disappeared with the First World War. In the decades following 1945 Methodists grappled – not unsuccessfully – with the problem facing all the churches: how effective could worship, theology, mission and service be in a society which, though its values were loosely based on Christian standards, had now become thoroughly secularized?

Theology

> *Jesus, confirm my heart's desire*
>   *To work, and speak, and think for thee;*
> *Still let me guard the holy fire,*
>   *And still stir up thy gift in me.*

The last forty years have seen the 'theological pendulum' swing to and fro. The radical era of the sixties, epitomized by the publication of Bishop John Robinson's *Honest to God*, seemed to a large section of the general public to cast a cloud over the authenticity of much traditional Christian belief. The truth was that Robinson was expressing what many Christians had believed for years, and Methodist scholars were quick to take advantage of the increased interest in religion that the debate provoked. The questioning of old assumptions was no bad thing. It encouraged people to be more honest and open, and to engage in an exciting exploration of theology and the Bible.

The next extract [78] is taken from the short study by two Methodist theologians, Frances Young and Kenneth Wilson, who were concerned that Christians in the 1980s should wrestle with the 'daunting but exciting task of theological enquiry'.[4] It is interesting to compare Frances Young's comments with those which John Wesley made nearly two hundred and fifty years before, concerning the use of scripture.[5]

---

78. What would it mean to allow the Bible to speak in its own way? In fact one of the things that critical study helps us to see is that, if we attend to it, the Bible speaks in many ways, and it is not appropriate to interpret every text by the same methods. Sometimes the Bible invites us to pray, sometimes it instructs, sometimes it tells stories; sometimes it chides, sometimes it rejoices. It is not in fact straightforwardly a history textbook any more than a physics textbook – indeed even those sections which do happen to be historical overlap and re-tell the same stories in more than one way. The stories told of the past are not concerned with the past for its own sake, but rather point to the present or the future, because they give people identity or hope. In other words, the Bible interprets events and actions and makes them relevant to those it addresses, and it encourages its interpreters to engage in the on-going discernment of God's will and purpose in their own history and their own lives, by matching them up, finding analogies, to the events and lives of which stories are told in its pages. Consciously or unconsciously those who live in the Bible are engaged in that kind of interpretative process.

Source: Frances Young and Kenneth Wilson, *Focus on God*, Epworth Press 1986, p. 20.

The radical era of the sixties gave way to a gradual resurgence of conservative thinking, though since then the area of debate has broadened considerably to include liturgical, liberation and feminist theology. In all of these fields Methodist theologians have made an important contribution which has been limited, as so often in the past, by their many other duties. The Methodist Church has always ensured that her servants have been fully occupied! It could be argued, however, that Methodism has made a greater contribution to church history than to theology, thanks to a renewed interest in Wesley studies and the development of Methodism – of which this book is a by-product!

One of the great issues facing Methodism, along with other 'mainstream' churches, is how to enable members with widely differing views to live and work together. Most Methodist congregations of any size contain a wide spectrum of theology and spirituality. Whether or not a church community can live in an atmosphere of mutual acceptance and trust, openly acknowledging that such sharp differences exist, is a test of its spiritual health and a challenge to its future unity. It may indeed prove to be one of Methodism's great strengths that it does not insist that its members adhere to narrowly prescribed doctrinal formulae. As the Deed of Union of 1932 proclaims, 'all those who confess Jesus Christ as Lord and Saviour and accept the obligation to serve him in the life of the Church and the world are welcome as members of the Methodist Church'.[6]

Worship

> *O for a thousand tongues to sing*
> *My great Redeemer's praise,*
> *The glories of my God and King,*
> *The triumphs of his grace!*

Over the last twenty or thirty years there has been a renewed interest in the purpose, shape and practice of worship as a result of what has become known as the Liturgical Movement.[7] This has led Christians of all denominations to rethink their liturgies and hymnody. The 'preaching houses' so characteristic of the previous century could no longer accommodate new patterns of worship. As a consequence, Methodist church buildings throughout the country have been modernized to reflect new developments.

In the Methodist Church the Liturgical Movement has led to a subtle but important shift of emphasis in Sunday worship. There has been a greater awareness of the importance of the sacraments, and the earlier custom of tagging communion on to the main preaching service has all but disappeared. Holy Communion is now (rightly) regarded as a normal and integral part of the Sunday service. Preaching has remained a vital part of Sunday worship without necessarily providing the climax to services, and most Methodists have become used to a three-fold structure consisting of preparation, the ministry of the word and response.

These changes in the approach to worship are reflected in the final version of the *Methodist Service Book* which was approved by Conference in 1974 as a replacement for the *Book of Offices* of 1936. A comparison of the earlier communion service with the more modern one is an illuminating exercise. The latter is far less introspective and has a much greater sense of celebration, thus becoming more truly a 'eucharist' (i.e. 'thanksgiving'). Some of the general instructions for the conduct of Sunday worship (without the Lord's Supper) are reproduced here [79].

---

79. This outline consists of three principal parts: The Preparation, including praise and penitence; the Ministry of the Word; the Response. Hymns should be inserted at appropriate points, as should the notices and the collection. Prayer may be offered extempore in any place where prayer is suggested.

The Preparation

Prayers of adoration (unless this theme has been sufficiently expressed in a hymn) and confession, with an assurance of God's forgiveness.

The Ministry of the Word

Readings of Scripture, normally not less than two. The lectionary offers a selection including the Old Testament, Epistle and Gospel, linked by a unifying theme; its use is strongly recommended.

The sermon should be so placed as to make clear its link with the Scriptures from which it arises.

One or other of the historic creeds might well be used in this part of the service.

The Response

Thanksgiving and Intercession in whichever order is thought fitting, concluding with Dedication of ourselves, and the Lord's Prayer. Principal subjects for a prayer of thanksgiving should be: God's work in creation; the revelation of himself to men; the salvation of the world through Jesus Christ; the gift of the Holy Spirit; anything for which at the particular time it is appropriate to give thanks.

Subjects for intercession should include: the universal Church and all its members; all men and the welfare of the world; all nations and all in authority; the concerns of the local community; those who suffer. It may end with thanksgiving for the departed.

The Dismissal should include one or both of the elements of blessing and commissioning for the service of God in the world.

Source: *The Methodist Service Book*, Methodist Publishing House 1975, pp. B18–19.

The Liturgical Movement has had an influence on Methodist worship in two other ways.

First, one can see a renewed sense of the importance of the Christian year, which has led to the greater use of the Lectionary. In 1992 the Methodist Church adopted a four-year lectionary, known as 'JLG 2'. The letters are an abbreviation of 'Joint Liturgical Group', and JLG 1 refers to an earlier lectionary of 1967. There has been a long history of consultation between the churches, but they have never reached total agreement on a single lectionary that all could use. The 1967 Lectionary was based on a two-year cycle of readings linked to the major Christian festivals of Christmas, Easter and Pentecost. Although some regretted that the new Lectionary did not have a 'theme' for each Sunday, it was felt that more flexibility had been created by the greater number of biblical passages which were now included.

Secondly, worship has moved from being almost entirely preacher controlled to becoming an act of celebration in which the *whole* people participate. It is now quite common for lay people to read lessons and lead prayers in Methodist churches. Some, indeed, have gone further and set up regular groups who share with the minister or local preacher in the planning and leading of worship.

Possibly the greatest challenge, similar to that posed by theological diversity, is the degree to which Methodism can accommodate the different styles of worship which have developed over recent years. Traditional worship has now been joined by more informal 'praise and prayer' services[8] reminiscent of early Primitive Methodism as well as by quieter, more reflective services in which meditation and, for example, music from Taizé, occupies a major part. The growth of all-age worship has presented another series of different, but related challenges to Methodist ministers and local preachers.

Perhaps the real distinction is not so much between structured and 'free' worship as between the relative importance which is attached to emotion and reason – the heart and the mind. This, of course, is an oversimplification, but Methodist churches up and down the country will only survive and flourish if their con-gregations can come to terms with the often conflicting expectations of their worshippers. I myself believe that this can only be done if a synthesis is achieved, though this demands great patience and sensitivity on the part of those who plan and conduct Sunday worship.

The ministry

> *Now then the ceaseless shower*
> *Of gospel blessings send,*
> *And let the soul-converting power*
> *Thy ministers attend.*

In recent years the Methodist Church has spent much time in developing its theology of ministry, both lay and ordained. Some would argue that it has never been entirely successful in this task.

The *Statement on Ordination* which Conference accepted in 1960 was intended to 'bring out the significance of Ordination' and 'to invite the Church to the further study of this vitally important matter'. In this respect Methodism was building on what it had said in 1932 and developing its understanding of the role and function of the ordained ministry, while at the same time attempting to avoid two extremes: on the one hand, the sacerdotal view – which sees the ordained person as a 'different being', endowed with special, supernatural powers – and, on the other, the understanding of ministry in terms of functions performed. Neither position is entirely satisfactory, though each has had its advocates.

Methodism's attempt to steer a middle course between the two approaches has stressed the representative role of ordained ministers. At the same time, their role and function in relation to those of lay people continue to be explored, and we can see how these issues emerged by reading an extract from the *Conference Statement on Ordination* of 1974 [80]:

80. 13. In what does this special calling consist? Unquestionably there are functions to fulfil, associated by long tradition with the ordained ministry and written into the ordination service. There are the preaching of the gospel, the celebration of the sacraments, pastoral care, the teaching office (this includes the theological task), and the leadership of the churches. But it would be inadequate to confine the special calling to a collection of functions. For one thing, they are largely shared with people who are not ordained – the local preacher, the class leader and the society steward witness to that. For another, some ordained ministers are not in a position to carry out all the functions, but their ordination is not questioned on that account.

14. To find a further category we go back to the rediscovery of the significance of the whole people of God. They are what they are because of the general calling to which we have referred. They are called, all of them, ordained and unordained, to be the Body of Christ to men. But as a perpetual reminder of this calling and as a means of being obedient to it the Church sets apart men and women, specially called, in ordination. In their office the calling of the whole Church is focused and represented, and it is their responsibility as representative persons to lead the people to share with them in that calling. In this sense they are the sign of the presence and ministry of Christ in the Church, and through the Church to the world.

Source: *Statements of the Methodist Church on Faith and Order 1933–1983*, Methodist Publishing House 1984, pp. 135–136.

Three further developments are worth noting. The concept of 'sector ministry' has been discussed at great length since the 1960s in order to find better ways of expressing the position of those whose main sphere of activity is outside the church but who are ordained and an integral part of the church's ministry.

Secondly, the ordination of women in 1974 was a major step, though it is worth remembering that in theory the way had been cleared in 1939. It was not until the 1960s that the idea was revived – only to be postponed until the situation concerning unity with the Anglican Church had become clear. By the 1990s the position and status of women ministers, while by no means ideal, had improved to the extent that a female 'Chairman' of District was no longer regarded as a novelty, and the first female President of Conference – Revd Kathleen Richardson – was accepted as an appointment which was long overdue.

Thirdly, at the Conference of 1993 in Derby Methodism took the major decision to recognize two orders of ordained ministry – the diaconal as well as the presbyteral. From the 1890s, women who felt called to the ministry of pastoral care and service – known as 'Wesley Deaconesses' – had become a familiar sight in many Methodist circuits, particularly inner-city missions. After 1974 there was, understandably, a decline in the numbers being recruited and many of the existing deaconesses offered for the ordained ministry. The order was actually closed for a time, only to be reopened to admit men as well as women. Once this decision had been made, the resolution of the 1993 Conference was inevitable. Wesley Deaconesses had always been accepted as members both of an order of ministry and of a religious order. This development, therefore, made both theological and constitutional sense.

In the post-war years the ordained ministry has become more settled, with the three-year pattern of itinerancy being gradually replaced by longer appointments. By the 1990s, a stay of eight or nine years has become by no means unusual. Since 1932, moreover, the role of the Chairmen of Districts has changed. They are now 'separated' in the sense that it is rare for them to have pastoral oversight of a local church, and their responsibilities consist primarily in exercising leadership over the whole range of district activities and caring pastorally for the ministers within their area.

Ministerial training has also changed a great deal since 1932. The 1980s saw an increase in the number of candidates coming forward, a trend which has happily been maintained. The theological colleges for their part have adapted the method and content of their training to meet the changing needs of modern times, and new patterns of non-residential training have been explored.

Structure

Author of faith, eternal Word,
Whose Spirit breathes the active flame;
Faith, like its Finisher and Lord,
Today as yesterday the same:

To thee our humble hearts aspire,
And ask the gift unspeakable;
Increase in us the kindled fire,
In us the work of faith fulfil.

Structures are a necessary part of any church. Complicated they may be, but without them no church can function efficiently. An interesting feature of Methodism has been the way in which its system has evolved over the years in order to meet the ever changing needs of its mission. It has been mentioned before that 'Methodism has been given to us by God bit by bit as it has been needed'.[9] We have already noticed how Methodism has adapted its worship and organization in the spirit of John Wesley himself, who improvised and adapted in order that the gospel might be preached and mission might be carried out more effectively. Indeed, Methodism has never had an immutable system of theology, churchmanship or government. Perhaps this has been one of its strengths.

The late 1960s saw the Methodist Church restructure its organization, with seven 'divisions' being given responsibility for its life and work.[10] (See Fig.3.)

An idea can be gained of the immense range of activities in which the various committees of local Methodist churches are engaged by referring to the diagram (Fig.4). In some ways the local committees parallel the connexional divisions in their areas of responsibility.

Thirty years later, however, it was felt by many that this had produced an unnecessarily large number of committees. In 1992 a move was made to simplify the connexional structure, with the aim of achieving greater efficiency at national level and given more freedom to local societies to organize themselves in ways which would best suit their own specific needs. Reproduced here are some excerpts from the report of

the President's Council to the Conference of 1992 [81]. These preliminary statements clearly show the seriousness with which structural changes have been viewed. The Greek word 'koinonia' which appears in paragraph 2.4 originally meant 'association' or 'partnership' in classical times. In the New Testament it is used to describe Christian fellowship.

81. 1.5 The Council has sought to see divisional structure and function within an overall view of the church's purposes and to ensure that its vision and judgement are consistent with those of the whole Methodist church.

2.4 The church exists to celebrate and proclaim God in Christ through the Spirit. Its koinonia has two focal points: worship and mission. Not only locally but nationally the church is structured for partnership in mission . . .

2.5 In Methodism something of this is expressed in our sense of being a connexion . . . Our emphasis on connexion is not just tradition or administrative convenience. It is about the sharing of resources, made available by the willing consent of the whole body, so that need in one part may be met and so that, in the mission of the church, any part may be the whole.

3.1 The present arrangements . . . go back to the 1970s and in recent years have proved less than adequate to a changed situation. Perceptions and relationships have changed and the sense has grown that what is needed is a more flexible and open system . . .

3.10 The evident need is for greater simplicity: an orderly framework which will provide room for future adaptation. There is no single correct way to structure any organization. When frustrations build up in an organization, however, there is a strong danger that structures, which are a means to ends, will become ends in themselves. So the desire is for a coherent structure that will set the church free to address it present needs and functions.

Source: The Methodist Conference of 1992, *Agenda*, Vol. 2, pp. 606–610.

The following year revised proposals were put forward, and it remains to be seen how successfully Methodism can adapt its structures. There is no doubt, however, that John Wesley himself – whose gift for improvization and whose willingness to embrace change provided such a notable precedent – would have regarded his twentieth-century followers as worthy heirs.

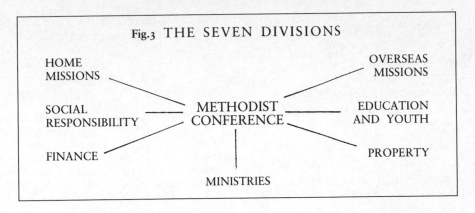

Fig.3 THE SEVEN DIVISIONS

HOME MISSIONS

OVERSEAS MISSIONS

SOCIAL RESPONSIBILITY

METHODIST CONFERENCE

EDUCATION AND YOUTH

FINANCE

PROPERTY

MINISTRIES

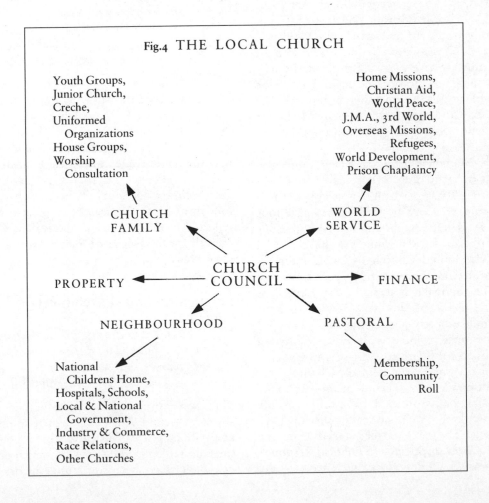

Fig.4 THE LOCAL CHURCH

Youth Groups,
Junior Church,
Creche,
Uniformed
    Organizations
House Groups,
Worship
    Consultation

Home Missions,
Christian Aid,
World Peace,
J.M.A., 3rd World,
Overseas Missions,
Refugees,
World Development,
Prison Chaplaincy

CHURCH FAMILY

WORLD SERVICE

PROPERTY

CHURCH COUNCIL

FINANCE

NEIGHBOURHOOD

PASTORAL

National
    Childrens Home,
Hospitals, Schools,
Local & National
    Government,
Industry & Commerce,
Race Relations,
Other Churches

Membership,
Community
    Roll

Mission

I would the precious time redeem,
*   And longer live for this alone,*
To spend, and to be spent, for them
*   Who have not yet my Saviour known;*
Fully on these my mission prove,
And only breathe, to breathe thy love.

The nature of overseas missions has changed considerably since 1932. As early as 1882 the Wesleyan Methodist Conference had decided that the West Indies should become an autonomous connexion. Although this particular development failed in the short term,[11] the pattern for the future had been set. British Methodism is now recognized as being one *small* part of World Methodism. The days of 'shouldering the white man's burden' have long since passed into history and overseas churches are acknowledged as having as much to give to us as British Methodism has to offer them. One of the highlights of the Conference each year is the introduction and welcome of representatives and visits from the many Methodist Conferences and United Churches throughout the world.[12]

The World Methodist Council which came into being in 1951 has tended to be dominated by American Methodists. It has performed a useful role as a consultative and advisory body over the past four decades, and fears that it might diminish Methodism's involvement in world-wide ecumenism have proved unfounded. The united Church of South India, in which Methodists have played a full part, was formed in 1947, to be followed in 1970 by the Church of North India. Indeed, Methodists everywhere have never been reluctant to participate in ecumenical ventures, and have joined with other Christian denominations to form United Churches in Canada, Australia, New Zealand, Sri Lanka and Ghana.

Much attention has been given to mission at home, and various statements on matters of faith and the practical outworking of Christian discipleship have been published. The next extract, taken from the paper entitled *Christian Social and Political Responsibility* which was adopted by the Conference of 1967, shows how Methodism responded to the challenge of secularism in the 1960s [82].

---

82. The primary content of the Christian faith is belief in the nature of God and in His purposes for man revealed through His acts in Jesus Christ; and in the human response of love to God in Christ. The consequence of this love is love for one's neighbour. But love, as it is defined and illustrated in the New Testament, is ... an activity directed towards one's fellows ... expressed only by involvement with them, whether this be in the immediate setting of the family or the wider context of the world ...

   The response of active love will vary according to circumstances. It may be prayer, sympathy, starting or supporting a housing association, serving on a trade union branch committee, giving help to a project that will aid the struggle against poverty or disease, or pressing for amendments to a Parliamentary Bill ...

Source: Declarations and Statements, The Methodist Conference, Division of Social Responsibility 1981, pp. 98–105.

The fact that the statement was issued from the Division of Social Responsibility is an indication of the degree of 'overlap' that exists. Though the apparent dichotomy between personal faith and social witness may remain in some minds, Methodism continues in its official statements to follow its founder's insistence that both are necessary if the church is properly to fulfil its mission. Tensions remain, however, and were reflected in the somewhat ambivalent way in which the call for a 'Decade of Evangelism' was greeted in some areas.

Ecumenism and church unity

Love, like death, hath all destroyed,
*   Rendered all distinctions void;*
Names, and sects, and parties fall:
*   Thou, O Christ, art all in all.*

The various proposals and developments in this area since the Second World War can be summed up as an alternating cycle of frustration and renewed hope. At the national level, the issues of ministerial status and episcopacy have been continuing themes. This can be seen in the response which the Methodist Conference of 1947 made to the overtures of Dr Fisher, then Archbishop of Canterbury [83]. In a sermon delivered the previous year he had invited the Free Churches to enter into conversations with the Church of England with a view to 'taking episcopacy into their system'. The Congregationalists and the Baptists declined, but the Methodist Church gave its guarded approval.[13]

---

83. The Methodist Conference also desires to express its sincere appreciation of the brotherliness and earnestness manifested in the Sermon preached by Your Grace before the University of Cambridge on November 3rd, 1946, in which you invited the Evangelical Free Churches to explore with our Anglican brethren how we might grow together into Full Communion. We, on our part, endorse your words that 'what we need is that, while the folds remain distinct, there should be a movement towards a free and unfettered exchange of life in worship and sacrament between them.' We recognise that in any growth towards Full Communion with the Church of England the most careful consideration will need to be given to Episcopacy, and we believe that we appreciate the importance which our Anglican friends attach to it as expressive of the unity and the continuity of the Church. A 'constitutional episcopacy' has long been in operation in the Methodist Church in the sense that its constitution provides for certain wider responsibilities of a pastoral nature within one and the same presbyteral order and fellowship, and, in view of the place to be taken by Episcopacy in this growth towards Full Communion, we are glad to be assured that no one dogma of it is expected. Moreover, we recall the development of conciliar government within the Church of England, and regard this as a helpful factor in the encouragement of closer relationships between that Church and the Methodist Church, whose government is essentially conciliar – through our local courts, the District Synods, and the Conference.

We, therefore, readily respond to Your Grace's appeal and to the spirit which has prompted it . . .

Source: Statements of the Methodist Church on Faith and Order, 1933–1983, Methodist Publishing House 1984, pp. 194–5.

After much discussion the Conference of 1969 approved a scheme which would have led eventually to organic union with the Church of England, but the proposal was not carried by Convocation with the required majority. Another attempt three years later met with exactly the same fate, despite strenuous efforts by the Archbishop of Canterbury, Michael Ramsey. The rejection of the various proposals of uniting with the Church of England has undoubtedly caused Methodists to rethink their position within the Church as a whole. Although negotiations between Methodists and Anglicans naturally received the greatest publicity, close links have been forged with, for example, the United Reformed Church, which was formed out of the Congregational and Presbyterian churches in 1972. Moreover, the Methodist-Roman Catholic conversations are now a well-established part of Methodism's attempt to understand and relate to the universal Church.

It is also worth noting that both formal and informal discussions between Methodists and Anglicans have inevitably been held on a number of levels. Those between the respective hierarchies have been paralleled – some would even say counterbalanced – by all kinds of local initiatives at the grass-roots. 'LEPs (Local Ecumenical Projects) involving shared premises and joint ministries, numbered over four hundred in the Methodist Church by 1987, while one-third of all United Reformed Churches had come into this category by that date.

The future

> He bids us build each other up;
> And, gathered into one,
> To our high calling's glorious hope
> We hand in hand go on.

We finish on an optimistic note. Part of this sense of constantly needing to reshape Methodism to meet the challenge of tomorrow can be seen in the production of *Hymns & Psalms* in 1983, on the fiftieth anniversary of *The Methodist Hymn Book*. In the Preface – an extract from which forms our next document – the Chairman (Richard Jones) and the Convenor (Ivor Jones) outline some of the considerations given by the committee to the work of compiling the new selection. It provides an interesting commentary on the way in which Methodists look positively to the future, and reminds us that the life of the Methodist people has been, and always should be, focused on worship [84].

---

84. Hymns and Psalms have been in the past, and still are today, distinctive features of Christian worship. They unite the intellect, the emotions, the will, and the voice, in the human response to God's grace; and they also point beyond our human faculties and abilities, for God addresses us in them, and through them applies the good news of Jesus Christ to our lives . . .

In compiling this hymn book, the committee has sought to respond to our changing times, and to produce a book which articulates the needs, the joys, and the fears of the contemporary world . . .

The compilers of this book believe that these aims can be greatly furthered by a hymn book which is rooted firmly in denominational traditions, and which makes available to all Christians the riches of classical, evangelical, catholic, and charismatic hymnody of the past and the present. By approaching God through them, and attending to God's word in them, may we all grow nearer to God, and in so doing grow nearer to one another in faith and fellowship.

Source: *Hymns & Psalms – A Methodist and Ecumenical Hymn Book*, Methodist Publishing House 1983, pp. vii–xi.

Methodism continues to live, as it did in John and Charles Wesley's day, with a number of inevitable tensions. Can it combine the virtues and strengths of a church with those of a society? Will it remain a 'broad' church or become a narrow one?[14] What part will the Methodist Church play in future ecumenical developments? Will it renew its attempts to unite with the Church of England or gravitate more to the Free Churches?

The final extract [85] is from a little book that quickly became a classic – *A Charge to Keep – An Introduction to the People called Methodists*. Its author, Dr Frank Baker, has been universally acknowledged as one of the most learned and prolific writers on Methodism this century. In the final chapter he looks to the future with optimism, and, although he was writing just after the Second World War, his words still ring true today.

---

85. We believe that for centuries to come both the student and the general reader will continue to be fascinated by the still unfolding story of the rise and development of Methodism . . . For that story is not one of unbalanced and evanescent revivalism – a mere religious flash in the pan. It reveals much that is of universal and permanent value. Whilst emphasizing the importance of each individual soul in the sight of God, Methodism has also given a firm lead in matters of public morality and of communal service. The tremendous impact on the world of its missionary zeal no one can gainsay – and no one can measure. Above all, Methodism is still alive. Indeed, simply because it is a living organism, continually adapting itself to meet changing conditions, some of the statements made about modern Methodism are out of date almost as soon as they are penned. Yet though conditions change, and details of organization with them, the heart of man remains the same, and likewise the essential content of Methodism's message. There is no doubt that a knowledge of our past can afford both inspiration and guidance for the opportunities of the future.

Source: Frank Baker, *A Charge to Keep*, Epworth Press 1947, p. 212.

For all its faults, the Methodist Church has survived – perhaps as an example of the miracle of God's grace. It bears little resemblance to the scattered collection of societies of the mid-eighteenth century from which it has grown. It has seen periods of decline and growth, division and reconciliation, and in spite of its failures, it faces the twenty-first century with optimism. I believe that Methodism will continue to maintain its spiritual vitality in years to come, and whatever contribution it makes to the universal church of the future, Methodists will continue to be, in Wesley's words, 'friends to all and the enemies of none'.

Time Line of Events

1939 Britain at war

1945 End of the Second World War; United Nations Organization founded

1957 Ghana becomes the first European colony in Africa to achieve independence

1958 Anglican-Methodist 'Conversations' begin

1962 First session of Vatican II opens in Rome

1963 *Honest to God* published

1964 Beginning of Local Ecumenical Projects

1969 Neil Armstrong steps on to the moon's surface

1972 Congregationalists and Presbyterians join to form the United Reformed Church

1973 Yom Kippur War between Israel and the Arabs; closure of the Suez Canal

1974 The Methodist Church ordains women presbyters

1975 Publication of the *Methodist Service Book*

1976 Failure of Covenant Proposals between Methodists and Anglicans

1979 Margaret Thatcher becomes Prime Minister

1983 *Hymns & Psalms* published

1986 Methodist diaconate opened to men as well as women

1989 Revolutions in Central and Eastern Europe

1990 End of Communism in the USSR

1992 First female President of the Conference

1993 Methodist Conference recognizes two orders of ministry

For Discussion

1. What was your immediate reaction on reading extract 78? How can Bible study be made more lively?

2. How would you go about reconciling two groups within your church who disagree fundamentally about patterns of Sunday worship?

3. In what sense is an ordained minister a 'representative'?

4. What do you feel are the hallmarks of a healthy church?

5. What qualities make a good hymn?

6. How far would you agree or disagree with the author's comments in the final paragraph?

Glossary of Terms

ADHERENT Someone who, while not being a full member of the Methodist Church, has an informal connection with a local Methodist community.

ANAMNESIS The act of remembrance in Holy Communion, though the word itself means more than simply 'remembering'. Rather, it carries the sense of re-presenting before God what Christ has done in such a way as to make it a reality for those present.

ANGLICAN Usually synonymous with 'the Church of England'. The word has also come to mean a church tradition which had its origins in the English Reformation at the time of Henry VIII and Elizabeth. This tradition can be found in churches throughout the world that were founded by the Church of England.

ANTEPAST A poetic expression, usually found in older hymns, meaning a foretaste or something to whet the appetite.

ANTINOMIANISM Literally 'against the law'. An approach to Christian living which minimized the place of laws and regulations (e.g. the Ten Commandments) and instead stressed the importance of the Spirit's guidance. 'Antinomians' emphasized faith alone over against Christian behaviour or 'works'.

ARMINIAN From Jacob Arminius (1560–1609) who opposed Calvin's teaching concerning predestination. He insisted that all people can be saved, but only by the grace of God. His teaching had a profound influence on the Wesleys.

ARTISAN A skilled workman, such as a tailor or weaver.

ASSESSMENT This is the money contributed by each local church, usually according to its size, to meet the overall cost of running the Methodist Church and maintaining its ministry.

ASSISTANTS Wesley's senior helpers who were ordained ministers. Later they became known as superintendent ministers.

ATONEMENT The reconciliation (literally, 'at-one-ment') between God and humankind, which was achieved by his Son Jesus Christ. Over the centuries different theories have arisen which try to explain how this is possible. Some focus on the sacrificial nature of Christ's death on the cross, some on his victory over evil, and others on the 'moral' force of God's love at work through Christ. No one theory explains this reconciliation completely, but each contributes something to our understanding.

AUGUSTINIAN From St Augustine (354–430), perhaps the most famous of the Early Church Fathers. His best known works were the *Confessions* and *The City of God*. An opponent of Pelagius (see below), his teachings were dominated by his belief that humanity's original sin could only be countered by the grace of God. He should not be confused with St Augustine, the first Archbishop of Canterbury, who lived in the sixth century.

BALLOT The vote. In British politics the secret ballot was introduced in 1872.

BANDS Similar to 'classes' (see below), except that they were smaller and composed of members who were considered to be more advanced in faith.

'BENEVOLENCE FUND' The modern term for the 'Poor Fund' (q.v.).

'BOWELS' In Hebrew culture this was the seat of the emotions – the heart being thought to control the will. Hence the term 'bowels of mercy' to describe a strong feeling of compassion.

CAMBRIDGE PLATONISTS These were an influential group of churchmen who gathered at Cambridge in the latter part of the seventeenth century. They developed a strong link between mysticism and reason, and held that spiritual truths could be understood by a combination of an individual's reason and his or her personal experience of God's indwelling spirit.

CAMP MEETINGS The outdoor revivalist meetings, somewhat akin to field-preaching in the eighteenth century, which marked the beginning of the Primitive Methodism as a breakaway movement. The first was held in 1807.

CANDIDATE A lay person who has offered him or herself for the ordained ministry of the Methodist Church.

CANON The original Greek word meant literally, a 'measuring rod', and came to refer to something that was correct or authoritative. It is now a term describing the Bible, which is a collection of those books that were accepted as having sufficient authority to be included.

CATECHISM A system of instructing new Christians in matters of faith and doctrine. It consists of a series of questions and responses concerning basic aspects of belief, the nature of the church, and so on.

CATHOLIC   The universal Church. Often used as an abbreviation for the Roman Catholic Church, although, strictly speaking, this is not correct.

CENTRAL HALLS   Multi-purpose buildings mostly found in city centres which were intended to act as a focus for urban mission as well as worship.

CHAIRMAN OF DISTRICT   A minister placed in charge of a district, responsible for its overall leadership and for the pastoral care of its ministers. He or she chairs the district synods.

CHARISMATIC   From the Greek word 'charism', meaning 'grace'. The term 'charismatic' refers specifically to the movement in the church that emphasizes the gifts of the Spirit. Charismatic worship is found particularly in Pentecostal churches, though it has become widespread among many Christian denominations. Its main characteristics are: the absence of formal liturgies, a high degree of congregational participation, stress on corporate extempore prayer, singing and movement, prophecy, and speaking in tongues.

CHURCH   Today we think of the word in two senses. 'Church' can mean both the universal institution and also an individual church in a particular location. In the eighteenth century 'church' in common speech invariably meant the Church of England.

CHURCH COUNCIL   The managing trustees of a local Methodist church. Meeting at least twice a year and consisting of both representatives from the main church groups and elected members, it has oversight over the whole life of the church.

CIRCUIT   A group of Methodist churches linked together at local level. Circuits are grouped together in districts, which form the Methodist Connexion.

CLASSES   Small groups of Methodists meeting together for prayer, Bible study and fellowship. In many areas they have been replaced by house groups.

CLASS TICKET   Now replaced by an annual ticket as proof of membership and as a reminder of the privileges and duties of being a member of the Methodist Church. It was originally given each quarter to class members as a ticket of entry to meetings.

COMMUNICANT   A person receiving Holy Communion.

THE CONFERENCE   The central governing body of Methodism which meets annually in July. Most of its members are elected representatives – lay people and ordained ministers – from the Districts, though some are ex-officio. It meets in two separate sessions but final authority on most matters lies with the Representative, rather than the Ministerial Session.

CONGREGATIONALISTS   A Protestant group emerging from the Reformation which believed in the autonomy of the local church. Eventually they joined with the Presbyterians (q.v.) to form the United Reformed Church.

CONNEXION   The national network of Methodist churches comprising of local churches, circuits and districts, linked together in progressively larger units.

'CONVINCING' (GRACE)   Sometimes written as 'convicting' (grace). Wesley used it in connection with repentance, to remind his readers that the grace of God works in the heart of an individual at the earliest stages of coming to faith.

COVENANT SERVICE   Usually held early in January, it is a service in which Methodists rededicate themselves to God's service for the coming year.

CPD   Short for the 'Constitution, Practice and Discipline of the Methodist Church', a manual which contains its rules and regulations, laid out in a series of 'standing orders' or instructions. CPD can be amended only by the Conference.

CURATE   Historically, the word means an Anglican clergyman who has care of a parish. In practice a curate is one who assists a vicar or who takes temporary charge of a parish when it is vacant.

DEACON   Literally, 'a servant'. In the Methodist Church, a member of the diaconal order is a man or woman who has been set apart for a full-time ministry of service. In the Church of England it denotes the third rank of ordained ministry below that of bishop and priest, a person usually being a deacon for a short period of time prior to ordination as a priest.

DEACONESS   In Methodism, before the diaconate was opened to men, the term referred to a member of the Wesley Deaconess Order which was founded in 1890. Deaconesses had both a pastoral and an evangelistic ministry, sometimes working alongside ordained ministers, sometimes independently.

DECADE OF EVANGELISM   The decision, embraced by all leading Christian denominations, to designate the 1990s as a special period of evangelistic outreach.

DEED OF DECLARATION   Approved in February 1784, this made Conference the legally constituted governing body of Methodism.

DEED OF UNION   The document, signed by the Primitive, Wesleyan and United Methodist connexions in September 1932 marking their formal union.

DEISM/DEISTS   Originally this word was used in contrast to Atheism (belief in the existence of no god) and Polytheism (belief in many gods). In the eighteenth century, however, it referred to a group of thinkers in England who applied the principles of the Enlightenment to religion. They believed that there was a divine creator, but that he remained aloof from the world. Deists, therefore, expressed doubts concerning aspects of Christian doctrine that depended upon revelation –

e.g. the Trinity, Christ's incarnation, miracles, the authority of the Bible, and the reality of immortality.

DENOMINATION   A group of people called by the same name. The term describes a religious organization that is more formally developed than a sect but not yet recognized as an independent church, though nowadays it often has a less specific meaning.

DIACONATE   The order of deacon. In the Methodist Church, along with the presbyterate (q.v.), it now constitutes the two recognized orders of ordained ministry.

DIOCESE   The area governed by a bishop.

DISSENTER   All those eighteenth-century Protestant groups in Britain who were not Anglican and who refused to adhere to the various Acts of Parliament which laid down the rules for conformity to the Church of England.

DISTRICT   There are currently thirty-three Districts in the 'home stations' of Methodist Church, i.e. England, Scotland and Wales, each of which consists of a number of circuits.

DIVISIONS   In the late 1960s Methodism was restructured, with seven 'divisions' being responsible for different areas of its life and work. They are: Home Mission, Overseas Mission, Ministries, Social Responsibility, Education and Youth, Finance, and Property.

DOMESTIC SYSTEM   The method of production (for example of woollen cloth) based on small units (usually families) working from home. With the onset of the factory system it went into steady decline, though in some parts of the country it still survives in the form of local cottage industries.

ECUMENISM/ECUMENICAL   The term originates from the Greek 'oikoumene', meaning 'the whole inhabited world'. It describes the movement, particularly in the twentieth century, which seeks understanding and cooperation between churches in a spirit of unity.

ELECTUARY   Prescribed medicine made into a syrup by, for example, the addition of honey.

THE ENLIGHTENMENT   A blanket term covering a movement of ideas in the eighteenth century. Enlightenment thinkers claimed that knowledge could be achieved through reason, observation and experiment (cf. Deism/Deists).

'ENTHUSIASM'   Used in Wesley's day as a term of abuse for any form of religious extremism. The label 'Enthusiast', therefore, indicated that a person was regarded as a fanatic.

THE ENVELOPE SCHEME   A method of regular Sunday giving which enables a church to plan its future income. Each week members place their offertory in specially dated envelopes, and the church stewards keep a confidential record of the amounts given.

EPISCOPACY   The office of bishop. The concept of the historic episcopate, in which bishops today are believed to be the successors of Peter and the apostles, has been a major bone of contention between the Church of England and the other Protestant churches.

ESTABLISHED   Usually denoting the Church of England which, unlike the Free Churches (q.v.), was established by an Act of Parliament. The Church of Scotland, however, is also an established church. Moreover, *all* the churches are controlled by Acts of Parliament.

EUCHARIST   Literally, 'thanksgiving'. One of the names given to the sacrament of Holy Communion.

EVANGELICAL   A loose term having a number of different meanings. In the nineteenth century it described an informal group within the Church of England who were known for their piety and who laid great stress on the need for personal conversion and the spreading of the gospel. In this century it refers to Christians who emphasize the importance of the doctrine of justification, evangelistic outreach and the authority of scripture.

EVANGELISM   The proclamation of the gospel. From the Greek 'euaggelion', meaning 'gospel' or 'good news'.

'EXPERIMENTAL'   In the eighteenth century it described an approach to faith that was related closely to a person's experience. The twentieth century equivalent would be 'experiential', but this loses the sense of testing which John Wesley believed was necessary.

EXTEMPORE   A sermon or prayer given without the help of notes, sometimes impromptu, is said to be delivered 'extempore'.

'FLY SHEETS'   Anonymous tracts, almost certainly written by James Everett, which were highly critical of the Methodist hierarchy in the 1840s.

'FORWARD MOVEMENT'   The attempt by Methodists in the early twentieth century to reach the unchurched, particularly in urban areas. Its strategy, underlining the need both to spread the gospel and to engage in social mission, involved the building of city-centre missions. It has sometimes been described as 'combining the sacrament with the soup ladle'.

FRANCHISE   Another term for 'the vote'.

FREE CHURCHES   A general term describing Nonconformist churches.

FULL CONNEXION   When a man or woman is 'received into full connexion' at the Conference, he or she is accepted as a minister of the Methodist Church. This process, confirmed by a standing vote, takes place prior to the person's ordination.

FUNDAMENTALISM   Fundamentalists believe in the verbal inspiration of scripture and therefore in its supremacy as the inerrant word of God. Consequently, they insist on the literal interpretation of the Bible.

GENERAL CHURCH MEETING   A meeting, held at least once a year, which is open to all people whether members or not, though only members can vote. It elects Church Stewards and representatives to the Church Council.

HELPERS   Mr Wesley's preachers.

HERRNHUT   The centre of the Moravian revival in Saxony.

HOUSE GROUPS   The modern equivalent of the classes, which are not necessarily in the pastoral care of a class leader.

THE HUSTINGS   A platform from which candidates seeking election to local or national office would deliver public speeches.

HYMNS & PSALMS   The present Methodist hymnbook. Published in 1983, it superseded the *Methodist Hymn Book* of fifty years earlier.

INCUMBENT   An Anglican clergyman who has charge over a parish.

INDEPENDENT   A term used until about the end of the eighteenth century for a Congregationalist. (q.v.)

'INDIFFERENTLY'   Impartially, without any special regard or favour. Today the word has another sense altogether, and implies a lack of any strong feeling about an issue.

INTERCESSIONS   Prayers on behalf of others, whereas petitions are normally thought as being for those who are offering prayer.

ITINERANT   The term used to describe ministers who travel around the country, staying in one circuit for a limited period of time. Today a minister is invited for an initial period of five years, whereupon his or her term can be extended.

JLG   Short for 'Joint Liturgical Group', the ecumenical body which has drawn up successive lectionaries.

JUSTIFICATION   The word was used by St Paul to express God's forgiveness and 'acquittal' of sinners. It came into theology as a term for part of the process of salvation, and has been interpreted in various ways. John Wesley equated it with the idea of 'acceptance' and 'pardon', and used it to describe the change in the relationship between a person and God, in which God took the first step.

LAITY   Another term for lay people, in contrast to the ordained clergy.

LATITUDINARIANISM   An attitude common in the eighteenth century which emphasized the virtues of practical religion at the expense of doctrine. 'Latitudinarians' believed that doctrines did not matter so much as living a moral life in accordance with the gospel. They allowed, therefore, a certain amount of 'latitude' in the interpretation of Scripture and Christian doctrines.

LAY PASTORAL ASSISTANT   The term by which lay workers were known (see below).

LAY WORKER   A lay person who is appointed to a circuit for full time paid service. Formerly known as 'lay pastoral assistants', they can sometimes have pastoral oversight of a single church.

LEADERS' MEETING   The forerunner of the Church Council in Methodism, i.e. the governing body of the local church.

LECTIONARY   The system whereby selected readings are appointed for use in worship throughout the Christian year.

'LEGAL HUNDRED'   The hundred specified members of the Methodist Conference as drawn up by the Deed of Declaration of 1784 (q.v.).

LEP   Short for 'Local Ecumenical Project'. This is formed when Christians from different denominations agree to co-operate formally in some way in a particular locality – for example, in the shared use of premises, amalgamating Sunday services, or the holding of joint membership.

'LIGHTNESS'   As used in the eighteenth century it simply meant a tendency towards frivolity.

LITURGICAL MOVEMENT   Originating in France in the mid-nineteenth century and spreading throughout Europe across all denominations, this arose from a general desire to renew the worship of the church. It stressed the importance of the sacraments and the observance of the Christian Year, but at the same time placed renewed emphasis on the value of preaching.

LITURGY   Literally, 'the work (of the people)'. It originally meant either the formal services of the church contained in the Book of Common Prayer (as opposed to private devotional prayers) or, occasionally, the eucharist itself. Nowadays the term can denote any formal order of worship.

LOCAL PREACHER   A lay person who preaches and leads worship, mainly in his or her own local area. In Wesley's day, some of the lay preachers were itinerant.

LOCAL PREACHERS' MEETING   The quarterly meeting of all local preachers in a particular circuit (which ordained ministers also attend), in which business is dealt with and matters of faith are shared. In modern Methodism it is more usually – and more accurately – known simply as the 'Preachers' Meeting'.

LOVE-FEAST   A service in which bread is broken and water drunk from a common cup. Methodist love-feasts included hymn singing, testimonies and prayers.

LUDDITES   Named after their leader, Ned Ludd, they were originally a group of Yorkshire labourers who smashed new textile machinery which threatened their livelihood. The term has come to describe any opponent of new technology.

MANSE   The Methodist equivalent of a vicarage, i.e. the house which, owned by the circuit, is the home of the minister and his or her family.

MASS   The celebration of Holy Communion or Eucharist in Roman Catholic churches, though it is possible to hold a Mass without communion.

'MECHANIC'   Nothing to do with car maintenance! In the eighteenth century it was generally a term of contempt, referring to a person, usually of limited education, who was engaged in manual labour.

MINISTER IN LOCAL APPOINTMENT   An ordained minister in the Methodist Church who is not itinerant, who does not live in a manse or receive a stipend and who sometimes has part-time secular employment.

MINUTES OF CONFERENCE   The Methodist 'year book' in which the main decisions of the previous Conference are recorded and which contains details of the Methodist Church, addresses of ministers and so on.

MORAVIANS   Originally known as the Church of the Brethren, founded in fifteenth-century Germany. A Protestant group closely linked to Lutheranism, they experienced a revival under Count Nicholas von Zinzendorf in the 1720s and were probably best known for their piety.

MYSTICISM   This has been a widespread approach to religion in general, not just Christianity. Mystics believe that it is possible to know God in this present life through personal religious experience, the highest state of which is sometimes described as a 'mystic marriage' with God. Christian mystics have laid great stress upon prayer, humility and charity as the outward sign of their spirituality. In seventeenth-century England the chief exponents of mysticism were to be found in the group known as the Cambridge Platonists (q.v.).

NONCONFORMIST   A general term referring to Protestant denominations not belonging to the Established Church. It was first used to denote those groups refusing to conform to the Act of Uniformity of 1662 (q.v.).

'ON NOTE'   This refers to a man or woman who has been given a 'note' to preach and thus who embarks on the first stage in becoming a fully accredited Methodist Local Preacher, by accompanying a more experienced preacher and taking an increasing part in leading worship.

'ON TRIAL'   A Methodist Local Preacher who is engaged in study and training before becoming fully accredited is said to be 'on trial'. The next step after being 'on note'.

OPEN TABLE   The term used to describe the Methodist policy of allowing 'all who love the Lord Jesus Christ' to participate in Holy Communion, irrespective of whether they are members of the Methodist Church.

'OPINIONS' Religious views distinguishing various denominations. Wesley used the term to mean the attitudes which he considered to be over and above the basic minimum necessary for a genuine faith in Christ.

ORDINANCE Literally, 'that which has been ordained' (by God). Wesley described the means of grace – prayer, reading the Bible, and receiving Holy Communion – as 'ordinances', since he felt that observing them was a matter of obedience.

PASTORAL VISITORS The present-day equivalent of class leaders. Men or women who have a number of members and adherents in their pastoral care.

PATRONAGE The right exercised by a person to appoint someone to a particular office. In the eighteenth century members of royalty, the aristocracy or powerful politicians and churchmen could, as 'patrons', exercise influence in this way. Many church offices were 'in the gift' of an individual. Often a wealthy landowner was able to control local elections because the majority of voters were his tenants. This possibility only finally disappeared when the secret ballot was introduced.

PELAGIAN From Pelagius, an English theologian and teacher who lived in the late fourth and early fifth century. He asserted that, because God had given men and women free will, they could choose whether or not to accept salvation. His greatest opponent was St Augustine, and his teachings were generally condemned by the church because it was felt Pelagius was encouraging salvation by works.

'PETERLOO' The name given to the tragedy at St Peter's Field, Manchester in August 1819, in which eleven demonstrators were killed and four hundred wounded as the result of action taken by local magistrates. The name derives from the battle of Waterloo four years previously.

PETITIONS Prayers of supplication, usually for those offering prayer.

PIETISM A movement that began in sixteenth-century Germany which sought to reinvigorate (Protestant) spiritual life by encouraging the practice of prayer, Bible study and contemplation.

THE 'PLAN' The Circuit Preaching Plan gives details of all the services held each quarter in a Circuit, and the names of the preachers planned to conduct worship in each of the churches. When a Local Preacher becomes fully accredited, he or she is sometimes said to have 'come on full plan'.

'POOR FUND' A fund from which gifts of money are made to those in special need. Today it is more usually termed the 'Benevolence Fund', and is formed from separate collections taken during the sacrament of the Lord's Supper.

'POOR STEWARDS'   The original name given to Communion Stewards, because they had charge of the 'Poor Fund' (see above).

PREACHERS   Originally the word referred to those men appointed by Wesley who could either be ordained ministers (of the Church of England) or laymen. In the nineteenth century 'the preachers' more often than not meant the ordained Methodist ministers. In modern times the term applies equally to ordained and lay men and women.

PREDESTINATION   The doctrine which teaches that God knows, and has decreed, who will be saved. It was developed by St Augustine (354–430), the key biblical passage being Romans 8.29. In the Reformation era the doctrine came to be associated with Luther and (especially) Calvin's teachings, though the latter laid great stress on the importance of assurance and human responsibility. The elect – those predestined to be saved – are, therefore, to strive to live holy lives rather than passively to accept the privilege of salvation. The theory of 'double predestination' is the doctrine taken to its logical extreme, i.e. that if some only are saved, then, inevitably, some must be preordained to damnation. It should be pointed out that Christians who accept the doctrine do so because they believe that *all* of sinful humanity deserves damnation, and that it is a sign of God's infinite love and mercy that at least some are saved.

PRESBYTER   The name given to an ordained minister of word and sacrament. Now used in Methodism to distinguish between the presbyteral and diaconal orders of ministry.

PRESBYTERIANS   Protestant groups arising from the Reformation who organized the government of their churches through a system of presbyters and elders, though patterns vary widely. Their doctrines are usually Calvinist in emphasis. In 1972 English Presbyterians joined with the Congregationalists to form the United Reformed Church.

PREVENIENT GRACE   'Prevenient' literally means 'going before'. Put in simple terms it is the capacity, possessed to a greater or lesser extent by every individual, for responding to the love of God. Wesley denied that anyone was devoid of the grace of God – which he sometimes referred to as 'natural conscience' – though he felt that many people stifled it as they grew into adulthood. 'No man sins because he has not grace,' wrote Wesley, 'but because he does not use the grace which he hath.'

PREVENTING (GRACE)   Another word for prevenient (grace).

PROTESTANT   Those churches adhering to the principles of the Reformation of the sixteenth century. Although it can denote any non-Catholic church, some Anglicans prefer not to think of themselves as Protestants – rather, as Catholics who are not at present in communion with the Church of Rome.

PURITANS   A blanket term describing the more extreme English Protestants who were dissatisfied with the Reformation settlement under Elizabeth. They laid great emphasis upon the authority of scripture, preaching and Sunday observance, and attacked elaborate forms of worship and anything that resembled 'Popery'.

'QUICK'   Literally, 'alive'. In the eighteenth century, to 'quicken' meant to 'enliven'.

QUIETISM   A passive kind of spirituality which played down the part of human activity and responsibility. At best it was a tranquil resting in God; at worst it denied the value of social action and even, in its extreme form, the importance of corporate worship.

'RANTERS'   A nickname given to Primitive Methodists.

RATIONALISM   In the eighteenth century, it meant an appeal to the use of the mind in matters of faith. Rationalists in Wesley's day held that certain things could be known about God by reason alone. Some went as far as claiming that reason could prove the existence of God.

RECTOR   In the Church of England, the incumbent who receives the tithes from the parish, as opposed to a vicar (see below) who does not. Today, neither in fact receives tithes!

REFORM ACT   An Act of Parliament extending the franchise. The first was passed in 1832 and was followed by further acts in 1867, 1884, 1918 and 1928. By the 1918 act women over the age of thirty received the vote for the first time.

REFORMATION   The great religious revolution of the sixteenth century that began with Martin Luther in Germany, though some would say it began earlier. Criticism of the Roman Catholic Church in general and the papacy in particular led to both movements of reform and schism within the church as a whole.

REFORMERS   A loose term describing the leaders of the Reformation, such as Luther, Calvin and Zwingli.

REGENERATION   The process whereby the image of Christ is formed in an individual. In other words, spiritual rebirth. Many high churchmen in Wesley's day believed that infants were 'regenerated' spiritually at their baptism.

RUBRIC   Statements of rules or instructions (originally written in red ink) concerning religious procedures, specifically concerning liturgy and worship.

SACERDOTAL   Although it can simply mean 'priestly', the word is often used in a pejorative sense to describe an excessive priestly influence over people or situations.

SACRAMENTALIST   A Christian who lays great stress on the observance of the sacraments, especially Holy Communion.

SANCTIFICATION   The continuing of God's work in the heart of a Christian, following justification (q.v.). As a process of growth in holiness, it marked a *real* change in an individual's character and life.

SECT   Although the word can be used in a variety of senses, in the context of religion it means a subdivision of a denomination. Usually, the term describes a group which is looser and less formally organized than a denomination (q.v.).

SECTOR MINISTER   A Methodist minister who, while being an ordained clergyman and subject to the discipline of Conference, exercises his or her ministry outside.

SECULARISM   An ideology that advocates the removal of religious influence on society. For example, nineteenth-century secularists believed that education should be allowed to develop independently of the church, and controlled only by the state.

SEE   Another term for a diocese (q.v.). The word comes from the Latin *sedes*, meaning 'seat', of the Bishop.

'SENSIBLE'   In the eighteenth century it did not mean 'wise' or 'practical' as it does in today's usage. Rather, it referred to the senses, i.e. human perception. See, for example, the line from Charles Wesley's hymn: 'and sensibly believe' (Document 48).

'SEPARATED'   In Methodism this refers to present day Chairmen of Districts who do not have pastoral oversight of a specific local church.

'SIT DOWN'   A Methodist minister who has reached retirement age is given permission to cease 'travelling' and 'sit down'.

SIX YEAR RULE   It is the usual practice for most office holders in the Methodist Church to serve for six years at any one time.

SOCIETY   The basic Methodist 'unit'. When Wesley's followers met together, they avoided using the term 'church' in order not to give the impression that they were competing with the local parish church.

SPECULATIVE   When used in the eighteenth century by John Wesley and others in connection with theology, it meant 'theoretical', 'based upon reflection', and did not have the sense of 'guesswork' that it does today.

STANDING ORDERS   The numbered rules and regulations of the Methodist Church to be found in CPD.

STANDING VOTE   The method of voting in the Methodist Church when important decisions need to be made, for example, when Conference approves candidates for ordination.

'STATIONS' Circuits and other appointments to which ministers are assigned by the Conference. They can be home and overseas.

STEWARDS In the Methodist Church today, church stewards are lay people elected to be responsible, with the minister, for the life of the local church. Circuit stewards oversee the welfare of the ministers and churches in a circuit. The term can also apply to lay people who perform certain duties relating to the celebration of Holy Communion (communion stewards), the welcoming of people into church on Sundays (door stewards), or the care of church buildings (property stewards).

'STILLNESS' Often used in a similar sense to 'quietism' (q.v.). It was one of the main features of Moravian piety, and arose from an over-literal interpretation of the text 'Be still and know that I am God' (Ps. 46.10). Those who advocated 'stillness' maintained that corporate acts of prayer and worship – even Bible Study – were unnecessary until a Christian was completely purified. Otherwise they might be seen as attempts to gain God's favour.

SUPEREROGATIONISTS Another nickname given to members of the Holy Club, because they were accused of trying to outdo their fellow Oxonians in good works.

SUPERINTENDENTS Superintendent ministers, formerly known as 'assistants', are senior ministers placed in charge of a circuit.

SUPERNUMERARY An ordained minister who has reached the age of retirement.

SYNOD The meeting, at district level, of ministers and lay people in the Methodist Church. It can also refer to any important church gathering, such as the General Synod of the Church of England.

TAIZÉ The Protestant religious community in France set up by Brother Roger which has exerted a wide influence on liturgy and worship, and is perhaps best known for its music and chants.

TEMPERANCE Although the word strictly means 'moderation', the Temperance Movement advocated complete abstinence from intoxicating liquor.

39 ARTICLES The statements of doctrine set out by the Church of England which defined what was acceptable as orthodox, as opposed to the teachings of Roman Catholicism on the one hand and Protestant positions (for example, Puritanism); on the other. They first appeared in 1563.

TOLERATION ACT Introduced in Britain in 1689, granting freedom of worship to dissenters under carefully laid down conditions.

'UNDISTINGUISHING' The same as 'indifferent' (q.v.).

UNIFORMITY ACTS   Along with a whole series of other Acts of Parliament in the seventeenth century, their aim was to ensure the loyalty of the clergy to the Church of England. They did this by defining what was acceptable. The last one in 1662 required all clergy to declare their public adherence to the Book of Common Prayer and make a declaration of loyalty to the king. It has been estimated that nearly 2000 dissenting clergy were forced to give up their livings.

UNITARIAN   A person who rejects the doctrine of the Trinity and who denies the divinity of Jesus Christ. Some Unitarians maintain that Christ *became* divine at his resurrection.

URC   Short for 'United Reformed Church', which came into existence in 1972 as a result of the uniting of the Presbyterian and Congregationalist Churches.

VATICAN II   The Council called by Pope John XXIII in 1962, whose aim was to renew the spiritual life of the Roman Catholic Church. It is probably remembered as much for its ecumenical vision as for its reform of Catholic liturgy, teaching, and organization.

VICAR   In the Church of England, an incumbent of a parish where the tithes are allocated to some other person or institution, for example, the local monastery. He performs the same duties as a rector (q.v.).

VOUCHSAFE   The word could either mean to 'guarantee', or, more usually in the eighteenth century, to 'graciously allow'.

WATCH-NIGHT   A nocturnal vigil involving prayers and hymn singing. In the Methodist Church today it often takes place on New Year's Eve, though this was not always the case.

APPENDIX 2

Suggestions for Further Reading

This is not an exhaustive booklist. It is simply a personal selection of books which will give you further background information or which you may wish to consult for more detailed study. In any case, many of the titles listed below have excellent bibliographies, particularly the final volume of *A History of the Methodist Church in Great Britain*. The shorter books which are more suitable for general reading have been marked with an asterisk.

General introductions to the historical background

For the years up to John Wesley's death

J. H. Plumb, *England in the Eighteenth Century*, Penguin 1950*
J. H. Plumb, *The First Four Georges*, Fontana 1966*
Roy Porter, *English Society in the Eighteenth Century*, Penguin 1982*

Probably the best studies. All are very readable, and the last concentrates on social issues.

Dorothy Marshall, *Eighteenth Century England*, Longman 1962

In the Longman History of England series. The series contain detailed, solid works by reputable authors, as do the relevant volumes from the Oxford History of England series, though the latter tend to be a little dry and are becoming rather dated.

The nineteenth and twentieth centuries

Asa Briggs, *The Age of Improvement*, Longman 1959
W. N. Medlicott, *Contemporary England*, Longman 1967

Good, recent surveys, many of which are suitable for the general reader.

Roger Fulford, *From Hanover to Windsor*, Fontana 1960*

Part of an excellent series of books on English sovereigns from the mediaeval times to the present day.

E. P. Thompson, *The Making of the English Working Class*, Penguin 1968

Provides a very scholarly, imaginative study of English social history from 1780 to 1832 which has a great deal to say about Methodism, though Thompson's Marxist leanings may not be to everyone's taste.

Surveys of church history

D. MacCulloch, *Groundwork of Christian History*, Epworth Press 1987*

Admirable but has less material on the modern period.

J. Comby and D. MacCulloch, *How to Read Church History Vol. 2: From the Reformation to the Present Day* , S C M Press 1986*

Blends historical narrative with a clear presentation of selected primary sources.

Rupert E. Davies, *The Church in our Times*, Epworth Press 1979*
Rupert E. Davies (ed), *The Testing of the Churches, 1932–1982*, Epworth Press 1982

Give valuable insights into the problems and challenges facing all Christian denominations over the past few generations.

Histories of Methodism

Rupert E. Davies, *Methodism*, 2nd revd edn, Epworth Press 1985*

The best single volume account.

Frank Baker, *A Charge to Keep*, Epworth Press 1947*

A classic short survey of the Wesleys and early Methodism. It is beautifully written, and, if seen in a second-hand bookshop, should be purchased immediately!

Jim Bates, *The Methodist Church*, Pergamon 1977*

A brief but informative introduction which is suitable for the newcomer.

W. J. Townsend, H. B. Workman & G. Eayrs (eds), *A New History of Methodism*, 2 Vols, Hodder & Stoughton 1909

The original standard history, and suitable for more detailed study. It is rather anecdotal but very useful, especially on the various off-shoot groups.

Rupert Davies, A. Raymond George & Gordon Rupp (eds), *A History of the Methodist Church in Great Britain*, 4 Vols, Epworth Press 1965, 1978, 1983, 1988

> Undoubtedly the best source for the reader looking for further material. The chapters consist of essays written by different authors on a wide range of topics, from general surveys to quite specialized themes. The final volume is a collection of edited documents and a bibliography that should satisfy the most ardent student of Methodism.

John Munsey Turner, *Conflict and Reconciliation*, Epworth Press 1985

> A series of detailed, well-researched essays on Methodism over the past two hundred and fifty years, with particular emphasis on Methodism's relationship with other churches.

John Kent, *The Age of Disunity*, Epworth Press 1966

> A similar collection of essays, is equally rewarding for the reader who wishes to delve deeper into nineteenth century Methodist history.

John and Charles Wesley

Biographies of John Wesley are plentiful, though less has been written about Charles.

John Wesley

Henry D. Rack, *Reasonaable Enthusiast: John Wesley and the Rise of Methodism*, Epworth Press 1989; 2nd edn 1992

> The most recent and is very detailed.

R. G. Tuttle Jr., *John Wesley: His Life and Theology*, Zondervan 1978*
S. E. Ayling, *John Wesley*, Collins 1979

> Examine Wesley's life from different perspectives. Both are comprehensive but the former is unusual in that part of the narrative is written in the first person from Wesley's own point of view.

R. Southey, *The Life of Wesley*, London 1829
C. E. Vulliamy, *John Wesley*, London 1931
V. H. H. Green, *John Wesley*, Nelson 1964

> All older but useful studies.

Maximin Piette, *John Wesley in the Evolution of Protestantism*, London 1937
Martin Schmidt, *John Wesley: A Theological Biography*, 2 Vols, Epworth Press 1962–73

Are both very scholarly works, more concerned with ideas.

Charles Wesley

Frank Baker, *Charles Wesley as Revealed by his Letters*, Epworth Press 1948*

Eminently readable and contains scholarly analysis based on original sources.

F. L. Wiseman, *Charles Wesley, Evangelist and Poet*, Epworth Press 1933*
F. C. Gill, *Charles Wesley, the First Methodist*, Lutterworth Press 1964

The two most detailed biographies of Charles. A modern study has yet to appear.

The Wesley Family

Maldwyn Edwards, *Family Circle*, Epworth Press, 1949*
Maldwyn Edwards, *The Astonishing Youth*, Epworth Press 1959*
Maldwyn Edwards, *Sons to Samuel*, Epworth Press 1961*

All eminently readable, yet based on sound research.

Theology and ideas

Albert C. Outler (ed), *John Wesley*, OUP 1964

In the *Library of Protestant Thought* series. This is a collection of Wesley's writings together with a great deal of discussion and analysis.

Albert C. Outler, *John Wesley's Sermons: An Introduction*, Abingdon Press 1991

Not really intended for the beginner – the author was one of the world's most eminent Wesleyan scholars – but will repay perseverance.

Rupert E. Davies, *What Methodists Believe*, 2nd edn, Epworth Press 1988*

An inexpensive guide to the essentials of the teachings of the Methodist Church, and will give you plenty of ideas for further areas to explore.

Leonard Barnett, *What is Methodism?*, Epworth Press 1980*

Gives a short but useful 'pocket' summary.

Michael Townsend, *Our Tradition of Faith*, Epworth Press 1980*
John Vincent, *OK, Let's be Methodists*, Epworth Press 1984*

The former is part of the *Refresher Courses for Preachers*. Both are short, thought-provoking studies of the way in which we can interpret Wesley's theology today.

John Stacey (ed), *John Wesley – Contemporary Perspectives*, Epworth Press 1988

A collection of recent essays by various authors. It is more demanding than the above titles, but gives some fascinating insights into Wesley's ideas and work.

J. E. Rattenbury, *The Conversion of the Wesleys*, Epworth Press 1938
Colin Williams, *John Wesley's Theology Today*, Epworth Press 1960

Both out of print, but are studies which have been sources of illumination to students of Methodism over the years, and are to be highly commended.

John Stacey, *Groundwork of Theology*, revd edn, Epworth Press 1984*

Probably the best recent introduction if you wish to move on to reading theology and Methodist doctrine.

Greville P. Lewis (ed), *An Approach to Christian Doctrine*, Epworth Press 1954*

Older, but extremely helpful, because at the end of each chapter the author gives a summary of one of Wesley's sermons, together with a short commentary.

Frances Young and Kenneth Wilson, *Focus on God*, Epworth Press 1986*

One of many recent works which will provoke thought, an extract from which you will have read in the last chapter. In addition to the authors already mentioned, the writings of Donald English, Colin Morris, Donald Soper, Neville Ward (who has written extensively on the subject of prayer), and Leslie Weatherhead – among many others – are also readily accessible.

The writings of John and Charles Wesley

John Wesley, *44 Sermons*, Epworth Press 1944
N. Curnock (ed), *John Wesley's Journal*, Epworth Press 1949*

Both are obvious and useful aids to study. Both have been reprinted at regular intervals.

James Holway, *Sermons on Several Occasions*, Methodist Publishing House 1986*

Provides a paraphrase which makes his sermons much easier to read, though purists might object! John Wesley's letters, sermons, journal and other writings are available, but best secured from libraries. The recent series of his works published by Abingdon Press, volumes of which are appearing at periodic intervals, are extremely expensive!

Frank Baker, *Charles Wesley's Verse*, 2nd edn, Epworth Press 1988*

    Makes for enjoyable and rewarding reading.

J. E. Rattenbury, *The Eucharistic Hymns of John and Charles Wesley*, Epworth Press 1948

    Is a classic work which has now been reprinted – but not by Epworth, though it is obtainable in this country. It is a rich resource for those particularly interested in hymnody and the sacraments.

No doubt you will find books not mentioned in this appendix which will prove of value. That is as it should be. It is interesting to note the number of titles which have been published by Epworth Press is an indication that Methodists are a reading people. You are, therefore, in good company.

APPENDIX 3

A Guide to Reading and Study

Many years ago as an undergraduate, I was with a group of students at a welcome meeting arranged by the local Methodist church. During the proceedings a very elderly member made the observation that, despite the difference in our ages, we all had something in common. 'I am a student too', he said. If I remember correctly, I smiled to myself in youthful ignorance of the truth behind his claim. Advancing years or lack of much formal education need not be a barrier to study. We are all capable of developing our potential.

If you are used to regular reading, and school or college days are still within memory, then much of what follows may seem rather obvious. If you consider yourself somewhat 'unlearned' – and you will not be alone! – then this study guide may not only help you to use this book but other reading which might be considered 'serious' as opposed to, say, popular fiction.

How to use *The Making of Methodism*

Each chapter combines narrative with short extracts from primary source material – that is, material dating from the particular time in question, as opposed to secondary sources which date from a later period. The documents are placed in boxes and numbered consecutively, with the original sources from which they have been taken placed at the foot of each box. A more detailed list of the sources used can be found in Appendix 2: *Suggestions for Further Reading*.

Contemporary documents are now much more readily available than a generation ago, and I hope that the extracts from primary sources will encourage you to delve deeper. Reading John Welsey's sermons is not quite the gruelling task that it is sometimes made out to be, not least because a version in modern English has been published: James Holway's *Sermons on Several Occasions*. The comments which appear alongside some of the books in Appendix 2 indicate my own impressions, but I hope they will make it easier for you to decide what kind of book to read next. Incidentally, it has been my experience that libraries tend to be under-used. Do not worry if your local library does not have the book which you require – it can be ordered for you at a very modest cost.

There is plenty of scope for you to use this book as a springboard for research into your local Methodist church. If you feel moved to go in this direction, you will be joining many ordinary people who have produced local studies which are a valuable resource for present and future generations.

Another way of using this book is in a group, taking either chapters or sub-sections as themes for an evening's discussion. The questions at the end of each chapter are simply suggested starting-points for reflection and conversation.

General reading techniques

If you are engaged in a course of study and have not done any serious academic work for some time, then the following hints concerning reading may prove useful. You will find that some of them will work for you, while others will not. That is fine. Each one of us reads in a different way, for different reasons. Take what you need, and leave the others with a clear conscience!

1. *There is reading, and reading!* Sometimes we find it useful to read a chapter rapidly, in order to gain a quick impression of the content before going any further. On other occasions a slower, more systematic approach is more appropriate. If you are following a correspondence course with set targets, it is probably better to set a time limit for your reading, rather than attempt a given number of pages in one sitting. Each of us reads at a different rate, which can vary according to the particular circumstances in which we are in, the time of day, or how tired we may feel.

2. Do not feel guilty about *reading only parts of books*. They are tools to be used. Some books are meant to be read from cover to cover, rather like a novel. Others are intended to be referred to, a section at a time, rather like a Sunday newspaper with all its parts and supplements. Another analogy is the DIY enthusiast's socket set, which provides a basic tool and a whole range of sockets for different applications. We have not wasted our money if we have bought a book that is used in this way over a period of time. It becomes an old friend to whom we return again and again for assistance.

3. *Reading documents* sometimes calls for special techniques, especially if they are long ones. Try going through the whole passage quickly in order to get a general impression, then again – more slowly this time – examining each section of the text in more detail. A third reading in one sweep will aim at examining particular things about the passage which are of interest, such as any marked inconsistencies in the argument, examples of exaggeration or poor logic, memorable insights, striking use of analogy, and so on.

4. It is worth trying to *summarize what a writer is saying* in a passage, and this is especially useful when reading documents, since the points may be expressed in unfamiliar language. People will develop their own 'retrieval systems' for future reference – it simply depends on the purpose of your reading. The test of any note-

taking method is whether we can gain a fair impression of what we have read by looking at our notes a couple of days later!

5. There are people who think that *marking a book* is sacrilegious. I am not one of them. Making notes in the margins and highlighting key words and sentences can both make future reference easier. Some people even use the blank pages at the end of the book to create an additional personalized index. The test of any method – and there are many – is whether we can look back at a chapter we have annotated and get the gist of its contents without having to read every word again.

6. Never be afraid to *consult dictionaries and encyclopaedias* if you are unsure of the meaning of a particular term. Not all books contain glossaries and writers do tend to slip into jargon! Whilst this can be infuriating at times, there are some technical terms which express a great deal in a single word or phrase. It is worth becoming familiar with the main ones. Every subject has its own 'language', and theology and history are no exception.

7. An author's *footnotes* need not be read in their entirety if you are reading a book quickly for pleasure, but they can clarify what the writer is saying or point to a particular source which you might want to consult at some later stage.

8. A book's *index* will help you find your way around a book quickly. It can also give a rough idea of the importance an author places on a subject or a person. Larger books have multiple indices with headings such as 'people', 'places' and so on.

A final point. Even though we may feel unqualified to express our own opinions, we should not hold authors in undue reverence. Naturally, we must never dismiss what a writer is saying unless we have clear evidence that he or she is utterly wrong. We should never be afraid, however, to make our own judgments and interpret material according to our own insights. They are valuable, too. The word 'academic' tends to frighten some people because they associate it with scholarship. This is a great pity. We are all students. As adults we may have stopped growing physically – at either end, if not in the middle! – but our minds are capable of absorbing new ideas for the whole span of our lives. We should never lose the confidence to tackle a new book. There may be fewer brain cells as we grow older, but for most of us there are sufficient untapped resources within our own minds to last a lifetime.

Notes

Introduction

1. All the verses at the beginning of chapters and chapter-sections are taken from Charles Wesley's hymns, some of which are in *Hymns and Psalms* which appeared in 1983, though they can all be found in the *Methodist Hymnbook* compiled fifty years earlier, both published by the Methodist Publishing House. The words are taken from the earliest version of the hymns.
2. From the Minutes of the First Annual Conference, held at the Foundery in London in June 1744.
3. In his *Sons to Samuel*, Epworth Press 1961, Dr Maldwyn Edwards writes that Charles had a 'lifetime habit of giving place to John' (p. 53).
4. Henry Rack, *Reasonable Enthusiast*, Epworth Press 1989, p. xvi.
5. Rupert E. Davies, *Methodism*, 2nd revd edn, Epworth Press 1985, chapter 1, entitled 'The Methodist Element in Church History'. This incidentally, was the main source used by students who followed the original *Methodism and Wesley Studies* course, on which this book is based.
6. Ibid., p. 21.

1. The England of the Wesleys

1. Herbert Butterfield, 'England in the Eighteenth Century' in Rupert Davies and Gordon Rupp (eds), *A History of the Methodist Church in Great Britain*, Vol. 1, Epworth Press 1965, p. 3. In this opening chapter Butterfield gives an excellent introduction to the eighteenth-century background.
2. For a brief definition of this and other terms likely to be unfamiliar, refer to the Glossary in Appendix 1.
3. See Glossary.
4. J. H. Plumb, *England in the Eighteenth Century*, Penguin 1950, p. 40.
5. Butterfield, art. cit., p. 19.
6. R. Porter, *English Society in the Eighteenth Century*, Penguin 1982, p. 65.
7. Attributed to the English philosopher Thomas Hobbes (1588–1679) who argued that an unwritten 'social contract' existed between members of society who shared a corporate responsibility for their mutual welfare. Without it, the quality of life of the lower classes would inevitably suffer.
8. In his influential (and controversial) work *The Reasonableness of Christianity* which appeared in 1695, Locke claimed the primacy of reason in the formation of doctrine and the interpretation of Scripture.

2. The Wesleys: Background and Early Life

1. There were four of these in all, the last being in 1662. It required all clergy to declare their public adherence to the Book of Common Prayer and make a declaration of loyalty to the King.
2. This is the number usually given, though there is some uncertainty, and even Samuel was not sure. There were three surviving sons: Samuel, John and Charles; seven daughters: Emilia ('Emily'), Susanna ('Sukey'), Maria ('Molly'), Mehetabel ('Hetty'), Anne ('Nancy'), Martha ('Patty') and Kezziah ('Kezzy'). Dr Maldwyn Edwards' books provide an fascinating insight into the Wesley family, particularly the daughters.
3. This and all subsequent extracts from Wesley's letters are taken from the standard edition of *The Letters of the Rev. John Wesley* edited by John Telford (8 vols), Epworth Press 1931.
4. Henry Rack, *Reasonable Enthusiast: John Wesley and the Rise of Methodism*, Epworth Press 1989, p. 50.

5. A reference to Zech. 3.2.

6. See Document 24 in chapter 4.

7. Robert G. Tuttle Jr., *John Wesley: His Life and Theology*, Zondervan 1978, p. 75 and pp. 227f.

8. See the Glossary.

9. The extract is taken from *The Journal of John Wesley* ed. Nehemiah Curnock, Standard Edition in 8 Vols, Epworth Press 1909 and reprinted in 1938. All subsequent extracts will be referred to by date only, to make it easier to locate the passages in other editions, e.g. the Abridged One Volume edition.

10. John's unkindness to his gifted but long-suffering sister Hetty, and his refusal to attend her funeral in 1750 is one of the more poignant instances of his undue severity. Charles was far more patient and understanding in his relationship with her.

11. Stanley Ayling, *John Wesley*, Collins 1979, p. 44.

12. Quoted by Frank Baker, *Charles Wesley as Revealed by his Letters*, Epworth Press 1948, p. 14.

13. Ibid.

3. *Wesley's Theology 1: His Sources of Authority*

1. Wesley preached only one sermon specifically on this doctrine: Sermon LIX 'On the Trinity' (John Wesley, *Sermons on Several Occasions*, London 1805, Vol. IV, pp. 21–31).

2. One of Dr Donald English's many memorable illustrations.

3. See Wesley's sermon 'The Nature of Enthusiasm' (op. cit. Vol. II, pp. 309–325) in which he analyses the various ways in which this 'dark, ambiguous word' is used. He points out that it is 'exceedingly rarely understood', and pleads the necessity for genuine religious zeal.

4. In chapter V of Rupert Davies and Gordon Rupp (eds) *A History of the Methodist Church in Great Britain* Vol. 1, Epworth Press 1965, pp. 173–4.

5. All the sermon extracts are from John Wesley, *Sermons on Several Occasions* (6 vols), London 1805. Most, but not all, can be found in the shorter collection: John Wesley, *44 Sermons*, Epworth Press 1944, which has been reprinted at regular intervals.

4. *From Georgia to Aldersgate Street*

1. See Document 12, ch. 2.

2. See the Glossary.

3. J. Telford (ed), *The Journal of the Rev. Charles Wesley, MA*, London 1909, Vol. 1, p. 16.

4. Ibid., pp. 87–88.

5. Robert Southey, *The Life of Wesley*, Longman, Hurst, Rees, Orme and Brown 1820, p. 55.

6. See chapter 7 for a more detailed explanation of this.

7. See chapter 6.

8. N. Curnock (ed), *Journal of John Wesley*, Epworth Press 1938, Vol. 1, p. 393.

9. F. C. Gill, *Charles Wesley, the First Methodist*, Lutterworth Press 1964, pp. 64f.

10. All these quotations are to be found in J. Telford (ed), *The Journal of the Rev. Charles Wesley, MA*, London 1909, Vol. 1, pp. 101, 123–4, and 131 respectively.

11. J. E. Rattenbury, *The Conversion of the Wesleys*, Epworth Press 1938, p. 85.

12. J. Telford (ed), *The Journal of the Rev. Charles Wesley, MA*, London 1909, Vol. 1, pp. 142–3.

13. Ibid., p. 139.

14. Ibid., p. 146.

15. Ibid., p. 149.

16. J. E. Rattenbury, op. cit., p. 84.

17. J. Wesley, *Sermons*, London 1805, Vol. 1, pp. 8–20.

18. See Document 8 in chapter 2.

19. From a sermon preached in Liverpool on 24 May 1988, the occasion being the 250th Anniversary Celebrations of the Wesleys' conversions.

20. For a full recent discussion of the significance of 24 May 1738, see Henry D. Rack, *Reasonable Enthusiast: John Wesley and the Rise of Methodism*, Epworth Press 1989, pp. 145–157. It was Piette coined the phrase 'moral conversion' when referring to 1725 (p. 43). Robert Tuttle's distinction between Wesley's 'religious' as opposed to 'evangelical' conversion has already been noted in chapter 2.

5. *Wesley's Theology 2: His 'Order of Salvation'*

1. M. Piette, *John Wesley and the Evolution of Modern Protestantism*, Sheed and Ward 1937, p. 445.

2. John Wesley, *Sermons*, Vol. 1, p. 5.

3. See the Glossary for a definition of these terms.

4. Paul used this expression on more than one occasion in his letters, the most relevant in this context being Rom. 5.14, and I Cor. 15.22.

5. J. Wesley, *Works*, Vol. VIII, p. 283.

6. Ibid., Vol. IX, p. 332.

7. H. Lindström, *Wesley and Sanctification: A study in the Doctrine of Salvation*, Epworth Press 1946, p. 35.
8. See the Glossary.
9. Ibid.
10. J. Wesley, *Sermons*, London 1805, Vol. 6, p. 9.
11. Ibid., Vol. 5, p. 110.
12. J. Wesley, *Letters*, Vol. 2, p. 118.
13. J. Wesley, *Sermons*, Vol. 1, p. 207.
14. For a fuller discussion of this, see H. Lindström, op. cit., pp. 93–4.
15. For example, in his sermon 'The Scriptural Way to Salvation'. Wesley says that 'repentance and its fruits are only remotely necessary, necessary in order to faith: whereas faith is immediately and directly necessary to justification.' (*Sermons*, Vol. 1, p. 351.) He does seem to be having difficulty here, in holding faith and repentance in tension.
16. J. Wesley, *Sermons*, Vol. 1, p. 74.
17. Ibid., p. 14.
18. Ibid., p. 297.
19. Ibid., pp. 294, 296.
20. J. Wesley, *Works*, Vol. VI, p. 74.
21. Colin Williams aptly summarized this aspect of Wesley's teaching. 'The holiness . . . of which Wesley speaks, is not a holiness judged by objective moral standards, but a holiness in terms of unbroken relationship to Christ the Holy One. The perfect Christian is holy, not because he has risen to a required moral standard, but because he lives in this state of unbroken fellowship with Christ' (*John Wesley's Theology Today*, Epworth Press 1960, p. 175).
22. Such as George Whitefield. Two letters to his brother in 1768 provide additional examples. Writing on 14 May, John complained that he was at his 'wits' end with regard to . . . Christian Perfection', and on 14 June wondered whether they should 'go on in asserting perfection against all the world' (*Letters*, Vol. 5, pp. 88, 93).
23. Wesley wrote to him on 2 November 1762, 'I dislike your supposing man may be perfect as an angel; that he can be absolutely perfect; that he can be infallible . . .' (*Letters*, Vol. 4, p. 192). Maxfield, one of the first lay preachers, became something of a fanatic and parted company with Wesley in 1763.
24. J. Wesley, *Works*, Vol. XI, p. 417.
25. Ibid., p. 423.
26. J. Wesley, *Notes on the New Testament*, Matthew 3.2.

6. *The Growth of Methodism to Wesley's Death*

1. John had all but been betrothed to a widow named Grace Murray, but a series of unfortunate events culminated in her marrying a rival, John Bennet, in 1749. The ceremony was conducted by Charles, who had been guilty of interfering in his brother's love life. John turned to another widow (Molly Vazeille), and their marriage was a deeply unhappy one – to such an extent that when she died in 1781, John failed to appear at her funeral.
2. In his journal Wesley refers to Zinzendorf's settlement as 'Hernhuth', but the spelling given is the one more usually found.
3. For example, the Moravian teaching concerning the doctrine of justification, their tendency towards secrecy and the rather autocratic nature of their leadership. Wesley's main point of disagreement lay in his opposition to their growing emphasis upon 'stillness'.
4. For the debate concerning predestination, see chapter 5, pp. 32f.
5. Dr Maldwyn Edwards has covered some of this ground, but for a very recent study see Paul W. Chilcote, *She Offered Them Christ: The Legacy of Women Preachers in Early Methodism*, Abingdon Press, Nashville 1993.
6. Henry Rack has examined this in some detail in his *Reasonable Enthusiast*, chapter VII. He concludes that persecution 'died away as the Methodists ceased to be unfamiliar, mysterious and dependent on strangers' (p. 275).
7. From a piece of unpublished research, which the author was kind enough to let me use.
8. Taken from the *Agenda* of the 1st Annual Conference of 1744.
9. Its full title was: *Primitive Physic, or an easy and natural Method of Curing Most Diseases*. It appeared in 1747, and was reprinted no less than 21 times, being bought in large numbers by Wesley's followers. Wesley gave away the proceeds from all his books, a sum estimated at £30,000. If we consider that an individual in Wesley's day could live comfortably on an annual income of £100, then this represented a small fortune. Wesley himself wrote in his journal in February 1782 that his own expenses amounted to 'neither more nor less than thirty pounds'.
10. Attributed to Dr Joseph Beaumont who was a contemporary of Wesley's. Quoted by Maldwyn Edwards in *A History of the Methodist Church in Great Britain* Vol. 1, Epworth Press 1965, p. 71.

11. There is a very interesting discussion of this in John Munsey Turner's *Conflict and Reconciliation*, Epworth Press 1985, pp. 16f.

12. Maldwyn Edwards, op. cit., p. 72. He adds an important footnote on the same page: 'The Plan of Pacification 1795 completed the process. It allowed a Society to have the Sacraments administered by Preachers authorized by the Conference.'

13. J. Wesley, *Letters*, Vol. VII, pp. 30–31.

14. J. Wesley, *Letters*, Vol. VII, p. 239.

15. Dr Frank Baker's view that Wesley made sweeping changes to the Book of Common Prayer has been challenged by Henry Rack in his recent biography of Wesley (op. cit., p. 510). The Articles which were left out in Wesley's revision were those with which Methodists had always found difficulty, i.e. the ones relating to grace and works (Article XIII), and predestination (Article XVII). The latter in particular was anathema to Wesley.

16. Quoted by Thomas Jackson, *The Life of the Rev. Charles Wesley, MA*, London 1841, Vol. II, p. 394.

17. J. Wesley, *Letters*, Vol. VII, p. 284.

18. This hymn is the only one used in the chapter and section headings which was not written by Charles Wesley. It has been included for obvious reasons.

7. *Wesley's Theology 3: The Means of Grace*

1. J. Wesley, *Sermons*, Vol. 1, pp. 247, 264–5; 'The Means of Grace'.

2. A. Raymond George, 'The People called Methodists – 4. The Means of Grace' in R. Davies and G. Rupp (eds) *A History of the Methodist Church in Great Britain*, Vol. 1, Epworth Press 1965, pp. 259–260.

3. A. R. George, art. cit., p. 263.

4. J. Wesley, *Works*, Vol. VIII, pp. 273–4.

5. J. Wesley, *Sermons*, Vol. 5, p. 335. The footnote appeared on the first page of the sermon.

6. The technical term for this is *anamnesis*. This Greek word means more than simply remembering what has happened in the past. It is difficult to translate, but has the sense of 'bringing into the here and now' that which is being commemorated.

7. From the *Methodist Service Book*, Methodist Publishing House 1975, pp. B12–B17.

8. E.g. Deut. 29.10–12, and instances in the New Testament (e.g. Acts) where whole households were admitted.

9. J. Wesley, *Treatise on Baptism*, Works, Vol. X, p. 191.

10. J. Wesley, *Letters*, Vol. 3, p. 36.

11. A. R. George, art. cit., p. 273.

12. Dr Frank Baker, in his recent study *Charles Wesley's Verse* (Epworth Press, 2nd edn 1988), has estimated the number of Charles' poems to be in the order of nine thousand. His hymns probably number over six thousand, though many of these consisted of short hymns of just a couple of stanzas. It is very difficult to be accurate.

13. F. Baker, *Charles Wesley as Revealed by His Letters*, Epworth Press 1948, p. 141.

14. Taken from *A Collection of Hymns for the Use of the People Called Methodists*, 1780 edition, Nos. 430, 113 and 206 respectively.

15. F. Baker, *Charles Wesley as Revealed by His Letters*, p. 150.

16. The hymns which are quoted in the text come from the 2nd edition which appeared, together with a new supplement, in 1780.

8. *Controversies and Divisions*

1. See chapter 6, p. 49.

2. In Wesley's eyes the preachers themselves were laymen, with a few exceptions. The distinction between ministers and laymen, which became more and more apparent as the century wore on, had never figured prominently in Wesley's own mind.

3. Dr John Walsh, in his chapter 'Methodism at the End of the Eighteenth Century' in *A History of the Methodist Church in Great Britain*, Vol. 1, Epworth Press 1965, pp. 284f., uses these terms to describe the 'two broadly differing views' that can be identified.

4. Dr Donald English, in an unpublished lecture given at Bristol in 1981.

5. Among these were: universal suffrage, voting by ballot and payment of Members of Parliament. The only demand made by those who drew up the 'Great Charter' of April 1848 which was not met was that general elections should be held annually.

6. Rupert Davies' *Methodism*, 2nd edn, Epworth Press 1985, and John Wilkinson's chapter 'The Rise of Other Methodist Traditions' in *A History of the Methodist Church in Great Britain*, Vol. 2, Epworth Press 1978, pp. 276f., both provide good introductions to the various breakaway groups.

7. There is little doubt that he was treated unjustly. No charges were levelled at his character, theology, or

conduct – Conference ejected him on the grounds that his writings were subversive.

8. By 1850 the total membership numbered just over 15,000.

9. Luddism became a general term for any movement opposing new ideas or technology. The Luddites – named after their leader, Ned Ludd – were groups of Yorkshire workers who reacted against industrialization by destroying stocking-frames and other machinery which threatened their livelihood.

10. E. R. Taylor, *Methodism and Politics, 1791–1851*, CUP 1935, p. 115.

11. From John Kent's chapter, 'The Wesleyan Methodists to 1849' in *A History of the Methodist Church in Great Britain*, Vol. 2, Epworth Press 1978, p. 222.

12. The mass meeting of some sixty thousand people at St Peter's Field, Manchester, in August 1819. The local magistrates attempted to arrest the leaders and were panicked into using a troop of hussars to clear a way through to the speakers. Eleven people were killed and four hundred injured. Coming so soon after Wellington's victory against Napoleon, it was understandable that the disaster should be nicknamed 'Peterloo'.

13. In his *History of the English People in the Nineteenth Century*, Ernest Benn Ltd, 2nd edn 1949. It was originally published in France in 1913 and first appeared in English in 1924.

14. Op. cit., p. 417.

9. *Towards Union*

1. The term 'Methodism' used in this chapter covers all the various Methodist groups unless named specifically. 'Wesleyan' denotes the Wesleyan Methodist Connexion.

2. Beatrice Webb, *My Apprenticeship*, Penguin 1938, p. 166.

3. Owen Chadwick, *The Victorian Church, Part II*, A. & C. Black, 2nd edn 1972; reissued SCM Press 1987, p. 270.

4. See chapter 8, pp. 67f. and Document 62.

5. This weekly newspaper was not the official organ of the Methodist Church and, in fact, caused as many ripples of disapproval in the Wesleyan hierarchy as it did in parliamentary circles.

6. This term came to be applied to all nonconformist denominations – the Glossary has a more detailed definition. The Oxford Movement, discussed briefly in chapter 8, helped push Methodism towards the other Free Churches.

7. Hughes' ideas found their fullest expression in his *Social Christianity*, published in 1889.

8. John Kent, 'Hugh Price Hughes and the Nonconformist Conscience' in *Essays in Modern Church History* ed. G. V. Bennett and J. D. Walsh, Adam and Charles Black 1966, p. 204.

9. J. M. Turner, 'Methodism in England 1900–1932' in Rupert Davies, A. R. George and Gordon Rupp (eds) *A History of the Methodist Church in Great Britain*, Vol. 3, Epworth Press 1983, p. 311.

10. The author's great-great-grandfather.

11. The purpose of Raikes' pioneering venture in 1780 was to prevent Sunday hooliganism when a pin factory near Gloucester closed.

12. The first state grant towards education was made in 1833. It amounted to the paltry sum of £20,000, a third of that spent on the upkeep of the royal stables.

13. In fact, this was not necessarily the case. Owen Chadwick argues that school board elections produced few permanent Anglican majorities (O. Chadwick, *The Victorian Church, Part II*, A. & C. Black, 2nd edn 1972; reissued SCM Press 1987, pp. 302–303).

14. The Bryce Commission of 1894, for example, invited the Wesleyan Conference to contribute to their report on secondary education.

15. F. C. Pritchard, 'Education' in Rupert Davies, A. R. George and Gordon Rupp (eds), *A History of the Methodist Church in Great Britain*, Vol. 4, Epworth Press 1988, p. 302.

16. The 'Tolpuddle Martyrs', as they became known, were six Dorset labourers who in 1834 were found guilty of administering illegal oaths, i.e. attempting to form a trade union. They were sentenced to transportation to Australia for seven years, though in 1836 they were pardoned and brought home.

17. See especially, R. W. Wearmouth, *Methodism and the Working Class Movements of England, 1800–1880*, Epworth Press 1937, and his later study, *Methodism and the Struggle of the Working Classes, 1850–1900*, Edgar Backus 1954.

18. The preachers designated by the Conference to these places were referred to as 'missionaries', even though they were not being sent to obviously 'heathen' areas.

19. See chapter 6.

10. Methodism since 1932

1. These figures are taken from George Thompson Brake, *Policy and Politics in British Methodism, 1932–1982*, Edsall & Co. 1984, p. 858.

2. Brake (op. cit.) points out that comparisons before and after 1968 are difficult because the way in which membership returns were made was changed. Nonetheless, the total of 585,123 for 1972 makes the overall trend pretty clear.

3. Rupert Davies, *Methodism*, 2nd edn, Epworth Press 1985, p. 163.

4. Frances Young and Kenneth Wilson, *Focus on God*, Epworth Press 1986, Foreword.

5. See chapter 3, Documents 13 and 14.

6. The Deed of Union: *The Constitutional Practice and Discipline of the Methodist Church*, Vol. 2, Methodist Publishing House 1993, p. 214.

7. See the Glossary for a brief definition of this term.

8. A general term describing a freer, less structured type of service in which choruses are sung, often accompanied by a modern group of singers and musicians, and in which the emphasis is more on an emotional response than that of the more restrained and structured 'traditional' services using formal liturgies.

9. This remark was made during a debate at the Methodist Conference of 1992 in Newcastle. Whether he knew it or not, the speaker was referring to one of the preachers in the 1836 Conference who claimed that 'Methodism came down from heaven, as it was wanted, piece by piece.' (See Gordon Rupp, *Thomas Jackson*, Wesley Historical Society Lecture, Epworth Press 1954, p. 41.)

10. The seven divisions were, Ministries, Home, Overseas, Education and Youth, Social Responsibility, Finance, and Property.

11. The West Indian experiment lasted just over twenty years and only came to a temporary end in 1904 because of financial problems. In terms of increased vitality and numerical growth, however, much progress had been made.

12. For example, in 1993 representatives from no less than seventeen autonomous Conferences were welcomed to the Conference at Derby.

13. Certain Methodist churches overseas, such as the United Methodist Church in the USA, have had bishops for many years. The key issue in Britain, however, was whether Methodism would adopt the *historic* episcopate, i.e. that bishops are part of a historic succession dating from St Peter.

14. The 1993 Conference's debate concerning human sexuality – the longest in the history of Methodism – showed that members were prepared to live with their differences and avoid a narrow dogmatism that would cripple the Methodist Church in future years.

Index